The Bread Lady's Quest

By

Jeanette Lavoie, R.N.

Dear Arlene,

Thank you for all the years of encouragement. God Bless You.

With all my Love,

Jeanette Lavoie

ISBN: 1-4107-2691-6 (e-book)
ISBN: 1-4107-2690-8 (Paperback)

Library of Congress Control Number: 2003091491

This book is printed on acid free paper.

Printed in the United States of America
Bloomington, IN

Cover design and artwork by Gigi M. Whitt
Illustrations by Gigi M. Whitt
"Golden Harvest" painting by Gigi M. Whitt
©Copyright 1999, used with permission

1stBooks – rev. 06/30/03

What Readers Say

"Jeanette Lavoie has done a service for our Lord in writing the book, <u>The Bread Lady's Quest</u>. I believe it will fulfill its intended purpose to draw those believers who read it closer to the Lord." Marvin J. Rosenthal, Executive Director of Zion's Hope Inc.

"With a thorough and accurate description of each ingredient that goes into bread-making, Jeanette Lavoie has revealed Jesus, as "The Bread of Life," in the most profound and complete way." Robert Pera is a baker and has been the owner-operator of Roma Bakery 35 years. Mr. Pera is the 3rd generation owner of this family business that supplies bread for restaurants in the Silicon Valley.

"<u>The Bread Lady's Quest</u> furnishes a treasure trove of sermons suitable for many occasions." Erna M. Holyer, author of <u>Wilderness Journey</u>, <u>Golden Journey</u>, and <u>California Journey</u>.

"Jesus said to them, 'I am the bread of life; he who comes to Me shall not hunger, and he who believes in Me shall never thirst.'" John 6:35

Dedication

This work is dedicated to my Lord and Savior, Jesus Christ. It is my hope that the "True Bread" that came out of heaven, Jesus, will satisfy your quest to discover the depth of meaning in the six words from Scripture that inspired this book:

"Jesus is the *Bread of Life!*"

Acknowledgments

My heart is full of gratitude to all the people who have prayed for me, encouraged my writing efforts, and sharpened my skills over the years. You have been like cheerleaders urging me on towards the finish line. Rather than risk omitting someone's name, I decided to list only one name, that of the late Liz Mullins. Since she is in heaven and I cannot thank her personally, I want the memory of her loving encouragement to be remembered here.

I give thanks to the teachers at Lutheran School of Our Savior in Cupertino, California, for allowing me to bake bread with the children and to share the beginning basic information that started my quest.

With a thankful heart, I remember those who read and commented on my manuscript, helped test my yeast experiments, and added their expertise. Your insightful feedback delighted my heart.

To the pastors, staff, and elders of Crossroads Bible Church in San Jose, California, I thank God for the faithful prayers, encouragement, insightful sermons, and worship music that provided food for thought as I pursued my writing efforts.

I praise the Lord for the youth leaders of Community Church in Santa Clara, California that I pray with every week before their youth group meeting. Your zeal for the Lord and passion to pray has been my inspiration for writing the devotionals in my book.

With much love and appreciation to my family for always believing in me.

And first and foremost, to the Lord Jesus Christ who makes all things possible by the power of His limitless strength.

Foreword

There are many choices available today regarding what we will "consume" - from food and groceries, to cars, clothing, and entertainment. People around us are on a search...a quest, trying to fill the "hole in their soul" and to satisfy the intense cravings of their heart. Jesus comes upon the scene of our life and very simply says: "I am the Bread of Life!" (John 6:35).

If we will take the time to examine His life, we soon discover it is only **this** "Bread" which can truly satisfy our quest for genuine fulfillment. Jeanette has certainly discovered this, through her journey along the pathway of life's struggles, difficulties, and challenges. If you will accompany her through this adventure you hold in your hands, you too can find this fulfillment.

In this wonderful compilation of devotional thoughts, recipes, Biblical insights, and ministry suggestions, we are constantly drawn to why Jesus used this metaphor of *bread* to depict for us Who He truly is! Jeanette reminds us that bread is one of life's "staples," as is a personal relationship with our Lord Jesus Christ. When we find this "Bread," we discover the essence of *eternal* life!

Let me encourage you to consume the contents of this book SLOWLY—enjoying each portion like a pull-apart coffeecake. Relish each bite, and savor the wonderful flavor and texture of each morsel before moving on to the next. For in this way, you will experience the tender promptings of the Holy Spirit, as He reveals to you insights never before seen. In the process, you will find your soul and spirit being fed with true "bread from heaven."

So...stay a while, take it in, pray about it - and leave refreshed, energized, and revitalized in the deepest part of your being. And then...return for more when the appetite is fully prepared. It will only grow sweeter awaiting your return visit!

Paul C. Zigan
Associate Pastor
Crossroads Bible Church
San Jose, California

Table of Contents

Introduction: A Recipe to Follow before You Begin this Reading Adventure xv

Prologue: The Bread Lady xvii

Chapter 1: Life-Giving Bread 1

Chapter 2: Separating the Wheat from the Chaff 17

Chapter 3: The Miraculous Kernel of Wheat 38

Chapter 4: Seeds to Sow 49

Chapter 5: Living Water 60

Chapter 6: One Egg: Three Parts 75

Chapter 7: The Milk of the Word 81

Chapter 8: Sweeter Than Honey 92

Chapter 9: The Oil of God's Presence 110

Chapter 10: The Salt of the Earth 133

Chapter 11: Beauty and the Yeast 154

Chapter 12: Taming the Beast 173

Chapter 13: Passover: A Picture of Redemption 188

Chapter 14: The Feast of Unleavened Bread 205

Chapter 15: Communion: God's Recipe for Peace 223

Epilogue: What Is *Your* Calling? 256

Appendix 267

Betty's Seven Grain Recipe 269

About the Artist: Gigi's Testimony 273

Notes 275

Introduction: A Recipe to Follow before You Begin this Reading Adventure

Dear Reader,

At the name Jesus, "the Bread of Life," the enemy trembles for therein lies the secret of living the abundant life. Like a Master Baker, the Savior desires to incorporate a unique set of ingredients into the dough of each believer's life so that His promise in John 6:35 may be fulfilled, "...he who comes to Me shall not hunger, and he who believes in Me shall never thirst." It sounds so easy; come, believe, and be completely filled and utterly satisfied. How then does this verse come to life when circumstances place us in the hot oven of suffering and we pray our witness will manifest the sweet aroma of "the Bread of Life?" This is an arduous quest, as believers live in a battlefield not a playground; yet, Scripture assures us that we will advance in His certain triumph towards our destiny.

"But thanks be to God, who always leads us in His triumph in Christ, and manifests through us the sweet aroma of the knowledge of Him in every place." 2 Corinthians 2:14

The Bread Lady's Quest explores this metaphor by adding facts about each ingredient in bread, sprinkling in Scriptural references, and mixing them together to find a connection to Jesus. Folding in poetry, songs, prayers, and personal testimony enhances the richness and allows the reader to capture each savory breadcrumb of truth providing food for thought. The devotionals allow the reader time to knead abstract concepts and transform them into practical recipes to use in everyday living. As the reader sifts through the material, he/she will find a treasure trove of mini-sermons to stir into everyday conversations.

Writing this book has been like opening up a very hot oven full of bread God has given me to sample. Follow this book like a recipe and you will get a taste of my journey. Are you running on empty? A loaf, a slice, a roll, a piece, a crumb, or even a whiff of Jesus' life-giving bread revives the faint of heart. Have you asked for your daily portion of Jesus today? As you read through this book and begin your own quest to learn more about Jesus, He will teach you how to allow Him to satisfy all your needs. Be confident of this, as surely as Christ rose from the grave, in the end all God's children will become like a piece of unleavened bread; the perfect image of Christ. Follow Jesus and the sensational fragrance that permeates the air will cause others to ask, "What are you baking today? Can I have a taste?"

In His Certain Triumph,

The Bread Lady

P.S. I believe that if we get the oven of our heart full of Jesus and allow the Holy Spirit to adjust the thermostat, the enemy will run for cover!

Prologue: The Bread Lady

Walking across the school parking lot one day, a kindergarten boy pointed at me and shouted with excitement, "Mommy, there's the Bread Lady!" In 1987, when I purchased a mill to grind grain to flour and a bread machine to speed up the kneading process, I had no idea that I would earn such a title. It began as I learned to bake bread and desired to share my new skill with my daughter and the children in her kindergarten class. The first year I taught the children to bake bread, I included a brief description of how each ingredient related to Jesus as "the Bread of Life." A few simple thoughts and supporting Scriptures set the kitchen of my mind cooking. Each time I baked bread with the children, I uncovered new hidden treasures of truth that I had not noticed before. The children's responses to the sounds, sights, and touch of baking bread turned my baking escapades into a ministry. Soon, I realized that I could not add any more material to my two-hour information-packed class so I began a file on each topic and dreamed of writing a book. What began as a simple gift of volunteering time at my children's school, ended up as a tool God has used to deepen and broaden my faith. Knowing that every word recorded in the Bible is there for a reason, I opened the Scriptures, searched for Biblical insights regarding each ingredient, pondered the process of baking bread, and began a fourteen-year quest in search of the depth and richness in the meaning of Jesus as "the Bread of Life." The wonder of what this would mean to a baker of bread gave me an appetite to feast on the Word of God, to pray for understanding, to satisfy my curiosity, and to find His will.

> "Thus says the Lord who made the earth, the Lord who formed it to establish it, the Lord is His name, call to Me, and I will answer you, and I will tell you great and mighty things, which you do not know." Jeremiah 33:2-3

"For now we see in a mirror dimly, but then face to face; now I know in part, but then I shall know fully just as I also have been fully known." 1 Corinthians 13:12

The disciples requested that Jesus eat in John 4:32-34, "But He said to them, 'I have food to eat that you do not know about.' The disciples therefore were saying to one another, 'No one brought Him anything to eat, did he?' Jesus said to them, 'My food is to do the will of Him who sent Me, and to accomplish His work.'"

In life, some mysteries remain unsolved and no one but God has the answers. Humility is the perfect teacher to prove that God is God and we are not. Imperfect as we are, He lifts our heads and invites us to sit next to Him at His feasting table. Here we are taught to crave heavenly delights, to be satisfied with the menu of His choice, and to discover the joy of worshiping in His presence. Just as food is necessary for our bodies, so too is feeding on God's Word essential to the survival of our souls. When Jesus lived on this earth, He embodied the living, breathing Word of God. In the desert, the Devil tempted Jesus to turn stones into bread to satisfy His hunger. Instead of performing a miracle, He hurled back a quote from the book of Deuteronomy to silence His tormenter, and He chose to wait for God the Father to attend to His needs.

"But He answered and said, 'It is written, MAN SHALL NOT LIVE ON BREAD ALONE, BUT ON EVERY WORD THAT PROCEEDS OUT OF THE MOUTH OF GOD.'" Matthew 4:4 (quote from Deuteronomy 8:3)

In general, the American culture does not know hunger because we learn to eat when we are yet not hungry. During my first years of college, so full of concerns over doing well in school, my taste buds were tainted with desires for chocolate-covered A's. For lack of time, I pushed aside the delicacies the Lord offered like vegetables on the plate of a picky youngster. As I shot up a quick prayer before a test, I hoped for the blessings with minimal effort. A finger's lick of frosting from the King's table was all I wanted. My persistent nursing school colleague Ellen, a completed (born-again) Jew, never gave up on me. After one year, I could no longer deny her invitations to the Nurses Christian Fellowship meetings she attended. Seated in a chair, amidst this circle of love, I feasted on the Word of God, tasted the sweetness of His loving-kindness, and shed hot tears during prayer time. God filled a barren, empty, lonely spot inside me with a taste of His presence. For me, to hunger after God at that moment, was to finally hear the empty growling sounds of my spiritual stomach. For the first time, I recognized how faint and spiritually malnourished I tested because of my failure to add the honey of God's Word to my bloodstream. Before, I worshiped God from a distance. Now I longed to be surrounded by His glory, feasting at His table, intently listening to God's Words as His invited guest, satisfied by the foods of His choice, filled to the brim with His love, lacking for no good thing. The song, "I Just Want To Be Where You Are," by Don Moen expresses the feeling for me. You can find it on his album entitled *Worship*.[1] Meeting God where He is and where He calls us to be is indeed a form of worship.

Moses spoke boldly to God and declared, "...If Thy presence does not go with us, do not lead us up from here" (Exodus 33:15). To thirst for God's presence is to desire to be where He is and to flee from the places where He is not. Repentant King David's desperate cry expresses the agony of separation.

"Do not cast me away from Thy presence, and do not take Thy Holy Spirit from me. Restore to me the joy of Thy salvation, and sustain me with a willing spirit." Psalm 51:11-12

Baking bread is a vehicle God uses to draw me closer to Him. The bread recipe I use in class (see appendix) is one from my friend, Betty Watson. It is an embellished version of the simple Jewish bread of old. Some of the ingredients mentioned in the Old Testament for baking bread are flour made from barley (or more expensive wheat), oil, yeast, and honey. From the basic ingredients in traditional Jewish bread, to the added mixed grains and seeds, water, egg, milk, and salt used with Betty's recipe, each tells a story that describes a different aspect of God's message of love. God has used the art of bread making to paint a picture of Jesus, to cause His Word to come to life, and to give me a new way of sharing my faith. Each Sunday, as I hold the elements of communion in my hand, the few quiet moments are never long enough to contain all the thoughts I have on this subject. The celebration of Easter and the commemoration of the Jewish feasts also stirs my heart in a new and fresh way. I invite you to follow along with me and to see how remarkable Jesus, "the Bread of Life," really is.

Devotional:

Personal Devotional: Each chapter includes a devotional to guide you through a personal or family time of prayer and reflection. Refer back to the chapter if you need more details. Most of the Scripture is printed in the main text; however, it is best to read each passage directly from the Bible. Examining the surrounding passages for each verse will help guard against taking God's Word out of context and coming to a wrong conclusion. Meditate on the verses for each category of prayer. Allow the verses to inspire your prayer time.

Praise – This is a time to focus on our amazing God and nothing else. Do not think about your troubles! Read John 6:35 and meditate on Jesus, "the Bread of Life."

Confession – Bring your sins before the Lord. May the agony of separation, due to sin, pull us back into His presence. Read Psalm 51:11-12 (a Psalm King David wrote after his sin with Bathsheba) and remember, sins rob us of fellowship with God like death separates us from a loved one who has died. The forgiveness Jesus offers to those who love Him is as joyous as knowing we will see our dear ones who are in heaven one day!

Thanksgiving – Thank God for providing everything we need to get us back into sweet fellowship with Him. Read Psalm 51:7-10 and 1 John 1:9.

Intercession – During this time, talk to God about what concerns you today. As you read these verses, John 4:32-34, Matthew 4:4, and Exodus 33:15, ask God to give you a hunger to do His will and a thirst for His sustaining presence as you serve Him.

Submission – The definition of submission is the act of yielding or surrendering your will to God so that His will can reign supreme in your life. An attitude of obedience, resignation (acceptance without complaint), and meekness (power under control) gives evidence that the act of submission is genuine. As you review your list of requests and spend time praying in the area of submission, focus on the last phrase in Psalm 51:12 "…and sustain me with a willing spirit." If King David had to ask God to sustain him with a willing spirit, then we should not be ashamed to do the same. Giving up what "I" want, to receive what "God" desires me to have, is not easy! That is why we need to ask for God's help.

Chapter 1: Life-Giving Bread

In Old Testament times bread was a basic food eaten at every meal, and it symbolized life itself.₁ To lack bread indicated the onset of hunger, which ultimately led to famine and certain death. When the prophet Elijah asked the poor widow to share her meal, these words exposed her dismal state, "As the Lord your God lives, I have no bread, only a handful of flour in a bowl and a little oil in the jar; and behold, I am gathering a few sticks that I may go in and prepare for me and my son, that we may eat it and die" (1 Kings 17:12). Elijah's response to this Gentile widow gave her a hope and a promise: "Do not fear; go do as you have said, but make me a little bread cake from it first, and bring it out to me, and afterward you may make one for yourself and for your son. For thus says the Lord God of Israel, 'The bowl of flour shall not be exhausted, nor shall the jar of oil be empty, until the day that the Lord sends rain on the face of the earth.'" (1 Kings 17:13-14)

In the New Testament, Jesus spoke of Himself as "the Bread of Life." He promised that those who act on faith by believing in Him would never go spiritually hungry and that simple belief in Him would also quench spiritual thirst. Just as physical hunger must be satisfied in order to sustain life and provide a level of comfort, so too must spiritual hunger. Investigating Jesus' birthplace and learning how Jewish feasts relate to Christ, while comparing Him to manna and the bread we eat, increases our appetite for His life-giving bread.

Birthplace of the King - Like manna that rained from above, Jesus, our everlasting eternal King, left His home in heaven to come to earth. How fitting it was for the "Lamb of God" - "the Bread of Life" - to be born in Bethlehem, whose name means, "house of bread." The specific district where the Savior took His first human breath was called Ephrathah, which

1

means "fruitful." This tiny area is the place where lambs were raised for sacrifice. In the prophecy of Micah, a glimpse of the purpose of His coming illumined the hearts of believers just as the star above the manger led the way for those seeking to find Him that first Christmas.

> "But as for you, Bethlehem Ephrathah, too little to be among the clans of Judah, from you One will go forth for Me to be ruler in Israel. His goings forth are from long ago, from the days of eternity."
> Micah 5:2

Jewish Feasts -The first four Jewish feasts - Passover, the Feast of the Unleavened Bread, the Feast of the First Fruits, and the Feast of Weeks - are all connected with an aspect of the ministry of Christ.2

Christ's Ministry	Day & Events	Connection to Jewish Feast	Bible Reference
Ministry to His disciples	Thursday evening, Jesus ate the Passover meal with His disciples.	The preparation for the Feast of Unleavened Bread (removal of all leaven) was completed before the sacrifice of the Pascal Lamb.	Exodus 34:25 Leviticus 23:5 John 13:18-30
Night & day of suffering.	Thursday, after the Passover meal, Jesus and His disciples went to pray.	Passover	Matthew 26:30

Christ's Ministry	Day & Events	Connection to Jewish Feast	Bible Reference
Jesus became our Passover Lamb.	Jesus' betrayal, arrest, and trials began and continued through the night and into the morning.	Passover	Matthew 26:47-27:1-26
Jesus died for the sins of the world.	Jesus was crucified on Friday, died at around 3 p.m., and was buried before sunset.		Matthew 27:46-60
The sanctification of Christ	Friday at sunset, Jesus is already in the grave.	The Feast of Unleavened Bread begins on a Sabbath Day.	Leviticus 23:6 Psalm 16:10 Luke 23:54-55
The Resurrection of Christ	Sunday morning Jesus arose from the grave.	The Feast of First Fruits goes from Saturday sunset to Sunday sunset.	Leviticus 23:9-14 Luke 24:1-8
Jesus left earth with a promise.	Jesus remained on the earth 40 days and then returned to heaven.		Acts 1:8-11
Just as promised, the Holy Spirit came to earth.	50 days after the Feast of First Fruits	The Feast of Weeks (Pentecost)	Leviticus 23:15-22 John 16:7-11 Acts 2:1-4

Passover is the Jewish remembrance of the twilight hour before God delivered the Israelites from the bondage of Egypt. Per God's instructions, an unblemished male lamb, sheep, or goat was sacrificed and the blood spread on the two doorposts and on the lintel (the horizontal section above the door) of their homes. By this act of obedience, God promised to spare the life of the first-born in that household thus protecting them from the last plague to fall on the land of Egypt. The women prepared unleavened bread, for yeast bread took too long to make, and the evening meal was eaten in haste, as they were to be ready to flee the land at Moses' command. The Passover celebration coincides with the day Jesus died on the cross and the redemption He accomplished at Calvary when He died in our place. Jesus, the only sinless (unblemished) one to ever dwell on the earth, fulfilled the demands of the law as it states, "...one may almost say, all things are cleansed with blood, and without shedding of blood there is no forgiveness" (Hebrews 9:22). The Apostle Paul, writing to the Corinthian church, calls Christ our "Passover" (1 Corinthians 5:7) and later explains what qualified Jesus to take the punishment for the sins of mankind:

> "He [God the Father] made Him [Jesus] who knew no sin to be sin on our behalf, that we might become the righteousness of God in Him." 2 Corinthians 5:21

The Feast of the Unleavened Bread begins the day after Passover, and unleavened bread is eaten for seven days. Seven is the Biblical number for perfection and knowing that the omission of yeast typifies the absence of sin, this is symbolic of the perfect and complete victory Jesus has over sin. The death and burial of Jesus occurred on Passover. Then, as the body of Jesus lay in the tomb, on the Feast of Unleavened Bread, His corpse remained exempt from the divine pronouncement all others face for the consequences of sin.

> "By the sweat of your face you shall eat bread, till you return to the ground, because from it you were taken; for you are dust, and to dust you shall return." Genesis 3:19

4

Marvin Rosenthal, President of Zion's Hope, connects the fulfillment of the prophecy spoken of by King David in Psalm 16:10 with the Feast of Unleavened Bread as he says, "it proclaims that Jesus' physical body would not experience the ravages of death while in the grave."3 Therefore, this feast reflects the sanctification of Christ; as God the Father set Him apart as pure and sinless.

> "For Thou wilt not abandon my soul to Sheol; neither wilt Thou allow Thy Holy One to undergo decay." Psalm 16:10

Even though our physical bodies are perishable, the hope and promise to believers rests in the knowledge that one day we will exchange the perishable (body tainted with sin) to the imperishable (unleavened like Jesus).

> "Behold, I tell you a mystery; we shall not all sleep, but we shall all be changed, in a moment, in the twinkling of an eye, at the last trumpet; for the trumpet will sound, and the dead will be raised imperishable, and we shall be changed. For this perishable must put on the imperishable, and this mortal must put on immortality. But when this perishable will have put on the imperishable, and this mortal will have put on immortality, then will come about the saying that is written, 'Death is swallowed up in victory. O death, where is your victory? O death, where is your sting?' The sting of death is sin, and the power of sin is the law; but thanks be to God, who gives us the victory through our Lord Jesus Christ." 1 Corinthians 15:51-57

The Feast of First Fruits is a precise picture of the resurrection of Jesus. He died on Passover, the Feast of

Jeanette Lavoie, R.N.

Unleavened Bread began the next day, and the third day after His death, He arose from the grave on the Feast of First Fruits! Compare the sequence of events that occurred the day Jesus became our Passover Lamb with the Jewish Sabbath that stretches from Friday evening to sunset Saturday. Jesus and His disciples ate the Passover meal Thursday night. Next, they proceeded to the Mount of Olives to pray (the significance of this will be covered under "'The Oil of God's Presence"). In the cover of darkness, the Roman soldiers, Judas the betrayer, and a multitude of others, participated in the arrest of Jesus. "And those who had seized Jesus led Him away to Caiaphas, the high priest, where the scribes and the elders were gathered together" (Matthew 26:57). As the false witnesses unsuccessfully testified against Him, Jesus kept silent. The high priest prompted Jesus to answer as he asked, "...I adjure You by the living God, that You tell us whether You are the Christ, the Son of God" (Matthew 26:63). Jesus' affirmative response provoked the high priest to tear his robes and shout; "He has blasphemed!...He is deserving of death!" (Matthew 26:65-66) "Now when morning had come, all the chief priests and the elders of the people took counsel against Jesus to put Him to death; and they bound Him, and led Him away, and delivered Him up to Pilate the governor" (Matthew 27:1-2). Judas' woeful confession, Pilate's wife's concerned warning, and Pilate's exasperated response as the crowd beckoned him to release the notorious prisoner Barabas and condemn Jesus to death, all point to the conviction of an innocent (unleavened) Man. On Friday, Jesus hung on the cross, died, and was buried before sunset.

> Judas, "I have sinned by betraying innocent blood." Matthew 27:4

> Pilate's wife, "...'Have nothing to do with that righteous Man; for last night I suffered greatly in a dream because of Him." Matthew 27:19

"And when Pilate saw that he was accomplishing nothing, but rather that a riot was starting, he took water and washed his hands in front of the multitude, saying, 'I am innocent of this Man's blood; see to that yourselves.' And all the people answered and said, 'His blood be on us and on our children.'" Matthew 27:24-25

"And it was the preparation day, and the Sabbath was about to begin" (Luke 23:54). The beginning of this Sabbath day coincides with the Feast of Unleavened bread and the Feast of First Fruits follows this day. Early Sunday morning, while it was still dark, Jesus arose from the grave. On this Jewish holiday, the people presented the first fruits of the barley harvest to the Lord by waving a sheaf of grain in front of the altar of the Lord. A sacrificial lamb accompanied by a grain offering of fine flour mixed with oil and a bit of wine fulfilled the requirements for this feast. Bringing the first of the crop symbolized the consecration of the entire harvest to God. The connection to Jesus, found in the words of the Apostle Paul, proclaimed that just as the resurrection is a sign that the sacrifice of Jesus pleased God the Father, so too will the harvest of believers be welcomed into the heavenly kingdom. For when God says it is good, it is good!

"But now Christ has been raised from the dead, the first fruits of those who are asleep. For since by a man came death, by a man also came the resurrection of the dead. For as in Adam all die, so also in Christ all shall be made alive." 1 Corinthians 15:20-22

The Feast of Weeks, also called Pentecost (meaning fifty) comes fifty days after the Feast of First Fruits. Along with sacrificial animals, grain (from the newly harvested wheat), and wine offerings, the people brought to the Lord two loaves of **leavened** bread made with fine flour. (Leviticus 23:15-22). God instructed that the bread be used as a "wave offering." Wycliffe Bible Encyclopedia defines a "wave offering" as, "the portions of the sacrificed peace offerings especially reserved for the priest and his family,...so called because it was "waved," i.e., moved towards the altar and back, as a symbol of presenting the offering to God and His returning it to the priest." 4 Thus, "waving" the bread symbolized an offering God received, accepted, and gave back to the priest. With that in mind and in connection to the Feast of Weeks, consider what this might mean to Jesus, who is called our high priest.

Jesus arose from the grave, spent the next forty days on Earth, and returned to His heavenly home with this promise; "...you shall receive power when the Holy Spirit has come upon you; and you shall be My witnesses both in Jerusalem, and in all Judea and Samaria, and even to the remotest part of the earth" (Acts 1:8). Ten days later, exactly on the Feast of Weeks, the Holy Spirit filled Jesus' waiting followers with the power to give birth to the church. (Acts 2) According to Marvin Rosenthal, "The two loaves brought to the Temple on the Feast of Weeks represented Jew and Gentile, now one in Christ with the advent of the Spirit's coming."5 The leaven in the loaves signifies the believer's sin; therefore, the waved offering must reflect God the Father accepting believers just as they are and giving them back to Jesus. Like the leaven buried in the bread, God knows the yeast of sin is mixed into the loaf of His imperfect church. Even so, God is willing to use imperfect people. Though the ashes from the sacrifice drifted away, the sweet aroma of the good that God transplanted into "the dough" of His church will linger in His holy temple forevermore!

Earthly vs. Heavenly - Food available on earth must be earned, purchased, and prepared. It provides momentary satisfaction to the flesh and to the continual demands of the physical body to sustain life. Perishable by nature, all products must either be consumed within a designated time or they must be discarded. In contrast, the spiritual food that God the Father provides through Jesus is free, eternally satisfying to the soul, and imperishable. Jesus proclaims that the greatest work a human being can do is to believe in Him - "the true Bread from Heaven."

As described in the gospel of John, Jesus performed a miracle by feeding 5,000 men plus women and children by using the five barley loaves and two fish offered by a small boy. The people were eager to make Jesus their king, yet not ready to swallow His message of a life-giving bread. The discourse by Jesus that followed compares earthly and heavenly food.

> "...'Truly, truly, I say to you, you seek Me, not because you saw signs, but because you ate of the loaves, and were filled. Do not work for the food which perishes, but for the food which endures to eternal life, which the Son of Man shall give to you, for on Him the Father, even God, has set His seal.' They said therefore to Him, 'What shall we do, that we may work the works of God?' Jesus answered and said to them, 'This is the work of God, that you believe in Him whom He has sent.'...Jesus therefore said to them, 'Truly, truly, I say to you, it is not Moses who has given you the bread out of heaven, but it is My Father who gives you the true bread out of heaven. For the bread of God is that which comes down out of heaven, and gives life to the world.' They said therefore to Him, 'Lord, evermore give us this bread.' Jesus said to them, 'I am the bread of life; he who comes to Me shall not hunger, and he who believes in Me shall never thirst.'" John 6:26-29, 32-35

Steps Towards God - A prodigal is one who is recklessly extravagant and characterized by wasteful expenditure. In the parable of the prodigal son, recorded in the book of Luke, the young man earned this title by his actions. He asked for and took his share of the estate from his father.

9

"And not many days later, the younger son gathered everything together and went on a journey into a distant country, and there he squandered his estate with loose living" (Luke 15:13).

With the money that satisfied the pleasures of his flesh now gone, he began to be in need and earned a living feeding swine (the lowest possible humiliation for a Jew).6   The first step towards reconciliation came as the young man recognized his need for food.   His next thoughts and words reflected the heart of a repentant sinner.

> "And he was longing to fill his stomach with the pods that the swine were eating, and no one was giving anything to him. But when he came to his senses, he said, 'How many of my father's hired men have more than enough bread, but I am dying here with hunger!' I will get up and go to my father, and will say to him, 'Father, I have sinned against heaven, and in your sight; I am no longer worthy to be called your son; make me as one of your hired men.'" Luke 15:16-19

The father's reaction symbolizes God the Father who is never in a hurry except when He runs with arms open wide to embrace, kiss, forgive, and welcome back a wayward son or daughter. The reason He was so quick about this task was because He had watched from a distance, patiently waited, and anticipated the homecoming. The rest of the story demonstrates God's abundant mercy and overflowing graciousness as He received the man back not in the expected position of a slave, but as a son. Sin is a disease to the soul that causes a loss of appetite for spiritual things. Acknowledging our transgressions to God and admitting our need for forgiveness is the first step towards reconciliation. As a well-balanced meal revives the body of one weak from hunger, God's forgiveness releases the tension and quiets the turmoil sin causes as He draws us to Himself.

"No one can come to Me [Jesus], unless the Father who sent Me draws him; and I will raise him up on the last day." John 6:44

"When I kept silent about my sin, my body wasted away through my groaning all day long. For day and night Thy hand was heavy upon me; my vitality was drained away as with the fever heat of summer. I acknowledged my sin to Thee, and my iniquity I did not hide; I said, 'I will confess my transgressions to the Lord'; and Thou didst forgive the guilt of my sin." Psalm 32:3-5

Bread from Heaven - God had led the people of Israel into the desert where they had no alternative but to trust in God to provide food or to murmur against Him.

"And He [God] humbled you and let you be hungry, and fed you with manna which you did not know, nor did your fathers know, that He might make you understand that man does not live by bread alone, but man lives by everything that proceeds out of the mouth of the Lord." Deuteronomy 8:3

For forty years God sent bread from heaven, called manna, to feed the grumbling people of Israel. Manna means "What?," for they had never seen anything quite like these white flakes that tasted like wafers with honey and cakes baked with oil. The following is a summary of God's instructions concerning this gift from above: Gather up only a day's portion for your families every morning before the hot sun melts the manna. Collect extra bread on the sixth day for God will send no food on the Sabbath. Bread saved until the next day will become foul with worms, but not that taken and prepared for the Sabbath. (Exodus 16)

11

God gave the people the bread of angels, yet they grew tired of the unchanging diet. They ground it, boiled it, and made cakes that tasted like those baked with oil. Manna pancakes, manna cupcakes, manna dumplings! As a complete food, manna provided all the essential daily nutritional requirements. This is a perfect parallel to the all sustaining power of Jesus - for feeding on "the Bread of Life" is never boring, always filling, and full of creative taste treats able to satisfy all who partake.

"Man did eat the bread of angels; He sent them food in abundance." Psalm 78:25

Manna Bread Had Limits - The Apostle John reminds the reader in Chapter Six of his gospel that those who ate manna in the wilderness still died. Jesus describes Himself as "the living bread that came down out of heaven." The phrases connected with this truth are: A bread that is imperishable, able to give life to those willing to take it in, and He calls it, "My flesh."

"I am the living bread that came down out of heaven; if anyone eats of this bread, he shall live forever; and the bread also which I shall give for the life of the world is My flesh." John 6:51

Ponder theories concerning Christ, consider books men have written about Him, and take the risk of missing the point. Seek for yourself what the Bible says, simply believe the truth of God's Word, and your quest to know Jesus will be satisfied. The testimony of His life, death, and resurrection represent the "true food" that is the sole source of eternal life. The Greek word for *eat* in John, Chapter Six, stresses a slow process of chewing and gnawing. Metaphorically, the habit of spiritually feeding upon Christ gives life to the soul as earthly food provides life to the body.

Feeding on Jesus by faithfully reading, chewing, and savoring His Word daily is imperative, for what is learned yesterday can evaporate with the morning dew or melt like the manna by noon. In like manner, what God showed me yesterday cannot sustain me if I reject the plate He sets before me today. When Jesus taught His disciples to pray He included the statement, "give us this day our daily bread." Jesus followed His instructions on prayer with the command not to worry, but to trust Him for our needs.

"Do not be anxious then, saying, 'what shall we eat?' or 'what shall we drink?'...your heavenly Father knows that you need all these things. But seek first His kingdom and His righteousness; and all these things shall be added to you. Therefore do not be anxious for tomorrow; for tomorrow will care for itself. Each day has enough trouble of its own." Matthew 6:31-34

Prayer:

Lord Jesus, without Your life-giving bread and thirst-quenching, living water, I cannot find peace with God. I long to be so close to You that I can feel your warm breath blowing in my hair like the wind. Draw me close, Lord, that the sound of Your beating heart might lead me in the right path. Give me an insatiable desire to be filled with the knowledge of Your Word that is stronger than the longing a starving person feels as a plate of food is finally set before him/her. Thank You Father for sending the "true Bread" from heaven. I believe Your food gives spiritual strength and maturity, physical power to resist temptation, emotional stability to bear up under trials, and wisdom to lead the way. Praise to You Lord God for, "Thou wilt make known to me the path of life; in Thy presence is fullness of joy; in Thy right hand there are pleasures forever" (Psalm 16:11). I want to stay in Your hand, enveloped by Your secure grip, Lord. When I feel the guilt of my sin pressing upon me, remind me of Your sweet forgiveness, so that I will not pull away from You. Thank You Lord, for I know I will forever remain Your child. Amen.

Poem:

Golden Harvest
By Christopher Vogt
age 13
Used with Permission

When you reap the harvest of your land
And a sheaf of wheat is in your hand
Remember Him who makes it grow
Him who makes the waters flow
You have no reason, no reason to run
Because He loves you, just like a son

Devotional:

Praise – Reflect on Jesus as the perfect, unblemished Passover Lamb as you read 2 Corinthians 5:21.

Confession – Read Hebrews 9:22 and Psalm 32:3-5 and remember Jesus is the reason we can confess our sins and find forgiveness before God the Father.

Thanksgiving – Thank God for the promise from Scripture that one day sin and death will no longer have any power over us! Read 1 Corinthians 15:51-57.

Intercession – Jesus proclaims that the greatest work a human being can do is to believe in Him. In order to do that, we must know who He is, what He did, what He will do, what He promises, and what He wants us to do. Read John 6:26-29, 32-35 and focus on this idea in your prayer time: "Lord, I ask You to increase my appetite for spiritual things. Give me the desire to spend time reading the Bible and praying so I can get to know You better."

Submission – Review John 6:26-29. What did these people come to Jesus looking for at first, food for their stomach or food for their souls? Examine the motives behind the personal prayers you lifted up during intercession. Trust Jesus with your needs, obey His directions, and the end result will have a lasting quality. Go to Him with a hidden agenda (pride, personal gain etc.) and this will spoil the blessing God had in mind. Ask God what He wants to accomplish in your life today and let Him have His way.

Chapter 2: Separating the Wheat from the Chaff

Peering between the cracks and knotholes of the fence that runs along the back of our home, our neighbor watched in silence as we faithfully watered and nurtured a puzzling crop of grass - no foxtails! - Or were they some exotic herb? One lazy summer afternoon, as we carefully harvested this mysterious crop, the question exploded from behind the back fence: "What is that? Is it wheat? Why would you be growing wheat in the city of Santa Clara?"

The reason for growing the wheat was to provide a visual illustration of Biblical truths in my various children's ministries. Pictorial presentations are powerful tools to aid children in grasping abstract concepts. If you would like to test your neighbor's curiosity, purchase a handful of hard winter wheat kernels from the local health food store, find a sunny spot, and plant your garden in January or early spring (if you live in California). In colder country, wheat is planted in the Fall before the first snow comes and lies dormant in Winter. At first, the wheat will look like fine blades of grass. Later, you will notice the heads of wheat pop out near the top where the plant starts to bulge. The wheat is ripe when the plant is golden yellow and the seeds are hard when bitten. You may want to find some foxtail plants and compare them to the wheat at various stages of development. Though the foxtails are similar in shape, color, and size to the wheat plant, the difference is obvious when the plants are full-grown. The head of the foxtail is flat and barren of edible fruit, while that of the wheat is firm and textured with a multiple array of seeds set one on top of the other. This illustration fits with the parable of the wheat and the tares. God knows His children and He will gather them into His kingdom. Be ready, for no man knows the day or the hour, but He alone.

"Allow both [wheat and tares] to grow together until the harvest; and in the time of the harvest I will say to the reapers, 'First gather up the tares and bind them in bundles to burn them up; but gather the wheat into my barn.'" Matthew 13:30

The following is a summary of how to share the richness of God's love using golden sheaths of ripe wheat. If you are unable to grow your own, wheat can be purchased in floral shops during the Fall season. Be sure to ask for dried wheat ripe unto harvest, not green wheat used in fresh flower arrangements.

Dissecting a Sheaf of Wheat:

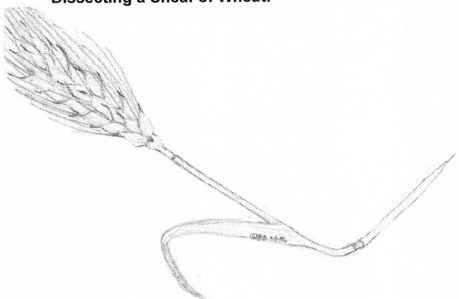

Beard: The long, slender, spindly tips protruding from the top of the sheave of wheat.

Stem: For fun, this part can be used to drink fluids. Just separate it from the head of the plant (includes the beard, wheat, and chaff), and cut off any elbow (a small, bulging, circular section causing bending) on the stem that would inhibit the flow. It works like any other straw.

Chaff: The chaff is the worthless, inedible part of the wheat stalk that covers each kernel of wheat. It is very light in weight and color. The psalmist who wrote the first Psalm used the image of chaff to describe the wicked. God calls the one who rejects Christ wicked; therefore, he/she cannot stand before God's holy presence for that person is guilty and without a Savior.

> "The wicked are not so, but they are like chaff which the wind drives away. Therefore the wicked will not stand in the judgment, nor sinners in the assembly of the righteous. For the Lord knows the way of the righteous, but the way of the wicked will perish." Psalm 1:4-6

> "For God so loved the world, that He gave His only begotten Son, that whoever believes in Him should not perish, but have eternal life. For God did not send the Son into the world to judge the world, but that the world should be saved through Him. He who believes in Him is not judged; he who does not believe has been judged already, because he has not believed in the name of the only begotten Son of God." John 3:16-18

Kernel of Wheat: This is the edible seed portion of the plant that can be crushed to make flour or, if planted, each seed can grow into a stalk of wheat yielding thirty or more seeds. The Bible likens believers to grains of wheat as Jesus promises that "...He will gather His wheat into the barn..." (Matthew 3:12). In the book of John, Jesus' words provide an analogy connecting a kernel of wheat (genuine believer who serves God obediently), with bearing fruit (the lasting results of

19

faithfully serving God). He concluded His remarks prophesying that He must die on the cross ("be lifted up") for the sake of all men. (John 12:32)

> "...The hour has come for the Son of Man to be glorified. Truly, truly, I say to you, unless a grain of wheat falls into the earth and dies, it remains by itself alone; but if it dies, it bears much fruit. He who loves his life loses it; and he who hates his life in this world shall keep it to life eternal. If anyone serves Me, let him follow Me; and where I am, there shall My servant also be; if anyone serves Me, the Father will honor him." John 12:23-26

The analogy holds that just as Jesus had to die so many could be saved, so must we die to our own self (wants and lusts) and live for Him more each day if a fruitful life is our heart's desire. I have taken many stalks of wheat, rubbed them between my fingers, and counted the amount of wheat that each one houses. Some heads of wheat are tall and full of a multitude of potential, while others carry a smaller number of seeds. Likewise, some believers are multi-talented and others have but a few special gifts. The quantity does not matter, but what is done with the gift reflects the motive behind the effort. Each seed placed into the ground, with God's blessing, will grow and bear fruit. Growth, by definition, demands change. The Bible calls this growth "the Fruit of the Spirit." Our joy is made complete when we seek to be of the same mind of Christ, allow Him to work in our lives, and obey His commands. Such a harvest is worth celebrating!

> "But the fruit of the Spirit is love, joy, peace, patience, kindness, goodness, faithfulness, gentleness, and self-control; against such things there is no law. Now those who belong to Christ Jesus have crucified the flesh with its passions

and desires. If we live by the Spirit, let us also walk by the Spirit." Galatians 5:22-23

"If therefore there is any encouragement in Christ, if there is any consolation of love, if there is any fellowship of the Spirit, if any affection and compassion, make my joy complete by being of the same mind, maintaining the same love, united in spirit, intent on one purpose. Do nothing from selfishness or empty conceit, but with humility of mind let each of you regard one another as more important than himself; do not merely look out for your own personal interests, but also for the interests of others. Have this attitude in yourselves which was also in Christ Jesus, who, although He existed in the form of God, did not regard equality with God a thing to be grasped, but emptied Himself, taking the form of a bondservant, and being made in the likeness of men. And being found in appearance as a man, He humbled Himself by becoming obedient to the point of death, even death on a cross...So then, my beloved, just as you have always obeyed, not as in my presence only, but now much more in my absence, work out your salvation with fear and trembling; for it is God who is at work in you, both to will and to work for His good pleasure." Philippians 2:1-8, 12-13

As we identify with Christ, allow Him to rule as sovereign over the sinful desires and passions of the flesh, and call upon the Holy Spirit to guide our walk, we will grow more and more like Him. The symbol of genuine faith finds proof in the quality of the fruit it bears. Good fruit reflects God's best. Bad fruit produces an image of man's efforts without the impression of God's handiwork. God, our creator, fully understands each person and knows how to teach us to separate His best from our worst. In similar fashion, a wheat farmer separates the desirable (wheat) and the undesirable elements (chaff) by a current of air - a process called winnowing. God's power, and the strength of His Word dwelling in our lives work like a winnowing device to give His children the ability to do what otherwise would be challenging and unattainable:

* To love others unconditionally.
* To exhibit joy and peace in all circumstances.
* To demonstrate patience when under pressure.
* To act with kindness without expecting something in return.
* To emulate goodness amidst the temptation to do evil.
* To cultivate faithfulness when others fail to keep promises.
* To practice gentleness rather than using force to manipulate the outcome.
* To allow God to be Lord of all thoughts, actions, and emotions, so the world will observe calmness, orderliness, and wisdom.
* To demonstrate the character of Christ that all conduct and speech would model self-control.

Separating the Wheat from the Chaff: In Biblical times, the wheat was separated from the harvested plant onto the hard threshing floor - a process called threshing. Either oxen trod out the grain or a threshing sledge was used to beat the chaff off the wheat. (Isaiah 28:24-28 and 1 Timothy 5:18) Flails (a hand threshing implement) or sticks were sufficient to beat out a smaller harvest. The farmer then winnowed the threshed grain by using a large pitchfork or shovel. (Matthew 3:12) He tossed the mixture into the air to permit the breeze to blow away the fine chaff and allowed the grain to fall at his feet. To further remove the bits of straw and other impurities, the grain required sifting through a sieve so that only the valuable wheat remained (Luke 22:31).

I will never forget the look on a young girl's face and her response as she watched me separate the wheat from the chaff and followed with her eyes as **only** the chaff fell to the floor as I gently blew on the plate. Her eyes widened as I asked the question, "The wheat (believers) stayed on the plate; what happens to the unbeliever (chaff) if he/she rejects Jesus and dies?" She blurted out the answer quickly, precisely, and without hesitation, "They go down to hell!"

> "...what must I do to be saved? And they said, 'Believe in the Lord Jesus, and you shall be saved, you and your household.'" Acts 16:30-31

The picture could not be clearer. Through faith in Jesus, we, like the wheat, rest safely in the palm of God's almighty hands. Would Jesus ever leave us or forsake us? God's answer is found in Hebrews 13:5-6 and is beautifully translated in Kenneth Wuest's book, <u>The New Testament: An Expanded Translation</u>. "...For He himself has said, and the statement is on record, **I will not**, **I will not** cease to sustain and uphold you. **I will not**, **I will not**, **I will not** let you down. So that, being of good courage, we are saying, The Lord is my helper. I will not fear. What shall man do to me?"[1] God knows that just as a mighty wind could blow both the chaff and the wheat away, those that love Him are in need of His secure protection. On the other hand, God will not protect the chaff from His winds of judgment. As the wind blows away the fragments of straw when the grain is winnowed, so too will the wicked (unbelievers) have no defense as they face judgment. Those who reject Jesus die in their sins. Like the chaff they are blown away from His presence forever.

Jesus and the Winnowing Fork: "And His winnowing fork is in His hand, and He will **thoroughly** clear His threshing floor; and He will gather His wheat into the barn, but He will burn up the chaff with unquenchable fire" (Matthew 3:12).

Chaff hides the wheat like a mask preventing the beauty of God's creation from shining through. Removing the excess chaff that stubbornly clings to a believer's life requires the Master Farmer's touch. Only when the winnowing process is completed is a believer ready for heaven. No small sliver of sin can escape the Savior's notice and sneak its way into heaven. When we are face-to-face with God our robes will be white and our hearts 100% pure. No matter if our kernel of wheat is robust or pint-sized, not one will be lost. All God's children will find their way home and **every sin and mistake** will go up in smoke.

> "For I am confident of this very thing, that He who began a good work in you will perfect it until the day of Christ Jesus." Philippians 1:6

Jesus Earned the Winnowing Fork - "But He was pierced through for our transgressions, He was crushed for our iniquities; the chastening for our well-being fell upon Him, and by His scourging (stripes) we are healed" (Isaiah 53:5). "He [God the Father] made Him [Jesus] who knew no sin to be sin on our behalf, that we might become the righteousness of God in Him" (2 Corinthians 5:21).

The sin of all mankind came upon Jesus and clung to Him like the chaff to the wheat. As the chaff is beaten off the wheat on the threshing floor, so Jesus willingly received the blows and sufferings of the cross to rid us of the burden of sin.

Jesus accepts each sinner. He willingly holds them in His tender grip because what He did at the cross cancels **all** past transgressions, covers **all** present transgressions, and goes ahead to prepare for **all** future transgressions. Once, and for all time, He took the punishment we deserve and shields His children from the pain of paying the ultimate penalty of sin on our own. Each temptation leading to sin has earthly consequences, and we must take responsibility for our actions. Choosing to place the undesirable (our worst) instead of God's best onto the threshing floor of our life has earthly ramifications. In Isaiah's parable of the farmer, he states, "Grain for bread is crushed, indeed, he does not continue to thresh it forever. Because the wheel of his cart and his horses eventually damage it, he does not thresh it longer" (Isaiah 28:28). Thus, the longer we allow a kernel of potential to remain covered in chaff, the greater the chance that a portion of that grain will be crushed. Jesus rose from the grave that no matter where we fail, we might come to know, His mercy and grace can still use any broken kernel of potential and spring it to life. The result of Jesus' awesome work on our behalf crushes Him like grain to flour and turns Him into our eternal "Bread of Life." For Scripture declares that someone must pay the price as it warns:

> "For the wages of sin is death, but the free gift of God is eternal life in Christ Jesus our Lord." Romans 6:23

> "For God has not destined us for wrath, but for obtaining salvation through our Lord Jesus Christ, who died for us, that whether we are awake or asleep, we may live together with Him." 1 Thessalonians 5:9-10

Do you feel the impact your sin caused Him today? Then partake of the life-giving truth that Jesus died for our sins. He lives to daily supply us with the sustenance we need to live for God, frees us from the weight of sin's crushing guilt, and offers us peace with God.

> Jesus said, "Greater love has no one than this, that one lay down his life for his friends." John 15:13

Farmer and Friend - What a friend we have in Jesus! We can feel safe in His presence. Freely, He invites us to pour our mixture of chaff and grain before Him. Since our Lord knows all things, in honesty, we are released from the burden of holding back our feelings. Those who trust God with every aspect of their life have nothing to hide, no need to fear, and His friendship to gain. The faithful, friendly hands of Jesus will sift the words, the thoughts and the intents of our hearts. He keeps what is worth saving and with a gentle breath of comfort, blows the rest away. This personal relationship, in its purest form, guarantees that our prayers will be heard, understood, and answered. Like a faithful, trustworthy servant, we can follow where Jesus leads because we know He has chosen to have a loving, caring relationship with those whom He calls His friends.

> Jesus said, "You are My friends, if you do what I command you. No longer do I call you slaves, for the slave does not know what his master is doing; but I have called you friends, for all things that I have heard from My Father I have made known to you. You did not choose Me, but I chose you, and appointed you, that you should go and bear fruit, and that your fruit should remain, that whatever you ask of the Father in My name, He may give to you. This I command you, that you love one another." John 15:14-17

Consider how delicately God dealt with Elijah the prophet. Elijah observed an amazing display of God's power as fire fell from heaven to consume his sacrifice to God, while the prayers of the 450 prophets of Baal fell on deaf ears. "And when all the people saw it, they fell on their faces; and they said, 'The Lord, He is God...' Then Elijah said to them, 'Seize the prophets of Baal; do not let one of them escape.'..." (1 Kings 18:39-40). As the prophets to this false god lay dead, the heart of Queen Jezabel burned with anger and she vowed to destroy Elijah. The prophet of the most high God ran in fear after receiving the death threat from the voice of a woman! Sitting under a juniper tree, Elijah prayed and "...requested for himself that he might die..." (1 Kings 19:4). God listened in silence, allowing Elijah to express his feelings. Perhaps from the strain of it all, he fell asleep. An angel of the Lord later awakened him, saying, "Arise, eat." After consuming the bread and water provided, he slept again. A second time, the angel said, "...Arise, eat, because the journey is too great for you" (1 Kings 19:7). The food and rest God provided gave him strength to travel to Horeb, the mountain of God. There God broke the silence and asked, "What are you doing here, Elijah?" God already knew what he would say; yet, He encouraged him to express his anguish in words,"...I have been very zealous for the Lord, the God of hosts; for the sons of Israel have forsaken Thy covenant, torn down Thine altars and killed Thy prophets with the sword. And I alone am left; and they seek my life, to take it away" (1 Kings 19:10). Next, God instructed Elijah to watch a spectacular display of the elements. "...And a great and strong wind was rending the mountains and breaking in pieces the rocks before the Lord; but the Lord was not in the wind. And after the wind an earthquake, but the Lord was not in the earthquake. And after the earthquake a fire, but the Lord was not in the fire; and after the fire a sound of a gentle blowing. And it came about when Elijah heard it, that he wrapped his face in his mantle, and went out and stood in the entrance of the cave. And behold, a voice came to him and said, 'What are you doing here, Elijah?'" (1

Kings 19:11-13) How patient is our God! He captured Elijah's attention using a quiet whisper, asked the same question, and listened to an identical response. Though the prophet's deep feelings remained unchanged, God knew verbal scolding was not in order and He recognized Elijah was now ready for a task. He sent him on a mission to appoint a new King and told him to anoint Elisha as prophet in his place. As God treated this prophet of old, so too will He meet our needs. God listens as we complain, hears as we ask, guides as we seek, teaches patience as we wait for Him to make a way, and prays for protection from the enemies winnowing fork.

The Enemy's Winnowing Fork - "Simon, Simon, behold, Satan has demanded permission to sift you like wheat; but I have prayed for you, that your faith may not fail, and you, when once you have turned again, strengthen your brothers" (Luke 22:31-32).

Satan's winnowing method works in reverse. He desires to infuse as much chaff into our lives as he can in order to render the believer powerless and the unbeliever hopeless. Sifting through a fifty-pound sack of wheat, I find a few malformed kernels that look like chaff-coated wheat. Examining these more closely, I discover that the chaff is very thick, hard, and will not rub away. Probing deeper, I discover that some are chaff through and through. Others do have a pale, brittle kernel inside that breaks apart in the process of digging out the kernel. I discard these for they are of no use in baking bread. In my mind, these represent either the unbeliever who has thoroughly rejected God or one whose heart is very hard and closed to spiritual matters.

Prayer:
Praise You, Lord Jesus, that You will not desert us when Satan desires to sift us as wheat. Your intercession for us is endless and the power of Your winnowing fork is unbeatable. Praise to You for Your great love, which sifts out the bad and

saves the kernel of good that was created in Your image. Thank You that Your promises are true. The prayers You submit on our behalf keep our faith from failing and, once we have turned from the error of our ways, You enable us to strengthen others. Amen!

"And God saw all that He had made, and behold, it was very good..." Genesis 1:31

Threshing the Mountains - Therefore, if you believe God is calling you to a task you feel unqualified to accomplish, or if there is a sin in your life that seems unconquerable, or a goal that will not be realized, remember this, God created all with a purpose in mind - nothing is impossible with God. Problems can rise up in our minds, becoming as large and impassable as a rugged mountain. Our God, who is greater than our fears, sends assurance through the prophet Isaiah:

"You whom I have taken from the ends of the earth, and called from its remotest parts, and said to you, You are My servant, I have chosen you and not rejected you. Do not fear, for I am with you; do not anxiously look about you, for I am your God. I will strengthen you, surely I will help you, surely I will uphold you with My righteous right hand...For I am the Lord your God, who upholds your right hand, who says to you, do not fear, I will help you. Do not fear, you worm Jacob, you men of Israel; I will help you, declares the Lord, and your Redeemer is the Holy One of Israel. Behold, I have made you a new, sharp threshing sledge with double edges; you will thresh the mountains, and pulverize them, and will make the hills like chaff. You will winnow them, and the wind will carry them away, and the storm will scatter them; but you will rejoice in the

29

Lord, you will glory in the Holy One of Israel. The afflicted and needy are seeking water, but there is none, and their tongue is parched with thirst; I, the Lord, will answer them Myself, as the God of Israel I will not forsake them." Isaiah 41:9-10, 13-17

Prayer:

Lord, when my fears overwhelm me and my anxious thoughts captivate my attention, let the power of Your righteous right hand holding me up bring me back to reality. When I choose to dwell in a land far from righteousness, speak to me in a quiet whisper until I can no longer ignore the sweetness of Your voice and must call upon You to save me. All praise, glory, and honor be to my Redeemer. Your help is not hollow or empty - it is new, sharp, and comes with double edges. Though in strength I may feel as feeble as a worm, the threshing sledge You prepare will enable me to pulverize my challenges. From troubles as large as Mount Everest to irritations as small as a molehill, You transform them **all** into plains I can hike through. I thank You God for the instruments of comfort and the tools of provision that shrink the size of my trials into manageable parts and carry the conquered fragments away by the winds of Your fearless love. For Your Word reminds me, "There is no fear in love; but perfect love casts out fear, because fear involves punishment, and the one who fears is not perfected in love. We love, because He first loved us" (1 John 4:18-19). May my eyes see and others recognize and consider and gain insight as well, that when the hand of the Lord begins to provide a solution, the impossible is no longer a worrisome concern. To God be the glory for the great things He has done. Amen.

Song:

As I consider the relationship God has with His children, compared to the intentions of the enemy (Satan), I feel blessed to be in God's loving hands! One of my favorite songs is, "Change My Heart, Oh God", by Eddie Espinosa.[2] The lyrics paint a picture of God being the Potter and man the clay. They remind me of how God carefully shapes us into the perfect vessel to accomplish His purpose. The words of this song, plus the knowledge I have gained from the study of wheat, inspired this song that I have written with my friends[3]:

May I Be Like You

Words by Jeanette Lavoie and Bev Ristow
Music by Bev Ristow and Greg Newlon

Copyright 1999 by Jeanette Lavoie, Greg Newlon, Bev Ristow

Jeanette Lavoie, R.N.

lead.   Re - move the   chaff   oh   God,_____

Make me   ev - er   new._____   Re - move   the

chaff,   oh   God,_____   May   I   be   like   You.

Devotional:

The following is a mini-devotional for Chapter 2 geared for children. If you do not have sheaves of wheat, use the illustrations from this chapter as a guide. Read the verses from the Bible, discuss the topics, and spend time praying through each section:

Praise: God's love is unconditional and He desires that none should perish. His love is not forced upon us; God gives us the choice to accept or reject His love.

Scriptures: John 3:16-18

Confession: Confession revives the soul! Let's see how, using a visual illustration:
1. **Dissect a sheaf of wheat** = Stem, head, beard, chaff, and grain.
2. **Chaff** = The worthless, inedible part that covers (hides) the grain. Represents those who reject Christ. Since all believers fall short of God's perfect standard, chaff reminds me of sin in general.
3. **Kernels of wheat** = Seeds that represent believers in Christ (Matthew 3:12). Not one will be lost as God's winds of judgment blow (Psalm One tells this story).
4. **Separate the wheat (believers) from the chaff (unbelievers) onto a plate.** Read Psalm 1:4-6 and Romans 3:23. Blow on the plate and ask, "What happens when believers and unbelievers (wicked) die and face God?" Notice that a strong wind is not needed!
5. **Sheaf of wheat** = Imagine new believers as seeds (kernels of wheat) that each mature into stalks of wheat ripe with opportunities to serve God. Each person has a different number of seeds (opportunities) in their stalk. Separate the wheat from the chaff onto a plate. Now you have a plate full of opportunities (seeds) swimming in a sea of chaff (the flesh)! Before you try to plant those

35

seeds, pray God will remove the chaff (sin) so that you can bear "good" fruit. Read John 12:23-26.

6. **Ahead of time, separate one head of wheat and glue both the wheat and the chaff onto a paper plate. With the children present, take another head of wheat and separate it onto another paper plate. Explain that these two plates of wheat with chaff represent either individuals or two Churches with all their seeds of potential. Blow on each plate and then ask these questions:** Which individual or Church will be more likely to bear "good" fruit? Why is it important to confess our sins? What kinds of feelings are stirred up as a result of sin? Sin can cause fear, turmoil, guilt etc. Confession revives the soul as it brings peace, freedom, joy, relief etc.

Thanksgiving: Read I John 1:8-9 and Romans 6:23. Thank Jesus for removing our sins! The feeling of joy that happens when our sin is gone revives our soul. Sin separates us from God and confession makes everything right. Someone who rejects Jesus is "spiritually" dead. The believer in Christ is "spiritually" alive. When believers sin they are still a child of God, but the consequences of sin make us feel like we are not "full" of life. Think of a person in the hospital who is near-death and the doctors bring him/her back to life. What a joy that is to the person and his/her family. The same is true when we confess our sins, admit we were wrong, ask God to (cleanse) remove our sins, and to help us change. This experience can be called a revival. Jesus can revive anyone! All we have to do is ask! Thank You Jesus!

The following are a few definitions of revival to use as food for thought as you pray:

1. Revival is being near-death and having your Savior restore you to life!
2. Revival is the stirring up of faith and the willingness to yield to the Holy Spirit among a people who were once cold and indifferent to God.

3. Revival is a "cold" faith that has said honest prayers and become "hot" (zealous for God).
4. Revival is missed when sinners cling to sin. Jesus loves us too much to let us stay that way.
5. Revival is signed, sealed, and delivered when all God's people are united in their passion to put God first and let go of sin.

Intercession:
Focus on these three topics during prayer time:
1. Help us to confess our sins quickly and always ask for God's help for everything we do so we can be a blessing to others.
2. Let each believer have a heart for the lost and a desire to pray that God would save them! Do not forget the image of the chaff (unbeliever) falling to the ground as the wheat (believers) remain safely on the plate (God's hands).
3. Help us make the most of every opportunity God gives us to serve Him.

Scripture: The following verse begins with "IF" for a reason! Read the verse and ask, "What do we have to do before God will hear our prayers, forgive our sins, and heal our land?"

"If my people, who are called by my name, will **humble** themselves and **pray** and **seek** my face and **turn** from their wicked ways, **then will I hear** from heaven and will **forgive** their sin and will **heal** their land." 2 Chronicles 7:14 (NIV)

Submission – Confessing our sins and obeying God is a conscious choice we must make every day. What will you choose to do today?

Chapter 3: The Miraculous Kernel of Wheat

"And when He broke the third seal, I heard the
third living creature saying, "Come." And I
looked, and behold, a black horse; and he who
sat on it had a pair of scales in his hand. And I
heard as it were a voice in the center of the four
living creatures saying, "A quart of wheat for a
denarius, and three quarts of barley for a
denarius; and do not harm the oil and the wine."
Revelation 6:5-6

The third seal of judgment declares famine in the
turbulent days spoken of in the Revelation given to the Apostle
John. In Biblical times, a denarius was equivalent to a day's
wage. The miraculous shelf life and the superb nutritional value
of wheat will make it a much sought-after food item during the
end times. Studying the characteristics, uses, and quality of
wheat creates another image of how Jesus ministers to His
people (symbolized by the kernels of wheat).

Shelf life - Whole kernels of wheat, protected from pests
and damage, will remain a useful food source indefinitely.
Genesis 41 records how Joseph stored up grain for seven
years, saving the nations of Israel and Egypt from the following
seven years of famine. "How long is the shelf-life of a kernel of
wheat?" "Is there a point where these seeds would no longer
be able to reproduce when planted?" These questions were
put to the test as I researched this commonly believed rumor:
"Upon the opening of King Tut's tomb, excavators found jars
filled with golden grains of wheat. These seeds lay dormant in
a cold, dark place for over 3500 years. Scientists planted them
and they grew!" In his book, <u>Pharaoh's Flowers: The Botanical
Treasures of Tutankhamun</u>, F. Nigel Hepper contends this is
false as he says, "Although the dry atmosphere of Egyptian
tombs has preserved in a remarkably complete state most of

the objects hidden in them, seeds rapidly become too dry to germinate."[1] Fresh seeds require some moisture to remain alive and the natural aging process is not well understood; therefore, the complete answer to these questions is still a mystery. What is clear is that the wheat that saved Joseph and two nations from famine remained viable for up to fourteen years.

The life span of freshly milled flour plummets dramatically. Crushed, unprocessed wheat, in its natural form, goes rancid quickly and must be used within three-five days or thrown away. Just as the protective outer covering of the kernel preserves the life of the wheat, so too Jesus promises to preserve His children. The glorious gospel of Jesus Christ is a treasure – a gift from God – that He places in the hearts of His frail, mortal children. Our earthen vessels are often weak and soft, but when Jesus inhabits the kernel of our soul, this part is hard as a rock. We will be afflicted in this life, but Jesus promises to hold us together. Though the outward man decay, our soul will stay intact: complete, impenetrable, untouched, undefiled, eternal. Satan can bite down as hard as he can into our flesh, yet all he will gain is a mouthful of broken teeth, for what Jesus holds together will not crumble! Our living Lord, the bread that gives life, actively protects believers from harm, offers to purge them from evil, provides that which is spiritually healthy on which to feast, and promises He will never forsake us.

"And He [Jesus] is before all things, and in Him all things hold together." Colossians 1:17

"But we have this treasure in earthen vessels, that the surpassing greatness of the power may be of God and not from ourselves; we are afflicted in every way, but not crushed; perplexed, but not despairing; persecuted, but not forsaken; struck down, but not destroyed; always carrying about the body of the dying of Jesus, that the life of

Jesus also may be manifested in our body." 2 Corinthians 4:7-10

"Therefore we do not lose heart, but though our outer man is decaying, yet our inner man is being renewed day by day." 2 Corinthians 4:16

Cleansing Power – Whole grain foods, high in fiber, have been touted as beneficial to promoting a healthy colon. Foods high in fiber are coincidentally often also rich in vitamins and minerals, low in fat, and low in calories. Fiber, such as the bran in wheat, is the portion of a plant that cannot be digested by the human intestinal tract. As it passes through the gastrointestinal tract, it adds bulk and roughage to the diet. Wheat bran can be purchased separately and, when consumed with adequate fluids, it is an effective tool to cleanse the colon by keeping the system regular. Foods made from freshly milled wheat have a higher fiber content than processed, store bought whole-wheat flour. Intestinal gas, cramping, bloating, and diarrhea can result if such foods are introduced too quickly into the diet of one not used to them. An old German saying, "If the farmer eats the bread while it is warm, he will remain poor; for there will be none left when later needed." And I will add, "If he eats the whole loaf in one sitting, his tummy will remind him of his mistake all night long." Just as the fiber in wheat helps our bodies expel waste products, Jesus desires to cleanse us of our sins and the poisonous side effects that plague such a lifestyle.

"If we confess our sins, He is faithful and righteous to forgive us our sins and to cleanse us from all unrighteousness." 1 John 1:9

Nutritional Value - The life-sustaining power of wheat has been proven through a well-known experiment. One group of rats was fed white bread only while the others feasted on wheat bread loaded with natural vitamins, minerals, proteins, fats, and starches. The results proved fatal for the former group. The other rats not only lived but thrived!

There are many ways of eating wheat. Cooking instructions are similar to that of rice: bring the water to a boil, then reduce heat, cover, and cook about one hour until softened. Cooked wheat may be used as cereal topped with honey and/or nuts for flavor. Crush it for use in baking bread and other sweet treats. Pop it in your mouth, wait for it to soften (to guard against broken teeth), chew and swallow, or let it linger in your mouth so that the gluten will become stretchy like a balloon and presto - you have homemade gum. Consuming wheat adds valuable nutrition to the human body (calcium, iron, phosphorus, magnesium, potassium, manganese, iodine, fluorine, chlorine, sodium, vitamin B-1, vitamin B-2, niacin, vitamin B-6, folic acid, vitamin E, and more). The entire kernel of wheat is surrounded by a layer of bran which supplies roughage (fiber) to the diet as well as vitamins, minerals, and protein. Wheat germ is the seed or embryo portion of wheat that takes up about 3% of the kernel. This is the life-giving part from which the wheat plant sprouts and is one of the richest known sources of B and E. vitamins. It also contains valuable proteins and fat. Endosperm is the inner part of the kernel consisting of starch and a small amount of protein. Though it comprises nearly 80% of the kernel, the endosperm is almost void of vitamins and minerals essential to our well being. White flour is made from this part of the kernel. Wheat does not have all the essential amino acids (building blocks of protein) that the body needs to function properly, as it is low in isoleucine and lysine. Adding a mixture of other grains (rye, brown rice, barley, millet, and whole oats) and eggs or milk make bread a complete protein. Of the grains mentioned, whole oats have a higher proportion of essential amino acids than the others do.

For Use or Storage – Wheat hidden away and forgotten will not provide fuel to the body nor add to the bounty at harvest time. If the purpose of storing grain is in anticipation of a time of famine or the threat of Y2K, then what has been saved will be available to meet needs. Just as each kernel of wheat has the potential to sustain physical life or multiply the harvest, believers must consider these two choices: Either we can remain dormant, nominal, on-the-fence "believers" who prefer to hide their faith in a jar, or we can allow Jesus to be Lord of our lives. The latter gives the Master Gardener free reign over the garden of his/her life. Such a one will flourish, for God's tool-shed is equipped with all manner of gardening techniques to ensure a healthy growth rate and a barn full of fruit.

> "Let your light shine before men in such a way that they may see your good works, and glorify your Father who is in heaven." Matthew 5:16

Planting – As a farmer plants a field of wheat, he recognizes that his efforts provide food in abundance; yet, the outcome depends on many factors. The seed part of the wheat plant springs to life after careful planting, diligent watering, watchful tending, and exposure to the sun-warmed soil of spring. Awakened from its dormant state, the slender green shoot presses its way up and out of the earth into the sunshine and the life of a stalk of wheat has begun. This process, called germination, heralds the beginning of a brand new creation. Eventually, the seed itself dies as the life within manifests itself as a stalk, roots, leaves, and finally a fully ripe golden sheave of wheat ready for harvest. Roots securely anchored in the ground, heads white and lifted up – the farmer must act quickly. An unexpected storm could result in the loss of the whole crop of one who chooses to rest at harvest time.

> "He who gathers in summer is a son who acts wisely, but he who sleeps in harvest is a son who acts shamefully." Proverbs 10:5

As a kernel of wheat goes through its cycle of life, so too does the believer in Christ. The term *germinate* is defined as, "to create, to cause, to come into existence." The kernel of wheat has already been shown to be symbolic of the believer in Christ. Thus the process of germination reminds me of the following truth:

> "Therefore if any man is in Christ, he is a new creature; the old things passed away; behold, new things have come." 2 Corinthians 5:17

As the seed of faith that God places in us germinates, the believer is reborn. Once just a dormant seed, now we are changed creatures and a tribute to the success and skill of God Almighty. Imagine new believers as seeds that mature into stalks of wheat ripe with opportunities to serve God. No two stalks of wheat are alike and each houses a unique number of seeds that is likened to the tasks and wonderful plans that God has for His children. God gives us the privilege of placing all the seeds in our stalk in the soil of His choice. After taking this step of faith, God does the rest. He calls upon us to labor in the field, but the resulting fruit is to His credit alone. When each kernel we were meant to sow has found its resting-place, our work on earth is finished. The shell or our body of flesh remains and turns to dust, just like the stalk of wheat minus the seeds. Meanwhile, our soul immediately flees to find refuge in God's presence; yet, the story of our life is not over. The seeds God has apportioned to each person will continue to burst forth in full bloom under God's creative direction and will continue to multiply beyond that which the mind of man can comprehend. Therefore, consider each gift God entrusts us with as a kernel of wheat – they are each a powerhouse of potential. Be faithful to labor in the field of God's choice, cast your seeds in God's appointed spot, and marvel at how God transforms a possibility into a reality. The greatest reward possible would be to hear similar words from our heavenly Father that two faithful servants received from the lips of their master in the book of Matthew:

"Well done, good and faithful slave; you were faithful with a few things, I will put you in charge of many things; enter into the joy of your master." Matthew 25:21

The sight of a field of amber waves of grain swaying from the warm breeze of a sunny summer day reminds me of worshipping the Lord. Some of us clap softly while others use a more lively approach. Both methods give Him the glory. Whether we are worshipping the Lord on the Sabbath, laboring in the fields of the world, or harvesting souls ripe and ready to become children of God – serving our Lord and doing His will is the food that provides fuel to sustain and grow our faith.

"And He was saying to them, 'The harvest is plentiful, but the laborers are few; therefore beseech the Lord of the harvest to send out laborers into His harvest.'" Luke 10:2

"Jesus said to them, 'My food is to do the will of Him who sent Me, and to accomplish His work.' Do you not say, 'There are yet four months, and *then* comes the harvest'? Behold, I say to you, lift up your eyes, and look on the fields, that they are white for harvest. Already he who reaps is receiving wages, and is gathering fruit for life eternal; that he who sows and he who reaps may rejoice together. For in this *case* the saying is true, 'One sows, and another reaps.' I sent you to reap that for which you have not labored; others have labored, and you have entered into their labor." John 4:34-38

Wheat as an Offering – Serving the Lord in some capacity, receiving His approval, knowing a reward is promised, and rejoicing in His presence, are all privileges available to the

44

faithful, diligent, willing child of God. A sweet reminder of why God's children qualify for blessings can be found by examining the Old Testament grain offerings. Leviticus Chapter Two discusses grain offerings of fine flour (from wheat or barley), mixed with oil, seasoned with salt, topped with frankincense, and free of yeast or honey. These were presented to the Lord as a tribute and reminder of His provisions of their daily food supply. Each ingredient highlights an aspect of the life of Christ:

> * The flour represents His well-balanced humanity and His willingness to be crushed for our sins.
> * The oil, as God's presence, symbolizes the Holy Spirit who overshadowed the Virgin. Mary at the incarnation. (Luke 1:35)
> * Salt is symbolic of Israel's covenant relationship with God.
> * The frankincense and the lack of yeast (symbolic of sin) declare the moral fragrance of His person.
> * The fiery sacrifice demonstrates His death on the cross.
> * The resulting sweet aroma rising heavenward proclaims His resurrection from the dead.

Jesus Christ – Wheat Supreme – Just as Jesus is the reason we are blessed, He is the necessary ingredient to perfect the quality of our efforts to please God. God provided all the children of Israel needed in the Promised Land to make a yummy loaf of bread:

> "For the Lord your God is bringing you into a good land, a land of brooks of **water**, of fountains and springs, flowing forth in valleys and hills; a land of **wheat** and **barley**, of vines and figs trees and pomegranates, a land of **olive oil** and **honey**...a land flowing with **milk** and honey." Deuteronomy 8:7-8 and 11:9

In Jesus we have all we need to do our best. Jesus, "the Bread of Life," is the spotless, unblemished, eternal Lamb of God. Therefore, all the ingredients of His bread are divinely pure, positively undefiled, and naturally in accordance to His perfect character. The wheat in His life-giving bread is stable and eternally resistant to decay. No modifications will ever be necessary and additives or artificial flavorings are never allowed. The nourishing value to mind, body, and soul goes beyond human comprehension. The bread Jesus offers cannot be bought or sold - rather He gives it as a gift to all that call upon His name. Those who partake will become so permeated with His presence that they will be living commercials and walking testimonies to the benefits of receiving His gift of life.

Factors Determining the Quality of our Bread - When purchasing wheat for whole grain bread baking, there are several factors to consider ensuring the best nutrition, texture, and flavor. These factors are organically certified wheat with strong gluten, high protein levels, and low moisture content. Either a lower gluten percentage in wheat, or a poor quality gluten result in either a crumbly texture and/or denser bread that tends to fall apart when making a sandwich. Grain kernels should be whole and not broken or cracked so that all the nutritional value will be protected and intact; thus, the oils will not become rancid due to oxidation as a result of exposure to the air. Wheat Montana Farms, a small family-owned-operated business, grows dependable wheat for the home bread-baker. Some kernels of wheat are planted, while others are destined to become flour for bread. A reliable source for purchasing wheat is necessary to bake the perfect loaf of bread. Likewise, Jesus provides the power to transform each miraculous kernel of "God-given-potential" into either a "spiritually" healthy loaf of bread (as in a believer's life) or fruit that will continue to multiply (as in good works that affect others). God provides the opportunities, Jesus supplies the power, and the Holy Spirit reminds us we are never alone! **Jesus is the reason believers are granted a season to reap the blessings of harvest time!**

Prayer:

Father God, You are the "Lord of the harvest." We call upon You to provide enough laborers to gather up every child of God and to cause every seed of potential to spring to new life. Harvest time requires a coming together of Your people, working as a team, laying aside differences, and accomplishing a common goal – to reap what has been sown.

Lord, strengthen and preserve Your people that we would have the power to do Your will. May the fruit of our labors be pleasing in Your sight. Praise to You Lord God, for when one person bypasses an opportunity You are faithful to provide another to finish the work for You are the "Lord of the harvest!" Amen.

"But do not let this one fact escape your notice, beloved, that with the Lord one day is as a thousand years, and a thousand years as one day. The Lord is not slow about His promise, as some count slowness, but is patient toward you, not wishing for any to perish but for all to come to repentance." 2 Peter 3:8-9

Jeanette Lavoie, R.N.

Devotional:

Praise – The character of Christ is our perfect example for godly living. Read Philippians 2:1-11

Confession – Just as the high fiber content of wheat cleanses the body, so too Jesus desires that we call upon Him to cleanse us of our sins. Before you confess your sins, try and quote 1 John 1:9 from memory. Now imagine, using all your senses, holding your sins in your hands and asking for forgiveness. Jesus, holy and pure, willingly picks up our disgusting, foul smelling sins. Jesus throws our sins into the depths of the sea, never brings them up again, and washes our hands until we are clean. Thank God Jesus is not afraid to get His hands dirty in an effort to purify God's children from all unrighteousness. God never refuses a sincere request for forgiveness no matter how big the sin – God can handle anything, so bring Him everything!

Thanksgiving – Given the proper environment, a kernel of wheat remains a fresh viable food source indefinitely. Once crushed, unprocessed wheat flour deteriorates rapidly. The kernel of wheat represents the believer in Christ (Matthew 3:12). Read Colossians 1:17, 2 Corinthians 4:7-10, and 2 Corinthians 4:16 and give thanks to God for His protection.

Intercession – Kernels of wheat are the seed part of the plant that springs to life once carefully planted, watered, and tended. Read through the "fruit of the Spirit," pick one that you need to work on, and pray for God's help to grow in that area. (See Galatians 5:22-25, Matthew 5:16, and 2 Corinthians 5:17)

Submission – In this category of prayer, you make the decision to submit to God's will for your life. The following is a sample of a prayer you might say: "Lord, let my heart's desire be to be more concerned about pleasing God than making myself or others feel happy." Spend time examining your life and consider how likely Jesus would be to say the words from Matthew 25:21, to you.

Chapter 4: Seeds to Sow

Tossing in a cupful of millet, sesame seeds, and the like into bread dough creates a crunchy texture pleasurable to the palate. The Word of God is like little seeds that God's people are meant to share with the world. They have the power to produce joy, change lives, and bear fruit as evidenced by people growing in their faith, belief, and trust in God. Those who sow these seeds of truth require God's power and patience as they labor in the fields of earth.

> "Now the parable is this: the seed is the word of God. And those beside the road are those who have heard; then the devil comes and takes away the word from their heart, so that they may not believe and be saved. And those on the rocky *soil are* those who, when they hear, receive the word with joy; and these have no *firm* root; they believe for a while, and in time of temptation fall away. And the *seed* which fell among the thorns, these are the ones who have heard, and as they go on their way they are choked with worries and riches and pleasures of *this* life, and bring no fruit to maturity. And the *seed* in the good soil, these are the ones who have heard the word in an honest and good heart, and hold it fast, and bear fruit with perseverance." Luke 8:11-15

Fruit - Seeds are the fruit of a plant or the product of one's labor. As they are scattered on the soil, the seeds will in turn yield fruit in due season. When a farmer plants his crops, he depends on many factors to produce a harvest. Proper soil conditions, skillful care, patience, and nature working with the timing of a symphony all play a role. In the beginning of King David's book of Psalms, God paints a portrait of a righteous man. In order to effectively sow gospel seeds, each person must first examine his/her own heart. Look to God's perfect timing for the fruit will not be ripe and ready until God says so. There are no shortcuts to reach to the finish of God's plan. The Holy Spirit quiets the heart with the assurance that fruit sown in the partnership with the Lord will yield greater blessings than that forced by the efforts of the flesh. Enjoying the process makes the waiting easier to tolerate while one waits for the fruit to ripen and the blessings to flow.

> "How blessed is the man who does not walk in the counsel of the wicked, nor stand in the path of sinners, nor sit in the seat of scoffers! But his delight is in the law of the Lord, and in His law he meditates day and night. And he will be like a tree firmly planted by streams of water, which yields its fruit in its season, and its leaf does not wither; and in whatever he does, he prospers." Psalms 1:1-3

> "Blessed is the man who trusts in the LORD and whose trust is the LORD. For he will be like a tree planted by the water, that extends its roots by a stream and will not fear when the heat comes; but its leaves will be green, and it will not be anxious in a year of drought nor cease to yield fruit." Jeremiah 17:7-8

The term "blessed" in the above passages is defined as "spiritually prosperous." Believers who depend on the Bible for guidance and who have confidence and trust in God will be genuinely rich in the ways that matter. Blessings are the fruit of sowing God's will. Such fruit is always good, pleasing, and perfect in God's sight. The writer of the book of Hebrews explains that perseverance precedes the fulfillment of God's promises; therefore, though the challenge of sowing seeds be severe, carry on, complete the task, do what God asks, and in due time God will deliver that which He has promised.

"For you have need of endurance, so that when you have done the will of God, you may receive what was promised." Hebrews 10:36

The prophet Jeremiah sends a warning to those who trust in fellow man, depend on self for strength, reject God's resources, and turn away from His will:

"Thus says the LORD, 'Cursed is the man who trusts in mankind and makes flesh his strength, and whose heart turns away from the LORD. For he will be like a bush in the desert and will not see when prosperity comes, but will live in stony wastes in the wilderness, a land of salt without inhabitant.'" Jeremiah 17:5-6

Planting God's will yields a lasting harvest. Sowing man's best efforts produces that which is cursed, barely noticeable, temporary, and eventually withers away like a desert bush.

Parable of the Sower - In Luke Chapter Eight Jesus spoke to a multitude of people using the parable of a sower who went out to sow his seed. Since the audience understood farming principles, this story captured their attention. In the parable, the sower is one who shares the Word of God. The soil is the human heart and the seed is the Word of God. The field is the world where four different kinds of soil are available for planting. Seed that falls on the roadside is trampled underfoot or gobbled up by the birds. This represents the person who rejects the truth before it has a chance to become absorbed into the soil of his/her hardened heart. Shallow-hearted is the best title for the rocky resting place of the next seed. These people joyfully hear the Word and then are quickly uprooted since their faith is not secure for a firm hold in turbulent times. The seed that fell amongst the thorns is in the cluttered, strangled heart that is too preoccupied with the pleasures, worries, and riches of this world to make room for God's seed of truth to flourish. Finally, good soil is found in the responsive heart that has been prepared by the Master Gardener (God). This individual is ready, eager, and willing to receive and accept the seed of God's Word.

God calls believers to spread the gospel to the ends of the earth. Expect a variety of responses along the way. Gardening is hard work! Watering, planting, weeding, pruning, and protecting against pests consumes a large portion of a farmer's day. Likewise, the magnitude of the task of sharing Christ with others can feel heavy and burdensome when one loses perspective. Acknowledging who is responsible for the outcome sustains faith and lightens the load.

> "And Jesus came up and spoke to them, saying, 'All authority has been given to Me in heaven and on earth. Go therefore and make disciples of all the nations, baptizing them in the name of the Father and the Son and the Holy Spirit, teaching them to observe all that I commanded you; and lo, I am with you always, even to the end of the age.'" Matthew 28:18-20

God's Victory - Barley and wheat are two seeds ground and used to bake bread. Both are included in God's description of the land set aside for the people of Israel. A curious story is mentioned from the life of Gideon as he spied the camp of Midian and overheard two of the enemies of Israel speaking concerning a loaf of barley bread:

> "...'Behold, I had a dream; a loaf of barley bread was tumbling into the camp of Midian, and it came to the tent and struck it so that it fell, and turned it upside down so that the tent lay flat.' And his friend answered and said, 'This is nothing less than the sword of Gideon the son of Joash, a man

of Israel; God has given Midian and all the camp
into his hand.'" Judges 7:13-14

God divinely placed Gideon within earshot of this
discussion. He had seen the tents of the enemy spread out in
the valley as numerous as a swarm of locusts. The
interpretation gave him confidence that God would give the
victory of the battle to the Israelites. In The Bible Knowledge
Commentary, by John F. Walvoord and Roy B. Zuck, they
state, "The barley bread aptly described the poverty-stricken
Israelites..." [1] They were poor by comparison; yet, none of that
mattered - the strength of God's right arm lay in the camp of the
Israelites. God's plan of attack no longer intimidated Gideon.
The Lord had previously told him to reduce his army from
32,000 men to 300! Now God informed Gideon that the battle
strategy called for the men to carry strange weapons of war -
trumpets to blow, pitchers of clay to smash, torches of light to
hold up high, and voices to cry out, "A sword of the Lord and for
Gideon." They confidently carried out the commands of the
Lord. Mass confusion, fear, and chaos filled the enemy. The
Midianites ran, crying out as they fled, and even turned on each
other with their swords. God's methods defy human
understanding, but His motives were clear from the beginning.
Underestimating the power of the Lord sets the stage for
defeat. Believing anything is possible with God as our general
builds faith. Victory recognized is victory possessed!

> "And the LORD said to Gideon, 'The people who
> are with you are too many for Me to give Midian
> into their hands, lest Israel become boastful,'
> saying' My own power has delivered me.'" Judges
> 7:2

Who gets the Glory - Gideon knew where the triumphal
glory belonged. Some New Testament saints forgot. The
people of Corinth boasted to one another regarding which man
God used to bring them to Christ. The Apostle Paul testified

that there was no room for pride in what man had done. God alone must be glorified!

> "I planted, Apollos watered, but God was causing the growth. So then neither the one who plants nor the one who waters is anything, but God who causes the growth. Now he who plants and he who waters are one; but each will receive his own reward according to his own labor. For we are **God's fellow workers**; you are God's field, God's building." 1 Corinthians 3:6-9

Fellow Workers – The Lord of the Harvest could accomplish His goals without us; yet, He chooses to allow His people be His partners in the process. As His personal representatives, God's children are called to make an appeal for the world to be reconciled to God through the message of Jesus Christ. The tasks He gives us are varied and uniquely suited to each person. Some people plant seeds of truth by preaching and teaching the gospel. Others water with care while meeting personal or spiritual needs. A high calling is bestowed on the warriors who sift their prayers into the soil of an otherwise impenetrable heart. Blessed indeed are the ones chosen to nurture the "good soil" of the heart receptive to the gospel. As His servants, what we sow we will reap. If we plant wheat, we will reap wheat and not rice. The same is true of the fruit of the Spirit. If we sow God's love, the bounty of the crop will be love. Those full of the joy of the Lord have the power to lift the downcast of spirit. An attitude of peace and trust in God will produce a calmness that defies human understanding. Patience teaches endurance. Kindness and a soft answer turn away wrath. Goodness, faithfulness, gentleness, and self-control reap blessings untold. Truth builds trust. These warnings from God's Word are worth pondering if one seeks to be fruitful in a spiritually barren land:

"Do not be deceived, God is not mocked; for whatever a man sows, this he will also reap. For the one who sows to his own flesh shall from the flesh reap corruption, but the one who sows to the Spirit shall from the Spirit reap eternal life. And let us not lose heart in doing good, for in due time we shall reap if we do not grow weary." Galatians 6:7-9

"According to what I have seen, those who plow iniquity and those who sow trouble harvest it." Job 4:8

"However, I consider my life worth nothing to me, if only I may finish the race and complete the task the Lord Jesus has given me - the task of testifying to the gospel of God's grace." Acts 20:24 NIV 2

Prayer:

Oh Lord, though the seed of our faith be small, You do not despise it. Oh patient, heavenly Father, You are the divine power source to us of everything pertaining to life and godliness. (See 2 Peter 1:3)

As Your children, we desire to be useful, effective, fruitful servants. Forgive us, Lord, when our doubts, fears, and selfish concerns interrupt the cycle of life and leave us barren and void of fruit.

Thank You, Lord Jesus, for dying for our sins, so that we are free to dwell in the land of promise and labor in fields yielding a lasting harvest. No matter what the condition of the field of souls, whether they are dry and in need of living water, cluttered with the weeds of worry and earthly concerns, laden with rocky stumbling blocks, or ripe and ready to harvest, we never work alone for You are with us.

May You cause the seed of faith You planted in our hearts to sprout and grow strong. Teach us how to sow the seeds You place under our care. By the mighty power of Your Word, Your children will produce spiritual offspring. For Your Word has the power to bring life into a spiritually barren heart. We give You all the glory for we know Your Word is true! Amen.

"For as the rain and the snow come down from heaven, and do not return there without watering the earth, and making it bear and sprout, and furnishing seed to the sower and bread to the eater; so shall My word be which goes forth from My mouth; it shall not return to Me empty, without accomplishing what I desire, and without succeeding *in the matter* for which I sent it." Isaiah 55: 10 -11

Devotional:

Praise – God gets the glory for everything good. Never underestimate the power of God to accomplish what seems to man as impossible! Read 1 Corinthians 3:6-9 and Philippians 4:13.

Confession – Examine your heart for areas of pride, for taking the credit instead of giving God the glory, and for rejecting God's best plan by considering ungodly advise. Read Jeremiah 17:5-8.

Thanksgiving – Read Isaiah 55:10-11 and Psalm 138:7-8 and thank God for keeping His promises.

Intercession – Believers are fellow workers with God. Working in partnership with God requires us to focus on the plan God has for us. Consider a task God has called you to do, meditate on Psalm 1:1-3, and add your own prayers to the following list:
1. Teach me to listen to wise counsel.
2. Give me the strength to reject the counsel of the wicked.
3. As I carry out God's plan, let me not run ahead or lag behind; rather, teach me to stay in synch with my Lord and King.
4. If I am bored or exhausted, reveal to me what I need to change about my daily schedule so that I may maintain a healthy balance of work and rest.
5. Strengthen me Lord; I do not want to wither my life away by failing to follow Your plan – I desire to bear fruit and to give You the glory!
6. Protect me from giving up when the going gets tough. Read Matthew 13:3-8. Only one-fourth of the seeds planted yielded a successful crop. God never said planting "spiritual" seeds would be easy!

Submission – Submit your time, talents, gifts, and resources for things of eternal value. We all want the "glorious" jobs, like leading a person ready to accept Jesus through the sinner's prayer; yet, God desires that we not neglect the "little" opportunities and the low profile jobs which play a significant part in the big picture. If today your friend does not come to Christ, but God enabled you to remove some "spiritual" weeds from that person's life – rejoice! As we are faithful to do our part, God will cause the increase in due time. Accept God's answers to your prayers and you will not be disappointed. Meditate on Galatians 6:7-9 and Acts 20:24 (NIV) as you pray.

Chapter 5: Living Water

In the baking of leavened bread, warm water activates yeast by causing it to spring to life, thus beginning the process of fermentation and the rising of bread. From a spiritual perspective, Jesus describes Himself as the source of a different kind of water that has the ultimate power over life and death.

Jesus said, "But whoever drinks of the water that I shall give him shall never thirst; but the water that I shall give him shall become in him a well of water springing up to eternal life." John 4:14

The water Jesus is speaking of represents the gift of eternal life that He offers to all mankind. Exploring the metaphor of water illustrates much more about God, His gift of life, and the guiding, penetrating, cleansing, restoring, reviving power of His presence.

Regular Water - All living things need to consume water daily for survival; yet, temporary satisfaction is all it can supply for thirst always returns. One can live for over forty days without food, but less than a week without water. The physical compound of water holds no power over spiritual life; yet, the lack thereof makes physical death inevitable. As for earthly wells, they have limits and the water level diminishes each time one draws out water.

Living Water - One drink quenches spiritual thirst for eternity. If we choose to partake of Jesus' living water, a well springs up in our lives filling the void in us with the presence of God's Spirit. This well is like none other and just as God's ocean of love can never be drained, neither can the well of living water ever run dry. Understanding the principles of water will shed light on the mysteries of God and His profound love for us.

Trinity – In his pamphlet, <u>The God of Israel: One God or Three?</u>, Mark Robinson states, "Our universe is essentially triune, consisting of three distinct but interrelated principles: time (beginning), space (heaven), and matter (earth). Everything in creation fits into one of these three categories."[1] By examining the structure, forms, properties, and uses of water, this illustration can be taken a step further to shed light on this dilemma: How can God be three Persons yet one Being? The analogy is that water is one substance, but can manifest itself in three very different forms - liquid, solid, and gas - and each has different properties. The triune God is much the same. The Father, Son, and Spirit manifest and work in different ways yet they are all of the same substance - God.

Molecular Structure - The one substance, water, is made up of a compound of three molecules, one oxygen and two hydrogen, whose chemical formula is displayed as H_2O. To me, the two hydrogen molecules symbolize the Father and the Spirit as they are both 100% God and 0% man. I liken

Jesus to the oxygen for He is 100% God and 100% man. He is the only one of the Godhead who came to earth in human form. Just as we cannot live without oxygen to breathe, so also are we unable to have eternal life without Jesus. Like the circle of a wedding ring, Jesus, as the O in the chemical formula for water, promises to keep His commitment to His bride (believers in Christ). When I am in the middle of Christ's circle of love, no one can get to me unless they go through Him first!

Liquid - The pure liquid form of water is wet, clear, odorless, and tasteless. Water found on earth often has suspended and dissolved impurities present making it unsuitable for consumption. Such water must be treated, filtered, and chlorinated to remove unwanted materials and to kill infectious microorganisms. Water in its pure form reminds me of the unseen Father God, His deity, and His love for us. He knew that just as we require water to survive, we needed to see His living water in action, so He showed us mercy by sending us His Son to walk on earth as a man and to demonstrate God through the senses of man.

"For God so loved the world, that He gave His only begotten Son, that whoever believes in Him should not perish, but have eternal life. For God did not send the Son into the world to judge the world, but that the world should be saved through Him." John 3:16-17

Solid - In the form of ice, water becomes hard and cold. As water freezes, the molecules move farther apart; thus water expands when frozen. To observe this process in action, fill a **disposable** plastic cup full of water, place it in the freezer, and watch the cup break from the pressure. I can grasp a piece of ice and hold it in my hand a while, but water slips away and cannot be held long. This image reminds me of Jesus. He took on human form to show us a tangible reality of who God is. At the cross, when Jesus became sin for us, God the Father and God the Spirit pulled away from Jesus like the molecules of water do when frozen. For the first, last, and only moment in time, God the Son was alone, for the Father cannot have sin in His presence. The cold signs of death and our sins held His body in the grave for three days. Then the warmth of life filled Him and He rose from the grave. The ice reflects the humanity of Christ, while the melting of ice back to liquid becomes living water and thus demonstrates His deity.

> "He [God the Father] made Him [Jesus] who knew no sin to be sin on our behalf, that we might become the righteousness of God in Him." 2 Corinthians 5:21

> "And about the ninth hour Jesus cried out with a loud voice, saying, 'Eli, Eli Lama sabachthani?' that is, 'My God, My God, why hast Thou forsaken Me?...And Jesus cried out again with a loud voice, and yielded up His spirit." Matthew 27:46, 50

In the book of John, Jesus declared His relationship with the Father and proclaimed His deity when He said, "I and the Father are one" (John 10:30). The word "one" literally means, "a unity, or, one essence." The Apostle Paul expounds on this truth in his letter to the Colossians: "And He [Jesus] is the image of the invisible God, the first born of all creation. For by Him all things were created, both in the heavens and on earth, visible and invisible, whether thrones or dominions or rulers or authorities - all things have been created by Him and for Him. And He is before all things, and in Him all things hold together" (Colossians 1:15-17). Jesus, the creator of **all** things, is the invisible God made visible!

Gas - Particles of water suspended in the air, such as steam, clouds, or fog, represent water in gas form. The gaseous state of water reminds me of the Spirit of God moving about freely in our lives. He is not held to the ocean nor bound to the ice caps, but able to go where the Father and the Son bid Him to go. Consider the water cycle in nature. Vapor condenses and comes down from the sky to the earth in frozen or liquid form and then rises back to the heavens by evaporation to repeat the whole process. You can feel the cool mist as it settles as tiny drops of water, but you cannot catch it, hold it in your hand, or confine it to a box - God the Spirit is much the same. Both the Holy Spirit and Jesus flow from the Father. Each member of the Trinity has different ways to communicate God's love; yet, the source or essence of deity is one and the same. In the past, the children of Israel observed God's presence as a visible cloud in the desert. The heat of the sun did not cause this cloud to evaporate and, neither will the Holy Spirit disappear once He has established residence in one's heart.

> Jesus said, "But I tell you the truth, it is to your advantage that I go away; for if I do not go away, the Helper shall not come to you; but if I go I will send Him to you. And He, when He comes, will convict the world concerning sin, and righteousness, and judgment; concerning sin, because they do not believe in Me; and concerning righteousness, because I go to the Father, and you no longer behold Me; and concerning judgment, because the ruler of this world has been judged...But when He, the Spirit of truth, comes, He will guide you into all truth; for He will not speak on His own initiative, but whatever He hears, He will speak; and He will disclose to you what is to come." John 16:7-11,13

Following God's presence - After God freed the Israelites from the bondage of Egypt, He led Moses and the people to set up camp near the Red Sea. "And the Lord was going before them in a pillar of cloud by day to lead them on the way, and in a pillar of fire by night to give them light, that they might travel by day and by night" (Exodus 13:21). The heart of

Pharaoh hardened as he regretted his decision to let his former slaves go. The army of Pharaoh then fled with their horses and chariots to chase after the people. Stricken with fear, the Israelites complained about their plight and lamented over God's battle strategy - for they appeared to be trapped between an impassable body of water and an angry army. God's spokesman, Moses, quieted the people's urge to grumble and prompted them to obey God's instructions.

"But Moses said to the people, 'Do not fear! Stand by and see the salvation of the Lord which He will accomplish for you today; for the Egyptians whom you have seen today, you will never see them again forever. The Lord will fight for you while you keep silent.' Then the Lord said to Moses, 'Why are you crying out to Me? Tell the sons of Israel to go forward.'" Exodus 14:13-15

Moses lifted up his staff, stretched forth his hands, and the sea divided, allowing the people to walk safely across on dry land. Symbolic of God's protection and heralding the imminent destruction of their enemies, God placed the pillar of fire and the cloud between the Israelites and the army of Pharaoh. God had the victory that day. The cloud by day and fire by night continued to be a visual manifestation of God's glorious, guiding presence during the subsequent forty years of wandering in the desert.

"Now on the day that the tabernacle was erected the cloud covered the tabernacle, the tent of the testimony, and in the evening it was like the appearance of fire over the tabernacle, until morning. So it was continuously; the cloud would cover it by day, and the appearance of fire by night. And whenever the cloud was lifted from over the tent, afterward the sons of Israel would then set out; and in the place where the cloud settled down, there the sons of Israel would

65

camp. At the command of the Lord the sons of Israel would set out, and at the command of the Lord they would camp; as long as the cloud settled over the tabernacle, they remained camped. Whether it was two days or a month or a year that the cloud lingered over the tabernacle, staying above it, the sons of Israel remained camped and did not set out; but when it was lifted, they did set out." Numbers 9:15-18, 22

If the cloud moved, they moved; if it stood still so, did they. Can you imagine setting up camp and not knowing whether you would stay in that spot two days or one year! Would you unpack your bags? If the cloud moved and you did not feel like packing, would you follow His leading and go anyway? It took many laps around Mount Sinai before the people learned to trust in God and went forward to possess the land that God had set aside for them. Are we any different? Drawing upon God's living water ensures that His purposes and promises will spring to life.

Effects of Water on Stone - As the waters of the deep wear away stones and its torrents wash away the dirt and dust of the earth, so too is the Lord able to penetrate the stony hearts of unbelievers. He destroys the rocky barriers that prevent His chosen ones from letting Him into their lives. Water cleanses the physical body, while the living water cleanses the soul.

Cleansing Property - The expression, "Little boys are noise with dirt on them" rings true. They often have sand spilling from their pockets, dried mud glued to their shoes, and sticky hands ready to receive a cookie. The outward body is easily washed with water and soap; however, the inward man requires living water and the Savior's bloody stain remover to cleanse sins. The Scribes and Pharisees of Jesus' day did not fool Him. To the world, they appeared to be holy, righteous, men of God; yet, the eyes of Jesus looked beneath the mask of beauty and found death and decay. The message of baptism illustrates a true picture of a changed life.

> "You blind guides, who strain out a gnat and swallow a camel! Woe to you, Scribes and Pharisees, hypocrites! For you clean the outside of the cup and of the dish, but inside they are full of robbery and self-indulgence. You blind Pharisee, first clean the inside of the cup and of the dish, so that the outside of it may become clean also. Woe to you, scribes and Pharisees, hypocrites! For you are like whitewashed tombs which on the outside appear beautiful, but inside they are full of dead men's bones and all uncleanness." Matthew 23:24-27

> "...God is light, and in Him there is no darkness at all. If we say that we have fellowship with Him and yet walk in the darkness, we lie and do not practice the truth; but if we walk in the light as He himself is in the light, we have fellowship with one another, and the blood of Jesus His Son cleanses us from all sin." 1 John 1:5-7

Baptism - Baptism by the Holy Spirit joins the believer to Jesus Christ, separating him/her from the old life and associating them with a new life. Water baptism symbolizes this truth. As we go down into the baptismal waters, we identify with His sufferings and death. Coming up out of the water reflects the resurrection of Jesus and the new life of which we make public testimony.

> "Or do you not know that all of us who have been baptized into Christ Jesus have been baptized into His death? Therefore we have been buried with Him through baptism into death, in order that as Christ was raised from the dead through the

glory of the Father, so we too might walk in newness of life. For if we have become united with Him in the likeness of His death, certainly we shall be also in the likeness of His resurrection, knowing this, that our old self was crucified with Him, that our body of sin might be done away with, that we should no longer be slaves to sin; for he who has died is freed from sin." Romans 6:3-7

Anyone can go through the waters of baptism, but the test of genuine faith becomes evident as we behold a person's life. Jesus, also called the "Word of God," longs to fill the hearts of His people with the full knowledge of God. As we allow the Word of God to wash us as water, a true cleansing within will be observed on the outside.

"Husbands, love your wives, just as Christ also loved the church and gave Himself up for her; that He might sanctify her, having cleansed her by the washing of the water with the word, that He might present to Himself the church in all her glory, having no spot or wrinkle or any such thing; but that she should be holy and blameless." Ephesians 5:25-27

Drink at the Quiet Waters - Like sheep, we are easily startled by the worries and concerns of the world. Praise to the Good Shepherd (Jesus) for providing a safe, comfortable, quiet sanctuary in prayer where we can come, drink, be filled, and have our soul restored. Nothing quenches physical thirst like pure water or spiritual dryness like living water. By comparison, earthly water is the dieter's guilt-free, zero-calorie choice while living water is rich in the flavor of God's grace, overflowing in mercy, and the key to guilt-free living.

"The Lord is my shepherd, I shall not want. He makes me lie down in green pastures; He leads me beside quiet waters. He restores my soul; He guides me in the paths of righteousness for His name's sake." Psalm 23:1-3

Planted by Streams of Water - When it comes to caring for plants, my forgetfulness ·often results in dried shriveled leaves and drooping flowers. I am always amazed at how a cup of water can improve their appearance. In the garden of the King, no living thing ever lacks for want of drink. His children get more than a sip of cool water. As we thirst after the knowledge of God, He will plant our roots by the streams; there we can soak up His Word as often as we choose in order to keep our spiritual water tank full. Our life with Jesus will be like a well-watered garden.

"How blessed is the man who does not walk in the counsel of the wicked, nor stand in the path of sinners, nor sit in the seat of scoffers! But his delight is in the law of the Lord, and in His law he meditates day and night. And he will be like a tree firmly planted by streams of water, which yields its fruit in its season, and its leaf does not wither; and in whatever he does he prospers." Psalms 1:1-3

A Cup of Kindness - By an act of kindness we can mimic God's goodness and demonstrate His love as Jesus did for the Samaritan woman He met at the well. He offered her a cup of living water without any prerequisite change in her life. While skeptical and questioning at first, she marveled at His responses and the water He offered began to come to life in her heart. She left her water pot, went into the city, and told the men, "Come, see a man who told me all the things that I have done; this is not the Christ, is it?" (John 4:29). Many lives were changed that day as the people accepted the gift and swallowed every last drop of the gospel truth. Be like the unselfish woman at the well and share the wealth with all who will listen. Bring your watering can filled with God's Word and sprinkle it with care wherever you go.

> "I [Paul] planted, Apollos watered, but God was causing the growth. So then neither the one who plants nor the one who waters is anything, but God who causes the growth. Now he who plants and he who waters are one; but each will receive his own reward according to his own labor. For we are God's fellow workers; you are God's field, God's building." 1 Corinthians 3:6-9

Once far away from God, His ocean of love swept me towards Himself. The more God revealed His love to me, the more secure I felt in His presence. Once cold as ice, God flooded my heart with warmth and kindness, melting my heart of resistance. Once my cup of sin looked clean on the outside, yet filthy and stained on the inside. By the mercy of God's only Begotten Son, Jesus thoroughly washed and cleansed my heart so that no spot or blemish remained for His discerning eyes to behold. Once I was alone; now God's Holy Spirit has taken up residence in the temple of my body. He is my Helper, Comforter, and the One who opens my eyes that I might distinguish right from wrong. As a channel guides water towards its destination, the Spirit directs me in all truth that I may reach the destiny of God's Promised Land. To God be the glory for the grace and blessings of today and the hopes awaiting my every tomorrow. Hope does not disappoint because His spirit of mercy has poured out the love of God within my heart. God withholds the judgment I deserve and showers me instead with His spirit of grace. He offers me what I could not earn - love and forgiveness for eternity.

> "I, Jesus, have sent My angel to testify to you these things for the churches. I am the root and the offspring of David, the bright morning star. And the Spirit and the bride say, 'Come.' And let the one who hears say, 'Come,' And let the one

who is thirsty come; let the one who wishes take the water of life without cost." Revelation 22:16-17

Jesus said, "...If any man is thirsty, let him come to Me and drink. He who believes in Me, as the Scripture said, 'From his innermost being shall flow rivers of living water.'" John 7:37-38

Prayer:

Most Sovereign Lord, man is often confused about the deity of Jesus Christ. Like driftwood floating aimlessly in a sea of opinions, some are never content to find a solid resting-place. Father God let Your Holy Spirit apply enough weight to the facts to secure the truth by the anchor of Your perfect Word. Lord Jesus, You are God manifested in the flesh who came to earth as an expression of the Father's love.

Lord Jesus, without You we would surely die in our sins and are like water spilled on the ground which cannot be gathered up again. Thanks be to God who desires that no one should perish. In Your divine wisdom, You give each one a glass of living water and leave us with choices. Take a sip, drink it all up, and take time to decide, or spill it on the ground. Praise God for teaching us that true love is never forced and is always willing to wait!

Lord Jesus, the living water You offer me is refreshing and inviting because You are the solid rock that keeps me cool when the pressures of life surround me. When life finds me floundering in a turbulent sea full of trials, revive me with the hope of Your promises, and remind me to drink deep and long from the well of water You placed inside me.

Lord, teach me to follow the cloud of Your Spirit as You direct my life. Anoint my pathway of choices by Your sweet presence that I might know the way. Sprinkle my life with salt to create a spiritual thirst within my soul that I might crave after Your living water and be satisfied. You make a way in the wilderness and provide a river oasis in the midst of my desert wasteland. Help me to run *to* You and not *from* You. I know You have a wonderful plan for my life, full of meaning and purpose, so help me stay on course with You. Teach me to worship You in such a way that my spirit will be like a sponge soaking up Your goodness, wisdom, and divine guidance - that I may discover Your will and follow Your leading. Make my crooked path straight. When I stray out from under the shadow of Your cloud, pull me back beneath Your umbrella of protection. Let Your presence go with me that I might find rest and let me forever echo the testimony of Moses when he said to You, "...If Thy presence does not go with us, do not lead us up from here." (Exodus 33:15). Amen.

Jeanette Lavoie, R.N.

Devotional:

Praise – Read John 4:14 and 2 Corinthians 5:21. Praise God for sending Jesus to be our Savior and the source of eternal life.

Confession – Are you ready to accept Jesus as your Savior today? If so, read Romans 10:8-11, pray, and God will satisfy your need. Do you have sins you desire to confess and be free of? Then read 1 John 1:5-9 and pray.

Thanksgiving – No matter how bad things seem, God is never without a plan. Read John 3:16-17 and thank God for His plan of salvation. Read Psalm 23 and thank God for His provision for all our needs.

Intercession – Spend time praying for family and friends who are not believers in Christ.

Remember to pray for Christian missionaries. Pray for wisdom to reach the lost, for strength to do their work, for a consistent profitable devotional life, for an awareness of God's presence in their life, for protection against illness, physical safety, and comfort in times of discouragement. Ask God to supply their financial needs and consider what God is calling you to do. Just because they are missionaries does not mean that their relationship with colleagues is perfect; therefore, pray for these relationships. Other areas of need are, for healthy marriages, wisdom in parenting, for strong friendships for single missionaries, and for older parents in the homeland.

Submission – Are you a believer in Christ that has not been baptized? Read Romans 6:3-7 and Matthew 28:18-20 and consider what God would have you do.

What is God asking you to do today? Are you willing to go with God? Are you tempted to run far from God's presence? Consider the testimony of Moses from Exodus 33:15 and pray as God leads.

Chapter 6: One Egg: Three Parts

Eggs give a golden color and add a cake-like texture to bread. They are commonly used in baking as a binder to hold the dough together. This is especially helpful in leavening grains low in gluten. Likewise, the Word of God binds together two undeniable truths: One, we are created in God's image. And two, in the miracle of creation, God acted as a plurality in unity.

> "Then God said, 'Let Us make man in Our image, according to Our likeness; and let them rule over the fish of the sea and over the birds of the sky and over the cattle and over all the earth, and over every creeping thing that creeps on the earth.' And God created man in His own image, in the image of God He created him; male and female He created them." Genesis 1:26-27

Which came first - the chicken or the egg? Scientists and philosophers have debated this subject for centuries. God is neither a chicken nor an egg; yet, the mystery of the Trinity and the question of life's beginnings are easier to explain by examining the parts of the incredible, edible egg! Just like God, the egg has three distinct and separate parts; yet, together they make up one egg. Each part of the egg has different ingredients, unique functions, and many uses.

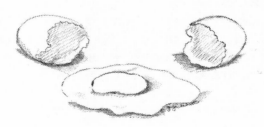

Shell - The chicken egg or ovum is encased in a white, hard, protective shell that prevents damage to the soft developing chick from the weight of the chicken's body during incubation. This reflects God the Father who completely surrounds and protects His maturing, growing child.

"Thou art my hiding place; Thou dost preserve me
from trouble; Thou dost surround me with songs
of deliverance. I will instruct you and teach you in
the way which you should go; I will counsel you
with My eye upon you." Psalm 32:7-8

Yolk - This perfectly round golden-yellow ball holds a rich, thick, gooey substance which is held together by a protective sack and provides nourishment for the developing egg. Puncturing the yolk of a fried egg and sopping up the liquid with a piece of bread is a common occurrence at breakfast tables around the world. Rich, creamy, sweet custard uses yolks for a glorious golden desert that slides down easily and is sure to satisfy hungry appetites. Both the shimmering sun in the sky and the yolk in the egg remind me of Jesus who was pierced for our iniquities and holds the key to eternal life in his nail-scarred hands.

"And this is eternal life, that they may know Thee,
the only true God, and Jesus Christ whom Thou
[the Father] hast sent." John 17:3

White - The albumen or egg white is the protein-containing, tasteless, low-calorie, additional food source for the developing chick. When making a fried egg, this part characteristically spreads out and fills the pan. Dieters enjoy guilt-free angel food cake since it requires only the whites for a divinely light, spongy, dessert treat. In like manner, once we declare our love for the Lord Jesus, the Holy Spirit fills the temple of our body and dwells in us from that day forward.

Sometimes we feel the presence of the Spirit and at other times He is barely noticeable; yet, He is always with us.

> "Or do you not know that your body is a temple of the Holy Spirit who is in you, whom you have from God, and that you are not your own? For you have been bought with a price: therefore glorify God in your body." 1 Corinthians 6:19-20

Airspace - There is a small airspace at one end of the egg between the shell and its contents. Perhaps an analogy would be that the airspace is the breath of life that God breathes into each new creation.

> "Then the Lord God formed man of dust from the ground, and breathed into his nostrils the breath of life; and man became a living being." Genesis 2:7

Prayer:

Praise to the one and only most awesome God, three in one - the Father, Son, and Spirit. The shell of Your all-encompassing love for us preceded our birth, for Your Word declares: "Thine eyes have seen my unformed substance; and in Thy book they were all written, the days that were ordained for me, when as yet there was not one of them" (Psalm 139:16). Your love is not hollow, for it is filled with that which is good and pure. Thanks be to Jesus for demonstrating God's love in human form and providing an answer for the burden of our sins and the yoke of our sufferings. As the yolk is in the middle of the egg, so too let Jesus be the center of our lives.

With gratitude we sing praises to God for allowing His children to be filled to the brim with the presence of His most Holy Spirit. Your patience and tender care toward us is undeserved; yet, we marvel at the grace and mercy You extend towards Your ungrateful brood of children as seen in the words of Jesus spoken through Matthew: "O Jerusalem, Jerusalem, who kills the prophets and stones those who are sent to her! How often I wanted to gather your children together, the way a hen gathers her chicks under her wings, and you were unwilling" (Matthew 23:37). We thank You Lord for Your gift of life and for Your unconditional love towards us. Amen.

Devotional:

Praise – The mystery of the Trinity is a concept which no one can fully comprehend. Search for yourself a few supporting Scriptures, find more on your own to compare, and ask God to help you discern the truth:

God the Father: 2 Peter 1:17

God the Son: Read John 1:1, John 8:58, John 10:30, and Revelations 22:7,12,13,20. Also, contrast Isaiah 45:21-24 with Philippians 2:5-11.

God the Holy Spirit: See Matthew 3:16-17, Luke 1:35, and Acts 5:3-4.

See the Father, Son, and Holy Spirit acting as one in creation in Genesis 1:26-27.

Review the following three passages, 1 Thessalonians 1:9-10, John 2:19-21, and Romans 8:11, and discover that all three had an active part in the resurrection of Christ.

Confession – Read what Jesus says about the people of Jerusalem in Matthew 23:37. As you lay your sins before God today, do not fear, for the words of Jesus are full of mercy, love, longing, and forgiveness.

Thanksgiving – Our God never loses sight of His children! Think of a personal example of how God surrounded you with His presence and protected you, kept you out of trouble, taught you something new, gave you wise counsel, and/or made you feel safe. As you read Psalm 32:7-8, thank God for surrounding yourself and loved ones with songs of deliverance!

Intercession – If there are things in Scripture that you do not understand or conflicts in the world that trouble your heart, pray for wisdom as you read James 1:5, Romans 11:33-36, Isaiah 55:8-9, and Romans 8:26-30.

Submission – The heart of Jesus broke as He spoke of the people, in Matthew 23:37, who killed the prophets God sent to them and were unwilling to allow Jesus to minister to them. Offering our petitions to God is called intercession. Letting go of our needs and allowing the Savior to provide comfort and support is an act of submission.

Chapter 7: The Milk of the Word

In the baking of leavened bread, milk can be substituted for honey, as lactose (milk sugar) is a food source for the yeast. Another benefit is that milk adds fat to keep bread fresh longer. Turning to a spiritual perspective, the milk of the Word is the foundation of new life in Christ Jesus.

Dipping my "Good Earth"® teabag into a cup of steaming water, I noticed a quote from Sir Winston Churchill on the tab. It read, "There is no finer investment for any community than putting milk into babies."[1] As the sole source of life for an infant, the supply of milk is necessary to the survival of the human race. Churchill's words set the stage for explaining what the Bible means when it uses the symbol of milk to describe the Word of God.

> "Therefore, putting aside all malice and all guile and hypocrisy and envy and all slander, like newborn babes, long for the pure milk of the word, that by it you may grow in respect to salvation, if you have tasted the kindness of the Lord." 1 Peter 2:1-3

Life-giving Essentials - The Apostle Peter extols the virtues of longing for the Word of God as babies hunger after their mother's milk. When an infant's stomach is empty, tears flow and crying fills the nursery until they taste their first drop of the warm, white liquid essential to their well-being. Baby's first food satisfies their total daily nutritional requirements to assure strong bones and a normal growth rate. In like manner, a foundation of the basic beginning elements of the Bible is the building blocks for discovering deeper truths. The milk of the Word is the Gospel message concerning Jesus. Peter stresses that these beliefs must be pure and not mixed up for spiritual growth to become evident. A new believer who feeds on the wholesome milk of God's Word will taste the kindness of the Lord. Those young in the faith can get sidetracked in distorted thinking if they spend more time listening to what others have to say about the Bible than researching truths for themselves. A group of early Christians were commended for checking out their preacher's teaching to make sure that what he said lined up with the Old Testament Scriptures.

> "And the brethren immediately sent Paul and Silas away by night to Berea; and when they arrived, they went into the synagogue of the Jews. Now these were more noble-minded than those in Thessalonica, for they received the word with great eagerness, examining the Scriptures daily, to see whether these things were so." Acts 17:10-11

First Things First - God promised Moses that He would lead the people of Israel into a good, spacious land. This implies there would be grassy fields to satisfy the cattle resulting in a bountiful production of rich milk. The second pledged food item was the abundance of honey. The order of these gifts is symbolic that first God would provide the essential and then the added extras. Moms have warned children throughout the centuries, "Eat your dinner or you will have no dessert." Mothers cannot be fooled! Those who sneak a sweet treat will be betrayed by the food remaining on their plate. Before the Israelites could taste the richness of the land, they needed to trust God like a baby who relies on his/her mother for milk. The first generation of Israelites were prohibited by God from entering into the Promised Land because they failed to believe God would enable them to conquer their powerful enemies and possess the land (Numbers 13-14). To make room for God, you must be willing to be like Joshua, Caleb, and the second generation of the Israelites who were willing to do what their parents were not; they chose to trust God and cross into the land of promise. The Father extends a similar invitation to all that would listen to His voice, respond positively to His message, and come to Him.

A Call to Salvation - The words of Isaiah Chapter 55 are a beautiful, poetic reminder that God's gifts are free and offered to all. Money spent on a counterfeit gospel is wasted. Listen to God and eat what He calls good. Give Him your ear and you will never be empty for His Words are always filling.

> "Ho! Every one who thirsts, come to the waters; and you who have no money come, buy and eat. Come, buy wine and milk without money and without cost. Why do you spend money for what is not bread, and your wages for what does not satisfy? Listen carefully to Me, and eat what is good, and delight yourself in abundance. Incline your ear and come to Me. Listen, that you may live; and I will make an everlasting covenant with you, according to the faithful mercies shown to David...Seek the LORD while He may be found; call upon Him while He is near. Let the wicked forsake his way, and the unrighteous man his thoughts; and let him return to the LORD, and He will have compassion on him; and to our God, for He will abundantly pardon. For My thoughts are not your thoughts, neither are your ways My ways, declares the LORD. For as the heavens are higher than the earth, so are My ways higher than your ways, and My thoughts than your thoughts. For as the rain and the snow come down from heaven, and do not return there without watering the earth, and making it bear and sprout, and furnishing seed to the sower and bread to the eater; so shall My word be which goes forth from My mouth; it shall not return to Me empty, without accomplishing what I desire, and without succeeding in the matter for which I sent it." Isaiah 55:1-3, 6-11

God desires to make the sullen deadness in the soul of an unbeliever come to life through the power of His Word. A friend seeking to put God first in her life proclaimed the following: "Since I have gone back to church, I feel a peace as never before. The extra measure of patience I have now surprises me!" Where once deafening silence resounded, now love, peace, joy and the like echoed in the depths of her heart.

Back to Basics - Reviewing the salvation message is food to the babe in Christ and a sweet reminder to the old timer to revisit the day he/she first tasted the kindness of the Lord. Gospel milk holds the key that saves all that believe. Mastering these concepts provides needed tools for the fledgling believer to share his/her newfound faith. To add, change, or complicate the truth heralds a stern warning from God.

> "Every word of God is tested; He is a shield to those who take refuge in Him. Do not add to His words lest He reprove you, and you be proved a liar." Proverbs 30:5-6

The simplicity of the message has the power to save even the youngest in years. The following is a summary of the main points and where you can find them in the Bible:

* Jesus is God. John 10:30; John 1:1
* God loves you. John 3:16-17
* Every human being has sinned and fallen short of God's perfect standard. Romans 3:23
* Jesus left His home in heaven to be born as a baby. Luke 1:26-35
* Jesus lived a perfect life and never sinned. 1Corinthians 5:21
* Jesus showed His love for us by being willing to take the punishment for our sins by dying on the cross. Jesus rose from the

dead on the third day. He is alive! 1
Corinthians 15:3-4
* If we believe in these basic truths, then we
are God's children. Romans 10:8-13
* Once we are the King's kids, He will never
desert us. Hebrews 13:5-6
* God forgives the sins of His children. 1 John
1:9

Food to Grow by - A newborn's sensitive digestive
system could not possibly tolerate steak and potatoes. Neither
would an adult be satisfied with a liquid diet for more than a few
days. As babies grow, the changes that their bodies undergo
prepare them to eat solid foods. To prolong them on a milk-
only diet past the allotted time would surely affect their growth.
The Apostle Paul expresses frustration with the stunted spiritual
growth of the church of Corinth, and the author of Hebrews
complains of much the same.

"And I, brethren, could not speak to you as to
spiritual men, but as to men of flesh, as to babes
in Christ. I gave you milk to drink, not solid food;
for you were not yet able to receive it. Indeed,
even now you are not yet able, for you are still
fleshly. For since there is jealousy and strife
among you, are you not fleshly, and are you not
walking like mere men?" 1 Corinthians 3:1-3

"For though by this time you ought to be teachers,
you have need again for someone to teach you
the elementary principles of the oracles of God,
and you have come to need milk and not solid
food. For everyone who partakes only of milk is
not accustomed to the word of righteousness for
he is a babe." Hebrews 5:12-13

The secret to spiritual maturity is to first build a solid foundation of the elementary teachings of the Gospel. Then, once this has been established, press upward to build precept upon precept. One of the participants in the *New Beginnings* class my husband is teaching presents a good case for these principles. "I felt funny joining your class at first because I have been a Christian for awhile. Yet, after I accepted Christ, I jumped into the middle of my Christianity. I imagined myself much like a Rubik's cube® turning in all different directions. I longed to gather myself together to be completely in line with God. I had learned a lot of information; however I needed a refresher class to go back and examine what I had learned. Only then could I make sure no essentials were missing, and review how all the pieces of the puzzle fit together."

God is the rewarder of those who diligently seek Him. Start at the beginning. Get involved with a New Believer's class. Ask lots of questions - never let fear or a limited knowledge of the Bible prevent you from asking questions. Use the Index in your Bible to hunt for passages that can answer questions you have on various subjects. And remember - there are no dumb questions. So ask away! And God will provide an answer for you.

King Solomon personifies wisdom in the Book of Proverbs. The wisdom of God speaks as a counselor and declares:

> "I love those who love me; and those who diligently seek me will find me." Proverbs 8:17

Prayer:

All-knowing heavenly Father, the words from the Bible are sweeter than honey for they have expressed Your invisible thoughts to us in written form. "Now to the King eternal, immortal, invisible, the only God, *be* honor and glory forever and ever" (1 Timothy 1:17).

Lord Jesus, the Scriptures declare that You are "the Word" (John 1:1) and that You are called "Emmanuel" which means "God is with us" (Isaiah 7:14 and Matthew 1:23). "And the Word became flesh, and dwelt among us, and we beheld His glory, glory as of the only begotten from the Father, full of grace and truth" (John 1:14). Thank You Lord Jesus for coming to earth to become the outward expression of God to mortal human beings, for Your Word proclaims:

> "No man has seen God at any time; the only begotten God, who is in the bosom of the Father, He has explained Him." John 1:18

> "And He is the image of the invisible God, the first-born of all creation." Colossians 1:15

When the disciples asked You to show them the Father, You said, "He who has seen Me has seen the Father" (John 14:9). Lord Jesus, like newborn babies long for the pure milk of the word, I thirst to know more of You each day. I believe You left

Your home in heaven to be born as a baby that we might see God in the flesh. You grew up to be a righteous man who never tasted sin – that You might show us the way of truth. Praise You for demonstrating Your love for us by dying for us while we were yet sinners (Romans 5:8). I believe that You rose from the grave and that You are alive! Thank You that all I have to do is ask and I can become Your child today. Like the chimes of church bells ringing over a hillside, let others see in my life and hear in my voice the joyful signs of a sweet new era beginning for me today. Amen.

"For God so loved the world, that He gave His only begotten Son, that whoever believes in Him should not perish, but have eternal life. For God did not send the Son into the world to judge the world, but that the world should be saved through Him. He who believes in Him is not judged; he who does not believe has been judged already, because he has not believed in the name of the only begotten Son of God." John 3:16-18

"But what does it say? 'THE WORD IS NEAR YOU, IN YOUR MOUTH AND IN YOUR HEART'—that is, the word of faith which we are preaching, that if you confess with your mouth Jesus as Lord, and believe in your heart that God raised Him from the dead, you shall be saved; for with the heart man believes, resulting in righteousness, and with the mouth he confesses, resulting in salvation. For the Scripture says, 'WHOEVER BELIEVES IN HIM WILL NOT BE DISAPPOINTED.' For there is no distinction between Jew and Greek; for the same Lord is Lord of all, abounding in riches for all who call upon Him; for 'WHOEVER WILL CALL UPON THE NAME OF THE LORD WILL BE SAVED.'" Romans 10:8-13

Devotional:

Praise – God is able to satisfy the soul that thirsts for Him. Read Psalm 63 in <u>The New American Standard Bible</u>, review the following outline of the passage, and spend time praising God.

> Psalm 63:1-4 - A desire which only God can fill.
> Psalm 63:5 – A decision to hunger for what God offers which will satisfy our needs.
> Psalm 63:6-8 – A devotion to God which becomes an all-consuming passion.

Confession – Verse five in the above passage describes "spiritual" satisfaction using the word marrow and fatness. Marrow is the soft, vascular, fatty tissue that fills the cavities of most bones. The chief function of marrow is to manufacture blood cells. Bones with marrow have vitality. Bones with dry marrow are dead. Keep these thoughts in mind as you read Ezekiel 37:1-14. The very dry bones in the prophet's vision reflect a hopeless, helpless state of affairs (see verse 11). God commanded Ezekiel to prophesy that He would resuscitate the captive Nation of Israel and bring them back to life (see verses 12-14). As you come to a time of confession, ponder these two thoughts: sin leaves us wanting like the lifeless, very dry bones. Only a passion and thirst for God can truly satisfy!

Thanksgiving – Read Psalm 63:7,9-11. Read these verses and discover that God gave this earthly King reason to rejoice! Add your own reasons to David's list as you pray.

Intercession –There is joy in the heart of our heavenly Father, when His children crave to know Him better. Take time to pray about your relationship with God. Who is God to you: a stranger, casual friend, intimate friend, best friend, and/or a respected, honored, heavenly Father? Whose words carry more weight, the advice of an earthly friend or the wisdom of

The Bread Lady's Quest

God recorded in Scripture? A hunger and thirst for God is a passion that requires time and energy to develop and nurture. Imagine various scenarios where a child chooses to cling to their parent's hand. As you bring your requests to God, use Psalm 63:8 and 1 Peter 2:1-3 as a guide to inspire you to cling passionately to the Lord.

Submission – Clinging to God's hand and allowing Him to lead you is an act of submission. Letting go of God's hand and choosing to find your own way is an act of the will. Whose hand are you holding? Which way are you going?

Chapter 8: Sweeter Than Honey

The sweetness of honey flavors bread and satisfies the appetite of yeast. As the process of fermentation continues, the flat piece of dough changes into a raised loaf of bread. In Psalm 19, Kind David extols the multiple transforming power of the Word of God. This master of poetry and song used a familiar metaphor to create an image capable of further illuminating the depth of his message. Perhaps, one day David reached into a beehive to partake of nature's sweetest food and the perfect illustration burst forth with these words:

> "The law of the LORD is perfect, restoring the soul; The testimony of the LORD is sure, making wise the simple. The precepts of the LORD are right, rejoicing the heart; the commandment of the LORD is pure, enlightening the eyes. The fear of the LORD is clean, enduring forever; the judgments of the LORD are true; they are righteous altogether. They are more desirable than gold, yes, than much fine gold; Sweeter also than honey and the drippings of the honeycomb. Moreover, by them Thy servant is warned; in keeping them there is great reward." Psalms 19:7-11

Fruitful Land - God repeatedly described the Promised Land of Canaan as "flowing with milk and honey" symbolizing its fruitfulness. The fields in ancient times must have been verdant with floral life for there to be an abundance of wild bees able to deposit honey among the rocks and trees. Honey is symbolic of whatever is pleasant and delectable. In contrast, milk is the figure of what is necessary nourishment rather than purely enjoyable. Appropriately, both milk and honey are used in Scripture to illustrate God's Word in both its life-giving essentials and its pleasant delights.

The Wonder of Honey - Reflecting on the glory of God in the mystery surrounding the manufacturing of honey gives testimony of the creator's handiwork. Mankind's attempts to substitute God's best with an artificial sweetener cannot fool most tastebuds. The products of the Lord cannot be duplicated and they each broadcast a silent yet evident demonstration of the splendor, creativity, and amazing talents of our awesome Jesus. Scripture declares, "All things came into being by Him, and apart from Him nothing came into being that has come into being" (John 1:3). The majestic creation is proof of an even more majestic creator, God. Bees alone were given the blueprint for honey. In a like manner, the Bible has been assembled by God to fit together with precise accuracy and purpose. When the men of old transcribed the Bible, they took care that every jot and tittle be copied without any mistakes. For each word recorded had a reason for being there. Just as each bee plays a part in the process of making honey, God directed the 66 Bible books to be penned by His chosen team of men. They each had different gifts, talents, and writing styles; yet, the message is knit together so well that the Master Editor (God) had to be the overseer of it all. In his book, <u>Evidence that Demands a Verdict</u>, Josh McDowell indicates that the Bible is unique because it involved forty authors and a span of 1600 years to complete.[1] Whether opening God's Word or a jar of honey, one can appreciate the patience and effort their creation took.

Molecular Structure and flavors - Honey is a viscous supersaturate sugar solution composed of 75% fructose (fruit sugar) and glucose in varying proportions. It has 17% water and the rest is a mixture of enzymes, oils, and other odds and ends. Carbohydrates are a quick source of fuel because they take less energy for the body to process and use. Nutritional information on labels of jars of honey proves they all contain pure 100% undefiled honey without additives or preservatives. Likewise, God proclaims His Word to be pure through and through; thus, it is worthy of our trust and enlightening to our eyes. Pediatricians warn new moms not to feed honey to their babies because, in its natural form, it can contain spores of a bacteria that are dangerous for infants under the age of one year; yet, it is completely harmless for adults and older children. This does not nullify the purity of honey; rather, it presses the point home that baby Christians first need a steady, firm, complete diet of the milk of the gospel before attempting to understand the richer passages.

When a spoon of processed sugar is compared with a spoonful of honey, there is no contest. Honey is twice as sweet and thus less of it is required to flavor baked goods. Golden gooey honey will cling to the sides of a measuring cup unless oil is measured in the same cup first. Likewise, the sweetness of God's priceless words stick to the soul of the one who spends time memorizing verses and treasuring them in his/her heart. The aftertaste of honey remains in the mouth longer than sugar as it coats the throat and fills the mouth with an explosion of flavor. Tasting the sweetness of the contents of the Bible takes God's children to the highest level of joy. God designed Scripture to fully satisfy His children so that we will lack for nothing if we look to His words to fill us. Examining the richness of God's Word is like finding a pot of Honey – God's gold – at the end and throughout God's rainbow book of promises. God's Word plus our life experiences, directed by His hand, work like the team effort of the honeybees to reveal His sweet love.

"And these things we write, so that our joy may be made complete." 1John 1:4

Teamwork - The honeybee is a social insect that can survive only as a member of a community. Laying eggs is the sole purpose of the queen bee. Drones are defenseless male bees that have no stinger. Their one function in life is to fertilize the queen. Sterile female workers are the guardians of the hive and fall into two categories. Young workers take on the domestic jobs of cleaning the hive, caring for the young, and building the honeycomb. Middle-aged field workers take on the more sophisticated task of collecting the pollen and nectar needed for making honey.

It is estimated that bees must visit two million or more flowers to collect enough nectar to make one pound of honey. Orchard farmers hire beekeepers to place hives amongst their blooming fruit trees. In an orange grove, as the worker bees go from blossom to blossom, they also gather and deposit pollen, which ensures fertilization by the process of pollination. The hive will be full of fragrant, orange-flavored honey, and the trees will yield a larger crop. This emulates God's promise that His Word will never return void and always multiplies and bears fruit when used properly.

Bees survive the winter as a result of the product of their labors. During each trip to the field, an individual bee collects nectar and pollen from just one kind of plant. Although they are deaf and mute, honeybees tell other workers the whereabouts of good sources of nectar by dancing in a certain way.[2] The scent of the pollen on the bee and the movement of the dance give clues as to the location and type of flower available.

Ed Brinkman is a beekeeper who sells honey at the Farmers Market in San Jose, California. He explains, "We place our hives near whatever type of plant is in season in order to offer many flavors."[3] It is hard to choose between raspberry, orange, sage, clover, eucalyptus, alfalfa, wildflower, and more. When asked if the bees have preferences, he replied, "If they are given a choice between clover and alfalfa, bees pick clover for obvious reasons. We have to force them to harvest nectar from alfalfa because every time they take in the sweet liquid, the flower bops them in the head!" Like the honeybee, mankind's human nature prefers to labor in fields where the reaping involves less pain and toil. By God's direction, as we labor in a difficult place and others follow by example, the work of our hands will produce a distinct "spiritual" fragrance. In all challenges of life we can be assured that we are not alone. God is with us and His precious word surrounds His children with strength for every task.

> "But thanks be to God, who always leads us in His triumph in Christ, and manifests through us the sweet aroma of the knowledge of Him in every place. For we are a fragrance of Christ to God among those who are being saved and among those who are perishing; to the one an aroma from death to death, to the other an aroma from life to life. And who is adequate for these things? For we are not like many, peddling the word of God, but as from sincerity, but as from God, we speak in Christ in the sight of God." 2 Corinthians 2:14-17

Sweet Protection - Nothing can harm the soul bathed in the sweetness of God's Word whose life's aim is to express the love of God through a life of obedience. In contrast, the world offers sugar- coated pills full of poison. The music of rock stars today speaks of sex, drugs, rebellion, despair and suicide. Laden with such bleak philosophies of life, nothing uplifting or positive can be found and lives have been prematurely lost to self-destructive behavior. God's Word is like a pure trustworthy love song written to protect us from false thinking, to keep us from the wrong path, and to uphold us when life's troubles threaten to make us faint with fear. In the book of Proverbs, wisdom is personified as a counselor. Wisdom speaks here and says: "My son, give attention to my words; incline your ear to my sayings. Do not let them depart from your sight; keep them in the midst of your heart. For they are life to those who find them, and health to all their whole body" (Proverbs 4:20-22). To read God's Word is to enter into His presence. To act on what He teaches allows us to step into the circle of His protection.

> "How sweet are Thy words to my taste! Yes, sweeter than honey to my mouth! From Thy

precepts I get understanding; therefore I hate every false way. Thy word is a lamp to my feet, and a light to my path. I have sworn, and I will confirm it, that I will keep Thy righteous ordinances. I am exceedingly afflicted; revive me, O LORD, according to Thy word. O accept the freewill offerings of my mouth, O LORD, and teach me Thine ordinances. My life is continually in my hand, yet I do not forget Thy law. The wicked have laid a snare for me, yet I have not gone astray from Thy precepts. I have inherited Thy testimonies forever, for they are the joy of my heart. I have inclined my heart to perform Thy statutes forever, even to the end." Psalms 119:103 -112

The sweet promise of Romans 8:1 extends a delectable assurance to the heart whenever past failures surface to haunt those forgiven by God's grace. Empowered by the honey of God's Word, embrace the sweet freedom that Jesus' sacrifice on the cross bought for His chosen ones: God's friendship, love, acceptance, and forgiveness. God's children will always be His "honey girls and boys" and nothing can tear His sweet love away from us!

"There is therefore now no condemnation for those who are in Christ Jesus. For the law of the Spirit of life in Christ Jesus has set you free from the law of sin and of death." Romans 8:1-2

The Perfection of Honey - Together, the components of milk (fat and protein) and honey (carbohydrates) comprise the three essential food types required for the human body to function. John the Baptist survived on a diet of wild honey and locusts. The law of the Lord, His will for us as revealed in Scripture, is connected to the adjective *perfect*. Webster's dictionary defines perfect as: "Being entirely without fault or defect (flawless); satisfying all requirements (accurate); corresponding to an ideal standard; faithfully reproducing the original (letter perfect), lacking no essential detail (complete); absolutely unequivocal (clearly leaving no doubt); of an extreme kind (unmitigated, being so definitely stated as to offer little chance of change or relief)."[4]

Covering all aspects of life, the perfection of God's Word is able to minister to our whole being. His reliable Word produces wisdom because it encompasses all the practical skills for everyday living. Imagine the power of allowing God's Word to reign so freely in our lives that we would be completely unhindered by our flesh. God's faithfulness would then produce the original letter-perfect image of God in us! Such a believer is a living, breathing sermon to the lost world.

To impact change in the lives of others, we must first place our faith in Christ and believe that Jesus can and will transform us. No one can boast perfection except God. The process of change is a minute-by-minute reality. Keeping the channels of our heart in tune with the frequency of God's Word allows His grace to redirect us when stuck on the station of the world or self. The Apostle Paul instructs the Church of Philippi concerning their obligations to follow Christ's example:

> "So then, my beloved, just as you have always obeyed, not as in my presence only, but now much more in my absence, work out your salvation with fear and trembling; for it is God who is at work in you, both to will and to work for His good pleasure. Do all things without grumbling or disputing; that you may prove yourselves to be blameless and innocent, children of God above reproach in the midst of a crooked and perverse generation, among whom you appear as lights in the world, holding fast the word of life, so that in the day of Christ I may have cause to glory

because I did not run in vain nor toil in vain."
Philippians 2:12-16

A Soothing Balm - A brew of hot water and lemon juice mixed with a generous spoonful of honey is an age-old remedy for soothing sore throats and taming a tickle in the back of the throat. If the Word of God had a label directing its use, it might read as follows:

Active ingredients: The living, breathing Words of the one and only true God.

Indications: "All Scripture is inspired by God and profitable for teaching, for reproof, for correction, for training in righteousness; that the man of God may be adequate, equipped for every good work" (2 Timothy 3:16-17).

Directions: Read daily or as often as necessary. Most useful if applied to daily life and memorized for quick, convenient access.

Warning: Use under the direction of the Great Physician (God) and the supervision of the Holy Spirit by prayerfully inviting Him to join the quiet times of studying His Word. Do not add to, change, or take His words out of context. "Every word of God is tested; He is a shield to those who take refuge in Him. Do not add to His words lest He reprove you, and you be proved a liar" (Proverbs 30:5-6). If problems persist or confusion remains, consult the counsel of godly men and women for additional prayer, support, and teaching. God's Word becomes sweeter as its usefulness and power is clarified. Keep within reach of children over the age of one (substitute milk for the younger ones).

Store: Treasure God's Word in your heart. Storing in hearts on fire for Jesus produces quicker, more lasting results than attempting to force them into hearts that are cold or lukewarm.

Source: Product of the triune God.

Distribution: All Christians are empowered by God and are directed to recognize the field of missionary possibilities.

Sharing God's Word with the lost is a privilege and a part of our job description.

Literally Sweet – In the book of Revelations, the Apostle John received instructions to consume a book of God's Words. Obediently, John went to the angel holding this book of judgment:

> "And I went to the angel, telling him to give me the little book. And he said to me, 'Take it, and eat it; and it will make your stomach bitter, but in your mouth it will be sweet as honey.' And I took the little book out of the angel's hand and ate it, and it was in my mouth sweet as honey; and when I had eaten it, my stomach was made bitter. And they said to me, 'you must prophesy again concerning the many peoples and nations and tongues and kings.'" Revelation 10:9-11

The prophet Jeremiah also received a message of woes, lamentations, and mourning because the people under his charge despised God's Word (Jeremiah 8:9). In contrast to the people who rejected God's stern message of judgment, he found the words, accepted (ate) them, and claimed it as a joy and delight because of His relationship with God.

> "Thy words were found and I ate them, and Thy words became for me a joy and the delight of my heart; for I have been called by Thy name, O Lord God of hosts." Jeremiah 15:16

When both men ate the Word of God, they symbolically received, absorbed, and processed the message as if it were food. The digestive process delivers food into the blood stream so the entire body can be nourished. As food is fuel to the body, the revelation of God's grace and the securities of His promises revive believers and sweeten lives. To the unbeliever, the pronouncement of consequences for sin produces a bitter response. Though God's Words may be pleasant to the taste, when they speak of judgment concerning sin they become bitter once digested. Blessings are welcomed and easy to swallow. If the revelation is chastisement, the result will feel heavy. Yielding to every bite of truth and every ounce of His will is always sweet in the end.

Too Much Honey - "Have you found honey? Eat only what you need, lest you have it in excess and vomit it…It is not good to eat much honey, nor is it glory to search out one's own glory. Like a city that is broken into and without walls is a man who has no control over his spirit." Proverbs 25:16,27-28

At first glance, this seems to be a strange proverb that King Solomon wrote because elsewhere we are exhorted to partake often of the honey of God's Word; however, filling our heads with the knowledge of God will not bear fruit if our motives are false. Feeding on knowledge for the sake of personal gain risks the sin of pride to run rampant in our lives. I have heard pastors give these two extremes: If you are too heavenly-minded, you may be of no earthly good. Likewise, if you are too earthly-minded you can be of no heavenly good. God is a God of order and balance and He demands the same of us. Better to know little and use it well than to know a lot and never use it in a practical way.

Taste and See - Bill has been a beekeeper for thirty years. In his family, they have three distinctly different reactions to bee stings. Bill tells this story, "When I get stung, I scream a little, a small red swollen spot forms at the sight, and it hurts for two to three minutes. My daughter has severe reactions and carries a syringe with an antidote to protect her against anaphylactic shock. At the age of eight, my son got a bee stuck underneath his protective head covering and it crawled all around his face. I instructed him to do what would have been hard for me, that is, 'hold very still while I slowly remove your hat and flick the bee off.' To this day, bee stings do not bother him at all."

Perhaps King David reacted similarly to the threat of worker bees guarding the hive as did Bill's son. As a shepherd boy, David deemed the risk of a bee sting no match for the craving he had for delicious, delightful, delectable honey. What obstacles stand in the way of your tasting the goodness of God's Word? Honey will not sweeten the bread unless taken out of the jar and spread. Likewise, we will never see God's goodness unless we try a taste and watch what happens. God's Word silences the voice of the accuser (Satan) causing him to shrink back in retreat.

When feeling faint over the security of your salvation, reach for a tall glass of gospel milk. To broaden understanding, dip your hand into the rich, deep, golden honey of God's Word. Let the jar of His delectable treasures flow into your heart so you will stand and testify to the truth of His message of Love.

"The angel of the LORD encamps around those who fear Him, and rescues them. O taste and see that the LORD is good; how blessed is the man who takes refuge in Him!" Psalm 34:7-8

Poem:

Sweeter than Honey
By Mary McSweeney
Used with Persmission

Sweeter than honey is God's book to me,
Full of blessed insights so pure and rich to see.
With His words in our heart we have nothing to fear.
Like honey to the soul, His wisdom we hold dear.

His precepts fill our hearts with love that is true.
As bees search for nectar, we find God in all we do.
Within the pages of the Bible you will find a home
That inspires and awakens like a busy honeycomb.

Prayer:

Thank You, Lord, that the Scriptures address all situations, answer any questions, comfort any pain or sorrow, and satisfy any sweet tooth. Across the oceans of time, Your Word is always relevant to any circumstance. It is sweet fuel to fight the fire, plentiful ammunition to battle the enemy, and the power source with which to gain victory.

Forgive us, Lord, when we forget to spend time reading the Bible. As a rainbow cannot be sustained without sunshine sprinkled with rain – so does neglecting Your Word weaken our faith and diminish our hope.

Pour the golden wisdom and Bible goodness into our hearts, O Lord, to secure the promise that our hope will not be cut off because our faith is not based on wishful thinking, but a sure thing! In a dry and weary land where there is no water and nothing yummy to eat, God You satisfy the soul that yearns for knowledge of God.

"If you say, 'See, we did not know this,' does He not consider it who weighs the hearts? And does He not know it who keeps your soul? And will He not render to man according to his work? My son, eat honey, for it is good, yes, the honey from the comb is sweet to your taste; know that wisdom is thus for your soul; if you find it, then there will be a future, and your hope will not be cut off." Proverbs 24:12-14

Heavenly Father, praise You that You treat us each as individuals. You know we all learn at different speeds and that comprehension varies from person to person. Let Your Holy Spirit guide us to take in only as much of Your Word daily as we can absorb, process, and practice.

Let us not be like the man who boasts of knowledge alone for such a one is like the cloud and wind without the rain. He cannot be fruitful or produce anything more than empty words.

When I am physically ill and only strong enough to read a few verses at a time, thank You for understanding and refreshing my soul even so. Amen.

"He who gives attention to the word shall find good, and blessed is he who trusts in the Lord. The wise in heart will be called discerning, and sweetness of speech increases persuasiveness. Understanding is a fountain of life to him who has it, but the discipline of fools is folly. The heart of the wise teaches his mouth, and adds persuasiveness to his lips. Pleasant words are a honeycomb, sweet to the soul and healing to the bones." Proverbs 16:20-24

"Therefore everyone who hears these words of Mine, and acts upon them, may be compared to a wise man, who built his house upon the rock. And the rain descended, and the floods came, and the winds blew, and burst against that house; and yet it did not fall, for it had been founded upon the rock. And everyone who hears these words of Mine, and does not act upon them, will be like a foolish man, who built his house upon the sand. And the rain descended, and the floods came, and the winds blew, and burst against that house; and it fell, and great was its fall." Matthew 7:24-27

Author's Personal Testimony of the Power of God's Word:

On a cold rainy day in January, 1994, fear gripped my heart like a vise and threatened to send me into a tailspin of anxiety. The first anniversary of my diagnosis of Bipolar Disorder drew near, and the return of some troubling symptoms cast my thoughts into past sorrows. My lips trembled as I noticed the water-stained Bible verse written on a 3x5 card and taped above my kitchen sink. I focused my eyes on the words, forced myself to read the verse out loud to aid my concentration, and inserted my name to personalize it.

"Do not fear, for I am with you [Jeanette]; do not anxiously look about you [Jeanette], for I am your God. I will strengthen you [Jeanette], surely I will help you [Jeanette], surely I will uphold you [Jeanette] with My righteous right hand." Isaiah 41:10

Like a special delivery Valentine from the lover of my soul, God placed the perfect message before me to calm me in that moment and to assure me of His loving, caring presence. Minutes later, I raced out of the front door to go and pick up my children from school. As I backed the car out of the driveway and then drove forward, a gigantic rainbow filled my field of vision with wonder and sealed God's promise of Isaiah as true for me. Later that month, twice I witnessed twin rainbows side by side. God's multicolored skyway love notes reminded me not to forget that His wondrous truths are always available to me; they have an answer for every question, and a comfort for every need! The great *I Am* who placed the bow in the sky holds me up with His righteous right hand. I know I am in His sure and tender grip because the Bible tells me so!

Jeanette Lavoie, R.N.

Devotional:

Praise – God loves us! The lover of our soul put His thoughts and feelings into words for us to read. The Holy Scripture tells the most romantic love story ever told. In honor of Valentine's Day, M and M's® say "I love you" in the colors that remind us of true love. White represents the purity of love, which is explained in 1 Corinthians Chapter 13. Red embodies the strength and power of an enduring, self-sacrificing love like none other. (See Ephesians 5:25-33 for details.) Pink is a combination of red and white which, when blended together, is sweeter than honey because it is the picture of the perfection of true love. (See Psalm 19:7-10) God's Words are sweeter than honey because they speak the truth and lack for nothing! Read the above verses, meditate on them, and tell God how much you love Him.

Confession – During this time of confession, read Psalm 19:11-14 and ask God to use Scripture to reveal hidden faults (sins of ignorance) and presumptuous sins (those that are deliberate violations). Consider the wisdom of Proverbs 30:5-6, be careful, and remember that God said what He said, as it stands for a reason.

Thanksgiving – Think of times when reading God's Word brought comfort, relief, direction, and/or joy. Have there been times when a memory verse flooded your mind at just the perfect time? Read 1 John 1:4 and Romans 8:1 and give thanks to God.

Intercession – Read Psalm 19:10 and Psalm 119:11. Ask God to allow your love for His precious Word to grow. Meditate on 2 Corinthians 2:14-17 and pray that you and other Christians will be the fragrance of Christ to a lost and dying world.

Submission – Read 1 John 4:7-21. Learning what God's love is like, how does it compare to the love you have found on earth? How does God's love compare to the love you have shown others? Have the words and actions of earthly love been satisfying or disappointing? God's love is unconditional. God's Word is true. God never lies or disappoints. God looks out for our best interest. Can you really say, "no," to a love like that? Is there a Scripture that you disagree with or has God asked you to complete a task that you have no desire or motivation to complete? Is there someone you should love, but you do not know how, or maybe you do not want to love him or her? God already knows what you are thinking, so tell Him what is on your mind and in your heart - do not hold anything back. Read Joshua 24:14-15 and decide today who you will serve; but as for me and my house, we will choose our loving, trustworthy heavenly Father who sticks to us like honey forever and ever.

Chapter 9: The Oil of God's Presence

Once again, the litany of the goodness spoken of regarding the land promised to the Jews includes yet another ingredient of bread, for it is called "a land of olive oil." Adding fat such as oil, butter, or vegetable shortening to dough creates a moist, rich-tasting, soft loaf. French breads, made with no fat, are dry and will begin to stale within a few hours because they lack moisture. Just as oil allows bread to remain fresh longer, the indwelling of God's Holy Spirit at work in the life of a believer keeps faith alive and new. The many faces of oil create a silhouette of the Trinity, demonstrate the functions of each person of the Godhead, and speak of the blessings of living in the presence of the Great *I AM*.

Anointing Leaders - In Bible times, kings, prophets, and priests were all consecrated or dedicated to God during a religious ceremony where their heads were anointed with oil. Only Jesus can claim to belong to all three categories of leaders. His title of Christ in the Greek and Messiah in the Hebrew means "The Anointed One," for He was set apart to fulfill the meaning of His name. Jesus means "Jehovah is Salvation."

> "And after being baptized, Jesus went up immediately from the water; and behold, the heavens were opened, and he saw the Spirit of God *descending* as a dove, and coming upon Him, and behold, a voice out of the heavens, saying, 'This is My beloved Son, in whom I am well pleased.'" Matthew 3:16-17

The word "descending" in the account of Jesus' baptism is defined as a consecration or dedication. The benediction from the Father and the anointing presence of the Holy Spirit began Christ's public ministry with a powerful demonstration of the Tri-unity of God. The joyous scene depicted here changed to sorrow in the garden.

Gethsemane - After Jesus and His disciples finished eating the Last Supper and singing a hymn, they went to Gethsemane in the Mount of Olives. The name means "oil press." Jesus retreated to this garden filled with olive trees to prepare for His imminent betrayal, suffering, and death on the cross. The men with Him were unable to follow Jesus' request to stay awake, watch, and pray with Him. Ultimately, Jesus was alone to face the cup of suffering representing God's grapes of wrath for the sins of all humanity.

> Jesus prayed, "Father, if Thou art willing, remove this cup from Me; yet not My will, but Thine be done." Luke 22:42

Then an angel from heaven appeared to Him, strengthening Him. The description of Jesus at this moment, as recorded by the physician Luke, is analogous to olives being pressed in order to release the expensive oil they hold. Jesus accepted the cost of healing mankind's broken relationship with God. The price tag was beyond human reach. No amount of money, no measure of good works, nor any sincere speech could suffice to pay the debt sins accrued. Thanks be to God for offering His immeasurably priceless free gift. Divine power enabled Jesus to fulfill the Father's request.

> "And being in agony He was praying very fervently; and His sweat became like drops of blood, falling down upon the ground." Luke 22:44

> "Surely our griefs He himself bore, and our sorrows He carried; yet we ourselves esteemed Him stricken, smitten of God, and afflicted. But He was pierced through for our transgressions, He was crushed for our iniquities; the chastening

111

for our well-being fell upon Him, and by His
scourging we are healed. All of us like sheep
have gone astray, each of us has turned to his
own way; but the Lord has caused the iniquity of
us all to fall on Him." Isaiah 53:4-6

The Power of the Spirit - Zechariah, an Old Testament
prophet, received a vision from the Lord. An angel asked him
to describe what he observed:

"...a lampstand all of gold with its bowl on the top
of it, and its seven lamps on it with seven spouts
belonging to each of the lamps which are on the
top of it; also two olive trees by it, one on the right
side of the bowl and the other on its left side.
Then I answered and said to the angel who was
speaking with me saying, 'What are these, my
lord?'" Zechariah 4:2b-4

The angel answered the question and Zechariah learned
that Zerrubbabel, a Jewish civic leader, would finish a Temple
to the Lord in this manner:

"...Not by might, nor by power, but by My Spirit,
says the Lord of hosts." Zechariah 4:6b

Examining the complete rendition of this vision suggests
that the oil (pouring from the fruit of the olive trees) which fills
the lamps is associated with the Holy Spirit. The Jewish priests
were responsible for keeping a perpetual light in the temple
lamps with clear, high quality olive oil, which burned with less
smoke than the cheaper kind. Zerrubbabel must have rejoiced
upon hearing that God's Holy Spirit would provide the oil in
abundance to keep the light of God's watchful eyes smiling on
this project dear to his heart. No mighty obstacle would be a
hindrance nor would human manpower accomplish the task; for

the all-sufficient Spirit of the living God would not let His lamp run dry!

The Light of the World - Consider an old-fashioned oil lamp as compared to how God's glorious light is spread. The lamp reflects the members of the kingdom of heaven, the fuel is the Holy Spirit, God the Father is the spark that lights the fire, and the resulting brightness illuminating the path is from Jesus who is "the Light of the World." His light draws us closer to Him and casts the darkness away to guard against our stumbling over obstacles. God's children are also given the same title and are commanded by Jesus not to hide their faith but instead to, "Let your light shine before men in such a way that they may see your good works, and glorify your Father who is in heaven" (Matthew 5:16).

> Jesus said, "...I am the light of the world; he who follows Me shall not walk in the darkness, but shall have the light of life." John 8:12

> "But the path of the righteous is like the light of dawn, that shines brighter and brighter until the full day. The way of the wicked is like darkness; they do not know over what they stumble." Proverbs 4:18-19

The Oil of Salvation – In the New Testament, Matthew records a parable that compares the kingdom of heaven to ten virgins who took their lamps and went to meet the bridegroom. Five prudent women took extra oil, while five foolish ladies did not. At midnight the bridegroom arrived to find five brides ready and waiting. The others were out searching to buy more oil. These foolish ones returned and found the wedding feast in progress. They sought admission but were denied entrance. The story ended with these words of warning from Jesus:

> "And later the other virgins also came, saying, 'Lord, lord, open up for us.' But he answered and said, 'Truly I say to you, I do not know you.' Be on the alert then, for you do not know the day nor the hour." Matthew 25:11-13

Though the passage does not specifically interpret the meaning of the oil, many commentators see it as representing the Holy Spirit and His work of salvation. Many profess a belief in the Savior; yet, God alone knows the heart. The lamp of God's salvation will never go out because the source of fuel is the bountiful, endless supply of the oil of His Holy Spirit. Praise to the Bridegroom, Jesus, for recognizing His own and for the invitation to be a part of His kingdom. Let us be found faithful and ready whenever He comes to take us home.

The Oil of Gladness - The oil of salvation precedes the oil of gladness. We could not discover the joy of living a life in partnership with God without Jesus first coming to conquer death and sin at the cross. The following Messianic prophecy mentions the Trinity in the first verse:

> "The Spirit of the Lord God is upon me [Jesus], because the LORD [God the Father] has anointed me to bring good news to the afflicted; He has sent me to bind up the brokenhearted, to proclaim liberty to captives, and freedom to prisoners; to proclaim the favorable year of the LORD." Isaiah 61:1-2a

Jesus quoted *only* the above portion of this passage while preaching in a synagogue in Nazareth and then proclaimed, "...Today this Scripture has been fulfilled in your hearing" (Luke 4:21). This implies that the rest of the prophecy is related to His Second Coming, and is as follows:

"And the day of vengeance of our God; to comfort all who mourn, to grant those who mourn in Zion, giving them a garland instead of ashes, the **oil of gladness** instead of mourning, the mantle of praise instead of a spirit of fainting. So they will be called oaks of righteousness, the planting of the LORD, that He may be glorified..." Isaiah 61:2b-3

The God of hope promises His anointed one, Jesus, will come again to exchange our mourning for the soothing, comforting oil of gladness. In place of the ashes, customarily put on one's head as a sign of mourning, we will wear a garland crown. That day will be a celebration of praise giving glory to God for we will learn the fullness of all that He has done. Without Christ, we are as dead as a stone bound to the roadways of earth. At the moment of salvation, God causes us to spring to life.

On Palm Sunday the people could not contain their joy as they cried out, "Blessed is the King who comes in the name of the Lord; peace in heaven and glory in the highest!" (Luke 19:38). They neglected to notice that when a King comes to conquer, he rides a horse; when he comes in peace, he rides a donkey. The Pharisees rebuked Jesus for allowing this display of worship. And He answered and said, "...I tell you, if these become silent, the stones will cry out!" (Luke 19:40) Unfortunately, the hearts of these people were not sincere. They wanted a King and not a suffering servant. Only "living stones" (those who have a personal relationship with God) are able to shout for joy for they know Jesus is both. The Apostle Peter calls us "living stones" (1 Peter 2:5). The laws of gravity no longer limit our thinking. Where once we were blinded, now we can see the marvelous fingerprints displaying God's handiwork. A stone is a lifeless object that is unable to move or make a sound on its own. Without God, we have as much power to create noise as a single stone resting on the desert sand. Men may reject believers, but God calls us chosen, precious, and alive with potential as we rest in His almighty hands. Dead stones remain silent and motionless. Living stones cannot be contained, will not be silent, and make a joyful noise as they move closer to each other and to their God!

"Therefore, putting aside all malice and all guile and hypocrisy and envy and all slander, like newborn babes, long for the pure milk of the word, that by it you may grow in respect to salvation, if you have tasted the kindness of the Lord. And coming to Him as to a living stone, rejected by men, but choice and precious in the sight of God, you also, as **living stones**, are being built up as a spiritual house for a holy priesthood, to offer up spiritual sacrifices acceptable to God through Jesus Christ. For this is contained in Scripture: 'BEHOLD I LAY IN ZION A CHOICE STONE, A PRECIOUS CORNER stone, AND HE WHO BELIEVES IN HIM SHALL NOT BE DISAPPOINTED.' This precious value, then, is for you who believe. But for those who disbelieve, 'THE STONE WHICH THE BUILDERS REJECTED, THIS BECAME THE VERY CORNER stone,' and, 'A STONE OF STUMBLING AND A ROCK OF OFFENSE'; for they stumble because they are disobedient to the word, and to this doom they were also appointed. but you are A CHOSEN RACE, A royal PRIESTHOOD, A HOLY NATION, A PEOPLE FOR God's OWN POSSESSION, that you may proclaim the excellencies of Him who has called you out of darkness into His marvelous light; for you once were NOT A PEOPLE, but now you are THE PEOPLE OF GOD; you had NOT RECEIVED MERCY, but now you have RECEIVED MERCY." 1 Peter 2:1-10

Sweet fellowship with God brings gladness. Sin, failure to spend time in prayer, neglecting the Scriptures, and/or difficult circumstances can cause a believer to pull away from God. The feeling that results is aptly described in the book of Job. In the midst of Job's sorrows, His deep longing for God and his desire to restore their previous relationship, is expressed here:

> "Oh that I were as in months gone by, as in the days when God watched over me; when His lamp shone over my head, and by His light I walked through darkness; as I was in the prime of my days, when the friendship of God was over my tent; when the Almighty was yet with me, and my children were around me; when my steps were bathed in butter, and the rock poured out for me streams of oil!" Job 29:2-6

Cream and olive oil are symbols of plenty. Job lacked the knowledge of why his spiritual, material, and physical prosperity appeared to have vanished like smoke in the light of the misery before him. His children, cattle, wealth, and health were gone. Only his wife (who suggested he "curse God and die"), three tormenting peers, and one young man were left. As if a lawyer building a case, Job defended his fine character in his lengthy last reply to his three older friends. "Then these three men ceased answering Job, because he was righteous in his own eyes" (Job 32:1). However, Elihu, a young witness to the entire confrontation between these men could not restrain himself. Scripture records the emotions that sparked these comments: "But the anger of Elihu the son of Barachel the Buzite, of the family of Ram burned; against Job his anger burned, because he justified himself before God. And his anger burned against his three friends because they had found no answer, and yet had condemned Job." Job 32:2-3

The wisdom of Elihu's speech highlighted these truths: God is greater than man is; He can do no wrong; He is aware of all things. The men of earth were plummeted into silence. Then God answered out of the whirlwind and built on what Elihu had said. Life is not always guaranteed to fill us with the fat of the land. Whether we are feasting on God's goodness - or if the butter of life's abundance has melted away - the love of God still speaks if we will unplug our ears and listen. Though dark clouds may surround and a slippery puddle lay ahead, know that God is still at work, always in charge, and forever on the throne.

> "God thunders with His voice wondrously, doing great things which we cannot comprehend." Job 37:5

Near the end of Job, four times God addresses Job as, "My servant Job." "And the LORD restored the fortunes of Job when he prayed for his friends, and the LORD increased all that Job had twofold" (Job 42:10). The secret to recovering his health and wealth did not come until he prayed. What God desires most is that we come to Him with all our needs.

The Shepherd's Oil - In Psalm 23, David pictures the Lord Jesus as a trustworthy shepherd. Philip Keller's book, <u>A Shepherd Looks at Psalm 23</u>, treats this passage with authoritative insights that the average urban dweller would never know. One insight is the use of oil to protect sheep from harmful insects and/or as a treatment for skin diseases.[1] These sensitive, easily frightened creatures cannot relax, sleep, eat, or drink freely unless ministered to by an ever-present, attentive, skillful, loving caretaker. The good shepherd anticipates every need and then spreads a feast before them to calmly enjoy in the face of danger.

> "Thou dost prepare a table before me in the presence of my enemies; Thou has anointed my head with oil; my cup overflows." Psalm 23:5

For a sheep, the enemy could be a real wolf. The danger believers face may be obvious or subtle. A minor twist of false doctrine can be accepted when it is clothed with an element of truth. Knowing the enemy is near creates fear, generates anxiety, and robs one of joy when a child of God forgets that the "Good Shepherd" is never caught off guard. Whether as lost and hurt as a wounded, isolated lamb, as meek as a sheep, or as stubborn as a ram, Jesus is prepared to act on our behalf. Experiencing God's anointing presence when surrounded by the trials of life causes the cup of joy to overflow. Jesus, our Deliverer, comes to the rescue as our weaknesses are exposed and our needs are placed into His care.

> "Surely goodness and loving-kindness will follow me all the days of my life, and I will dwell in the house of the Lord forever." Psalm 23:6

Healing Properties – Partaking of a balanced diet maintains healthy skin, for some fat is necessary to prevent dryness. Oil has long been used as a healing and moisturizing agent. When the rough winds of Winter leave skin dry and cracked, a small amount of olive oil softens and smoothes the discomfort. As oil penetrates through the top layers, it promotes healing.

In the parable of the Good Samaritan, Luke records the use of oil and wine to treat an injured man. This story of caring for a stranger in need with neighborly love and kindness patterns the character of Jesus, shows His heart for the lost and wounded, and illustrates the qualities He wants His children to emulate. The Good Samaritan, Jesus, and the injured man were outcasts and rejected by the Jewish leaders. Together they recognized what the Pharisees, Priests, and Levites disregarded - "...It is not those who are healthy who need a physician, but those who are sick" (Matthew 9:12). Jesus healed countless people who were hopelessly sick in mind or body, dined with sinners, and revived a few from the dead in order to give glory to God the Father. Yet the main focus of His first coming targeted the healing of sin and its effect on the human soul. John 3:16 is the most quoted verse of all time. However, the full impact is lost without including verses 17-18. Jesus earned the right to be the ultimate judge of the world when He took the punishment for our sins on the cross. He prefers we choose Him to be our Primary Physician as anything less permits Satan to behave like an **unlicensed** surgeon without the possibility of being sued for malpractice. As the "Great Physician" and the "Good Shepherd," Jesus is able to skillfully attend our every need because of His unconditional love.

> "For God so loved the world, that He gave His only begotten Son, that whoever believes in Him should not perish, but have eternal life. For God did not send the Son into the world to judge the world, but that the world should be saved through Him. He who believes in Him is not judged; he who does not believe has been judged already, because he has not believed in the name of the only begotten Son of God." John 3:16-18

Jesus the Great Physician - Jesus is the greatest physician because, as the creator, He understands the body and soul as no one else. He did not throw us together in a haphazard manner; rather, we were knitted together in our mother's womb with meaning, purpose, and tender care. The mold for each human being is unique and God kept each one for reference. Therefore, if a child is born with problems perplexing to man, God is not baffled and the diagnosis is always based in truth. A doting grandmother once said, "The doctor told me that my granddaughter would never draw a breath and most likely be a pure vegetable; however, he did not have a clue as to her potential. At thirteen months of age, I teased her and said, 'Grandma is too tired to read Bible stories tonight. Do you still want me to read to you?' Unable to speak from birth, my granddaughter made repeated quick movements with her eyes from me towards the bookcase that held God's precious words and back again. We will never know until heaven how much she understood in her short life, but the lessons she taught will remain in our hearts forever. Through this child, my eyes were opened to see God's power and my weakness. Her big gorgeous eyes were like a flashlight pointing me to God and helping me to understand that life is not in my control."

When this grandmother looked at her disabled granddaughter, she said, "I saw her as whole and complete. Others missed the radiance of the beauty God had built into her." The ultimate healing for this child came when her death brought her face-to-face with her Maker. No longer imprisoned by her body, she sees, hears, speaks, and leaps around the gardens of heaven having been completely saturated with the healing oil of God's presence and encompassed by the light and warmth of His radiant glory. One day, all God's children will receive this same freedom; thanks be to God for His gift of healing will be perfect in every way!

> "Thou wilt make known to me the path of life; in Thy presence is fullness of joy; in Thy right hand there are pleasures forever." Psalm 16:11

> "And I heard a loud voice from the throne, saying, 'Behold, the tabernacle of God is among men, and He shall dwell among them, and they shall be His people, and God Himself shall be among them, and He shall wipe away every tear from their eyes; and there shall no longer be any death; there shall no longer be any mourning, or crying, or pain; the first things have passed away.'"Revelation 21:3-4

Anointing by the Elders - The book of James contains the only verses, which directly address anointing the sick with oil by the elders of the church, for the purpose of seeking healing from God through prayers of faith.

> "Is anyone among you suffering? Let him pray. Is anyone cheerful? Let him sing praises. Is anyone among you sick? Let him call for the elders of the church, and let them pray over him, anointing him with oil in the name of the Lord; and the prayer offered in faith will restore the one who is sick, and the Lord will raise him up, and if he has committed sins, they will be forgiven him. Therefore, confess your sins to one another, and pray for one another, so that you may be healed. The effective prayer of a righteous man can accomplish much." James 5:13-16

Since there is no Biblical example, I will share from my personal experience. During a time in my life when I feared that an episode of my Bipolar Disorder threatened to surface, I turned to my doctor for medical attention and to the Elders of my church for anointing and prayer. If those who are sick do not take the initiative and let the Elders know, they will be unaware of the need. As the Elders expressed their caring concern and prayed for me, I felt a peace inside because they made it clear that I could call upon them at any time. Though I still have this condition, I believe that God really did hear the prayer of the Elders and that He is going to deal with my needs. I have already realized specific answers to my cry for help, especially in these areas of praise:

* Suffering has been my teacher to reach a deeper level of dependence on God than if I had no weaknesses to draw me to my knees.

* My medication keeps me stable, free from wild ups and downs, and without any return trips to the hospital since my diagnosis in 1993.

* Faithful friends hold me up with their prayers, letters, and visits when I feel like the cowardly Lion in the <u>Wizard of Oz</u> struggling to find my courage.

* God's power enables me to boldly witness of my past and present experience to those struggling with mental illness, especially to the women to whom I minister who suffer from postpartum depression and psychosis. The theme of my group, Christian Assistance for Postpartum, is a verse from Paul's second letter to the church of Corinth.

> "Blessed be the God and Father of our Lord Jesus Christ, the Father of mercies and God of all comfort; who comforts us in all our afflictions so that we may be able to comfort those who are in any affliction with the comfort with which we ourselves are comforted by God. For just as the sufferings of Christ are ours in abundance, so also our comfort is abundant through Christ." 2 Corinthians 1:3-4

I am blessed to finally be at the point where I can recognize how much more God uses me because of what I have been through than if all the days of my life had been bathed in butter. Sometimes God causes a tumor to miraculously disappear; other times he does not. Will God someday take me off of medication and free me of any bouts with mental illness in the future? I do not know, and maybe it does not matter. God has put me under the authority of my husband and my psychiatrist and they agree: "Let us not rock a boat that is sailing smoothly."

Mary's Expensive Gift - Six days before Jesus' death, Mary, the sister of Lazarus, broke an alabaster vial of costly aromatic oil in order to anoint the feet of Jesus. The fragrance of perfume filled the house. Judas, the betrayer, rebuked the waste by questioning, "Why was this perfume not sold for three hundred denarii [approximately a years wage], and given to poor people?" (John 12:5) Coming to Mary's defense, Jesus

123

replied that this act of loving devotion would be forever memorialized, "...Let her alone; why do you bother her? She has done a good deed to Me. For the poor you always have with you, and whenever you wish, you can do them good; but you do not always have Me. She has done what she could; she has anointed My body beforehand for the burial. And truly I say to you, wherever the gospel is preached in the whole world, that also which this woman has done shall be spoken in memory of her" (Mark 14:6-9).

Oil as Payment - God required the Jews to zealously give an annual tithe for the maintenance of their priests, the Levites. Three of the five provisions recorded for Ezra the Priest were ingredients in bread, thereby establishing the value and usefulness of wheat (400-600 bushels), oil (550 gallons), and salt (as needed) in the house of the Lord. Giving is most often thought of as being limited to finances. Reflecting on the concept of allowing the oil of God's Spirit to have His way in our lives is a form of tithing - for Jesus said, "If you love Me, you will keep My commandments" (John 14:15). When we do so, God is free to use our time, talents, and finances according to His good pleasure.

The Oil of Abundance - "Now a certain woman of the wives of the sons of the prophets cried out to Elisha, 'Your servant my husband is dead, and you know that your servant feared the LORD; and the creditor has come to take my two children to be his slaves.' And Elisha said to her, 'What shall I do for you? Tell me, what do you have in the house?' And she said, 'Your maidservant has nothing in the house except a jar of oil.' Then he said, 'Go, borrow vessels at large for yourself from all your neighbors, even empty vessels; *do not get a few.* And you shall go in and shut the door behind you and your sons, and pour out into all these vessels; and you shall set aside what is full.' So she went from him and shut the door behind her and her sons; they were bringing the vessels to her and she poured. And it came about when the vessels were full, that she said to her son, 'Bring me another vessel.' And he said to her, 'There is not one vessel more.' And the oil stopped. Then she came and told the man of God. And he said, 'Go, sell the oil and pay your debt, and you and your sons can live on the rest.'" 2 Kings 4:1-7

The prophet immediately responded to this frantic woman, calmed her with a task, and instructed her regarding the outcome. The rich life lessons that can be gleaned from this story are:

* Little becomes much if God is in it. She had nothing to begin with except a jar of oil.

* God's solution **always** requires us to exercise our faith as we trust in Jehovah Jireh; the Lord provides for those who acknowledge their dependence on Him.

* Our Lord wants us to offer Him our empty vessels, so He can fill them to overflowing. God's supply met her need and was as large as the woman's faith and obedience.

*Trusting God while living in abundance is easy. Doing the same in times of wanting is a stretch of faith. How many empty jars will you believe God to fill?

Prayer:

Amidst a stormy trial, Lord, make my life flow smoothly and undisturbed, like a river of oil. You are my captain, my champion, and my hero. Whether You shower me with blessings or teach me lessons during times of wanting; let me worship as Job did at the *start* of his sorrows and echo his amazing words, "...'Naked I came from my mother's womb, and naked I shall return there. The LORD gave and the LORD has taken away. Blessed be the name of the LORD.' Through all this Job did not sin nor did he blame God" (Job 1:21-22). Amen.

Prayer inspired by a grandmother's wisdom:

Dear Jesus, healer of my soul, use the oil of Your love to soften the callous hearts of my unbelieving friends and confounded doctors. Allow the soothing balm of the Holy Spirit to penetrate deep into my soul and change my life that I may become more like You. Praise You, oh Lord, for using a precious life that some deemed useless as a tool to sharpen a young grandmother's faith in a mighty God. As King Solomon proclaims in Ecclesiastes 3:1, "There is an appointed time for everything. And there is a time for every event under heaven." God, You hold the key to the meaning of each one of life's mysteries. You give wisdom to assist my mind in decision-making; You surround me with songs of deliverance to provide hope in times of need; Your comfort has healed my broken heart. I rejoice for giving one grandmother the wisdom to say, "Life is a performance for which I never had the opportunity to rehearse." Continue to train my eyes to see Your plan unfolding in the middle of any circumstance no matter how dark it seems. Praise to my Lord, the greatest physician, for You have a plan, You know which is the best treatment for me, and the end is not a mystery to You. "For Thou didst form my inward parts; Thou didst weave me in my mother's womb. I will give thanks to Thee, for I am fearfully and wonderfully made; wonderful are Thy works, and my soul knows it very well. My frame was not hidden from Thee, when I was made in secret, and skillfully wrought in the depths of the earth. Thine eyes have seen my unformed substance; and in Thy book they were all written, the days that were ordained for me, when as yet there was not one of them" (Psalm 139:13-16). Amen.

Devotional:

Introduction – Psalm 46 paints a picture of God being a very present help in times of trouble. Emotional, physical, or spiritual needs place believers on a faith journey to discover more of Jesus. In this quest, we long to find the Promised Land – a place where we can taste, in a practical way, what John 6:35 means in everyday living. The answer is not struggling to travel *to* God's presence, but to recognize believers travel *in* His presence. Distracted by the storms of life, feeling spiritually dry and alone are common complaints. God calls us to experience His presence in a deeper way as we come, pray, relax, and rest under His tender care. Oil sticks to a baker's hands when making bread and the skin soaks up the excess. In the same way, Jesus promises to always stay very close to His children, especially when danger is near. The illustration for the chapter, "The Oil of God's Presence," depicts the fact that our needs cannot exhaust God's divine power supply. As you meditate on Psalm 46 and pray in Jesus name, may God open your eyes of faith to experience how near and dear is God's help to us.

> May the oil of God's presence surround you with such power that the potent fragrance will choke the life out of the enemy!

Praise – The quality and quantity of time spent praising God sets the tone for the rest of the prayer time. In our home, my husband is the only one who loves board games. I spoil his fun by taking my turn, getting up, and saying, "I'll be right back." How often we approach praising God with the same distracted attitude. Burdens and prayer requests roll off the tongue in a steady stream; however, it is at the level of praise that God's power can break through in the most dramatic way. Set your trouble down, focus on Psalm 46:1, and add to these list of praises:

1. God is my refuge. No matter where I am, God provides shelter and peace amidst the storm.
2. God is my strength. Whatever circumstances I am in right now…I praise God because He can handle any situation:

Praise You God for remaining close to me as I struggle, instead of helping from a distance. Lord, whether I see You working on my behalf or not, I praise You anyway! God's power is unleashed amidst the praises of His people! Let us praise the Lord!

Confession – Read Psalm 46:2-7. The word, therefore, at the beginning of verse 2 is there for a reason. Since Psalm 46:1 is true, why is fear the most common reaction to life's troubles? Fear is the by-product of unbelief. Review this passage, search for God's reasons not to be afraid, and ask God to forgive any unbelief. The following prayer may be used as a guide.

The Holy Scriptures grant assurance to the faint of heart. Though catastrophic events occur, God's presence surrounds believers like a peaceful river; yet, my heart trembles with fear. God, forgive my unbelief. Revive my faith, Lord, and help me to remember:
DO NOT BE AFRAID – for there is nothing to fear!
DO NOT WORRY – for God can handle anything!
DO NOT BE CONCERNED ABOUT THINGS WHICH ARE NOT UNDER MY CONTROL – for there are problems only God is equipped to fix!

Forgive me, Lord, when I try to take over Your job. I can think of so many ways to deal with problems, but these plans fail because sometimes only You know what is broken. Thank You that I can find forgiveness and mercy in Your place of refuge, because Jesus died for my sins and rose victoriously from the dead. Grant me victory over my unbelief, in Jesus' mighty name. Amen.

Thanksgiving – Psalm 46:8-9 beckons believers to behold God accomplishing the impossible. Who else makes wars cease, enemies live in peace, and destroys weapons of destruction? Make a mental picture of a perilous situation. Imagine the oil of God's presence surrounding this trouble like a frame. Reflect on the promise that "all" is safe and secure in God's presence. May God use the following prayer to bring rest, relief, peace, rejoicing, and expressions of thanks.

Oh Lord, when the troubles of life seek to overwhelm me, thank You for Your ever-present help. Thank You for hearing my prayers, for lifting my burdens, for showering me with the gift of hope. Dear Lord, as I sit and wait on You, in the midst of these horrible circumstances, I remember another time when my hope vanished from sight – then – suddenly – my God broke through and everything changed forever! When my God moves, my circumstances do not have a chance! Forever will I be grateful that I have a BIG GOD!

Thank You for sending family and friends filled with words of comfort and wisdom. They tell me, "Things are not so bad; God is at work." Thank You God for filling my life with people who can see positive changes before I feel a difference. Thank You God for progress! In the name of Jesus, who is my wonderful, counselor, and mighty God! Amen.

Intercession – Psalm 46:10 begins with "cease striving" in the New American Standard Bible and "be still" in the New International Version. To strive and to be still are two opposing qualities. Words linked to the former are silence, at rest, motionless, and tranquility. The latter carries action verbs such as to quarrel; to struggle; to put forth-great effort to win a battle; or to fight against oppression. Be careful how you submit prayer requests in troubled times. Read Psalm 46:10 and take God's advice. Prayers which focus on the problem alone magnify the struggle and stimulate mental exercises to fervently labor in our own strength in an effort to find a solution. There is a key to finding rest and peace as we speak to the God whose voice causes the earth to melt; link each stressful detail with what we know to be true about God. The following outline gives examples to use in prayer:

1. My fervent prayers for this situation feel like the pangs of childbirth as I long for this pain to be gone so new life and joy can begin. (God knows all the details. God knows more than you know.) Dear Lord, though there may be no quick solution, You make wars on earth to cease; therefore, in Jesus' name, I ask You to clear my mind of the clutter of worry and win this raging war in my head. I place my "unquiet" mind in Your hands to become still by the power of Your presence.

2. Lord God, You speak to me not in an audible voice, but in impressions of the heart and mind as I read Your Word. Keep me quiet Lord so I can hear Your so-called "still small voice" guiding me. In troubled times You command me to behold the works of the Lord, cease striving, and know God. Help me honor these requests. In the rest of the passage, the words spoken as facts rather than commands amaze and thrill my heart. God's help is available. God is with us. We will not fear. We will not be moved. Oh Lord, I trust, in the name of Jesus, that Psalm 46 will become more than just words on a page, but the answer to my prayers.

Submission – In the midst of a depressing situation, the simplicity of saying, "Just let go of your burdens and silently trust in God's saving power," is hard to grasp. Worry tempts me to peer through a microscope called "details of trouble." The two identical verses in Psalm 46 (7 and 11) provide God's telescope of hope to enable the discouraged to peek up, out, and over the problem to catch a glimpse of God's point of reference. First, the God who commands the armies of heaven is with us. Second, the same God that Jacob believed in is our stronghold. Psalm 46:1 used the word refuge to indicate God provides shelter or protection from danger. A stronghold takes this meaning a step further. Fortified and having strong defenses, a stronghold is where a group of people, having certain views, attitudes, etc., congregate together. Are you unable to "be still" and give everything to God? Then you may still be lacking hope. The power to hope, the peace to be still, and the faith to believe are gifts which God gives to those who ask. So ask, and God will give you the strength to leave both your cares and worries at the foot of the cross.

> "Now may the God of hope fill you with all joy and peace in believing, that you may abound in hope by the power of the Holy Spirit." Romans 15:13

Chapter 10: The Salt of the Earth

Though optional in bread, salt is more than just a flavor enhancer. Too much salt leaves a bitter quality and inhibits yeast activity. Too little salt creates flat-tasting bread. One day I decided to leave the salt out of my bread dough. Such an omission had never presented a problem while baking cookies, zucchini bread, and the like; however, I never repeated this error again for I learned that salt inhibits the rising of the bread dough. The effect would not have been as obvious with the old-fashioned method of making bread by hand. My bread machine speeds up the process by kneading the finished dough on a higher speed for six minutes. This fully develops the gluten in the wheat, so that it will quickly become stretchy like a balloon and able to capture the carbon dioxide bubbles produced by the hungry yeast, causing the dough to rise. Only a relatively small amount of salt (1/2 Tablespoon) is required to slow the rising dough (8 pounds) in order to keep yeast (3 Tablespoons) under control. Leaving the salt out of the recipe allowed the yeast to go wild. As I attempted to form orderly loaves of bread, by squishing excess bubbles out, the dough refused to comply. The bread smelled as delightful as usual, but the finished loaves were lumpy and many slices had gaping holes in them. Eating a peanut butter sandwich with this unsightly bread created a gooey, sticky mess. Next time you slice through a loaf of French bread and find a big hole, remember - yeast is the beast responsible and either the bread baker did not form the loaves well or someone forgot to add the salt!

The spiritual application here is that yeast is a symbol of sin, and salt is the power God gives us to say "no" to sin and "yes" to His plan for our lives. Without including God's potent salt, we have nothing available but self to season our witness. If God is not involved, the outcome will be bland and ineffective. If God is on the throne of our lives, our testimony will be rich with flavor, oozing with potential, filled with His creative touch, and free to always draw upon His unlimited resources for help. Why are we so blessed? Because God has made a covenant with His people.

The properties, uses, and effect salt has on the earth and in the art of bread baking describes the spiritual reaction that occurs from the relationship God has with His children. Salt has long been useful for preserving food. When Vitamin C is added to a batch of bread, it also keeps the bread fresh longer. Therefore, both salt and Vitamin C portray a spiritual image of the effect of God's moral preservation on His people. As the Holy Spirit works in the life of a believer, God exerts His Fatherly discipline to protect His children from "going bad." By the time we reach heaven, the spoiled brat within the flesh of each of the King's children will be tamed.

As an antidote for corruption, the salt pouring from God's heavenly salt shaker makes us thirsty to overcome impurities and hungry to let God finish the work He began at our second birth. This salt becomes the crystallized evidence that God preserves, as proof that the character of Christ is played out in the life of each genuine believer.

> "For I am confident of this very thing, that He who
> began a good work in you will perfect it until the
> day of Christ Jesus." Philippians 1:6

The Chemical Compound of Salt - The process whereby salt is derived from the combination of two opposing elements opens the door to help us understand how the salt of Christ's character can empower a believer to live a life pleasing to God. The chemical compound for ordinary table salt is formed by the combination of two opposite substances, an acid (HCl) and a base ($NaOH$). When the two mix together, they produce salt ($NaCl$) and water (HOH). The reaction occurs because of the attraction between the negative hydroxyl ions ($OH-$) and the positive hydrogen ions ($H+$) leaving the negative chlorine ions (Cl-) and the positive sodium ions (Na+) to combine. Once completed, the process is irreversible because of the character of water. As the water evaporates, the crystallized salt is formed and then harvested for use.

Combining these thoughts together is reminiscent of the process that occurs when any human being gravitates towards God and welcomes Him to enter his/her life. A holy, perfect, and sinless (positive) God then willingly steps into the heart of a sinful (negative) people because of His unconditional love. Even though every human being falls short of perfection, God does not hold that against us. We are God's opposite, yet He makes a permanent commitment to His children for eternity and pledges His undying love! The reason for the security of this union lies in the character of God. Jesus did not wait until we were worthy enough to love before He sacrificed His life. The first line in the song, "Amazing Grace," sums up the fact that Jesus lovingly and willingly died for the wretchedness in us all. "Amazing grace! How sweet the sound - that saved a wretch like me!" [1]

"But God demonstrates His own love toward us, in that while we were yet sinners, Christ died for us." Romans 5:8

"Draw near to God and He will draw near to you..." James 4:8

Creates a Thirst - Salt enhances the flavor of foods and stimulates the need to drink fluids to balance the sodium level in the blood stream. As followers of Christ, we are titled "the salt of the earth." This means we are called to holy living.

"Blessed be the God and Father of our Lord Jesus Christ, who has blessed us with every spiritual blessing in the heavenly places in Christ, just as He chose us in Him before the foundation of the world, that we should be holy and blameless before Him." Ephesians 1:3-4

A spiritually "salty" Christian, following God's leading, will produce a curiosity and desire in the world around him/her to sample a taste of the source of their positive witness. As the old adage says, "You can lead a horse to water, but you cannot make him drink, unless you salt his oats!" If the salt you add is without flavor, your efforts have been in vain. Modern-day salt can sit in a shaker and never lose its flavor. However, in Jesus' day, salt came from ponds and contained minerals that would leach out the salt, rendering it tasteless and useless.

"You are the salt of the earth; but if the salt has become tasteless, how will it be made salty again? It is good for nothing anymore, except to be thrown out and trampled under foot by men. You are the light of the world. A city set on a hill cannot be hidden. Nor do men light a lamp, and put it under the peck-measure, but on the lampstand; and it gives light to all who are in the house. Let your light shine before men in such a way that they may see your good works, and glorify your Father who is in heaven." Matthew 5:13-16

"Therefore, salt is good; but if even salt has become tasteless, with what will it be seasoned? It is useless either for the soil or for the manure pile; it is thrown out. He who has ears to hear, let him hear." Luke 14:34-35

Combining the thoughts in the above two passages, Jesus admonishes believers to remain salty and never let their zeal for the Lord wane or lose its tang. In order to carry out our responsibility to be a moral preservative in the world, we must be willing to stand out as different. Just as salt enhances the flavor of food, the light of God's love shining in a dark place brings forth the ability to distinguish good from evil.

Yeast and salt are as opposite as sinful man and our most Holy God. As the salt in Biblical times lost its flavor, so too are human efforts ineffective without the power of the salt of God's character at work. Just as the salt keeps the yeast from getting out of control during the rising process, so too will God's salt preserve the character of His children. In his album, "Living in Jesus," Reggie Coates wrote the song, "Make it Shine." The chorus boldly proclaims, "You put the light in me, you've got to make it shine."[1] Reggie's songs always calm my anxious thoughts and allow me to take simple Bible truths to a higher level of comforting hope. The glorious gospel of Christ is like a treasure that God set in our hearts. The fire of God's love reflects off of this jewel, sending flashes of His light bouncing in every direction. The more territories of my heart that I surrender to Christ, the brighter the reflecting power of His light will be in my life. Listen to the focus of the Apostle Paul's message and the object of his concern to the church of Corinth:

> "For we do not preach ourselves but Christ Jesus as Lord, and ourselves as your bondservants for Jesus' sake. For God, who said, 'Light shall shine out of darkness,' is the One who has shone in our hearts to give the light of the knowledge of the glory of God in the face of Christ. But we have this treasure in earthen vessels, that the surpassing greatness of the power may be of God and not from ourselves..." 2 Corinthians 4:5-7

How amazing that our majestic Lord would choose to contain His most treasured gift in human, earthbound vessels. It is like trusting an ordinary cracked clay pot to keep the famous Hope Diamond safe and sound. Concerning salt, Reggie's song inspired me to write this chorus line, "You put the salt in me, Lord; you have to preserve the flavor." In the

Jeanette Lavoie, R.N.

Sermon on the Mount, Jesus presents the way of righteous living and encourages believers to be the salt of the earth. Followers of Christ must mimic Him in order to reach their full savory potential. First we must know who we were in our flesh alone and without our Savior:

> "...for all have sinned and fall short of the glory of God." Romans 3:23

Then we can praise God for who we are in Christ. Salt stands for permanence and incorruption, which is reflective of who Jesus is and what He desires we become.

> "For in Him [Jesus] all the fullness of Deity dwells in bodily form, and in Him you have been made complete, and He is the head over all rule and authority...". Colossians 2:9-10

> "Therefore if any man is in Christ, he is a new creature; the old things passed away; behold, new things have come." 2 Corinthians 5:17

Seasoning - In Chapter Six of his biography, Job defends his right to complain concerning his present circumstances. The following describes, in part, his lost zest for living as the spice of life eluded his grasp:

> "Can something tasteless be eaten without salt, or is there any taste in the white of an egg? My soul refuses to touch them; they are like loathsome food to me. Oh that my request might come to pass, and that God would grant my longing! Would that God were willing to crush me; that He would loose His hand and cut me off." Job 6:6-9

A low-salt diet may become necessary for health reasons; however, for many the joy of eating is missing when food is void of all salt. Job's will to live waned, for his relationship with God sounded distant and confusing at this point. He found no logical explanation for his multitude of sufferings. He pleaded with his tormenting friends to cease their hurtful accusations. In the end, Job no longer required intellectual answers to his questions. When one acknowledges God as sovereign, omniscient (all knowing), omnipotent (all-powerful), and omnipresent (present in all places at the same time) then a zeal for life can return. Why? Because of the assurance that God has everything under His control. The calmness and peace that follows will equip us to season our words with salt for every occasion.

> "Then Job answered the LORD, and said, 'I know that Thou canst do all things, and that no purpose of Thine can be thwarted. Who is this that hides counsel without knowledge? Therefore I have declared that which I did not understand, things too wonderful for me, which I did not know. Hear, now, and I will speak; I will ask Thee, and do Thou instruct me. I have heard of Thee by the hearing of the ear; but now my eye sees Thee; therefore I retract, and I repent in dust and ashes.'" Job 42:1-6

Speech Seasoned with Salt - To the Colossian church, the Apostle Paul exhorts believers to lace their words and actions with the character of salt. Each unbeliever we witness to will have a different tolerance and response to the testimony of our faith. Therefore, temper your discussions with the pure, penetrating wisdom from above. Protect your language from the corrupt or obscene. Season your life with prayer, spice your works with grace and mercy, and sprinkle a generous quantity of love to all who cross your path so that your efforts may not leave a fleshly aftertaste.

"Conduct yourselves with wisdom toward outsiders, making the most of the opportunity. Let your speech always be with grace, seasoned, as it were, with salt, so that you may know how you should respond to each person." Colossians 4:5-6

The Apostle Peter takes this a step further as he encourages those suffering persecution to always be ready to answer everyone who asks them to give an account of the reason for their hope. Those who dare to use God's salt shaker will enhance their efforts and make the most of every opportunity. One, who locks the spice of life in some hidden closet of their heart because they fear the response, will miss the chance to make a difference in someone's life.

"But even if you should suffer for the sake of righteousness, you are blessed. And do not fear their intimidation, and do not be troubled, but sanctify Christ as Lord in your hearts, always being ready to make a defense to everyone who asks you to give an account for the hope that is in you, yet with gentleness and reverence; and keep a good conscience so that in the thing in which you are slandered, those who revile your good behavior in Christ may be put to shame." 1 Peter 3:14-16

Supersaturated with Salt – As previously mentioned, the amount of salt used in bread baking and the omission of this spice can adversely affect the outcome. Correlating this principle to that of evangelism, Christians need to be seasoned, not smothered in salt, to be an effective witness. Offering the world a taste of gospel chips as salty as the sea can produce a gag reflex. When an unbeliever rejects Jesus, it should come as no surprise, especially if the testimony has been high on words and low in acts of loving-kindness. The absence of joy, peace, patience, goodness, faithfulness, gentleness, and self-control will further aggravate the problem. The Apostle Peter acknowledges that sharing faith in Jesus will not be easy; therefore, be ready before you speak, and do so with gentleness, reverence, and a clear conscience.

"To sum up, let all be harmonious, sympathetic, brotherly, kindhearted, and humble in spirit; not returning evil for evil, or insult for insult, but giving a blessing instead; for you were called for the very purpose that you might inherit a blessing. For, LET HIM WHO MEANS TO LOVE LIFE AND SEE GOOD DAYS REFRAIN HIS TONGUE FROM EVIL AND HIS LIPS FROM SPEAKING GUILE. AND LET HIM TURN AWAY FROM EVIL AND DO GOOD; LET HIM SEEK PEACE AND PURSUE IT. FOR THE EYES OF THE LORD ARE UPON THE RIGHTEOUS, AND HIS EARS ATTEND TO THEIR PRAYER, BUT THE FACE OF THE LORD IS AGAINST THOSE WHO DO EVIL. And who is there to harm you if you prove zealous for what is good? But even if you should suffer for the sake of righteousness, you are blessed. AND DO NOT FEAR THEIR INTIMIDATION, AND DO NOT BE TROUBLED, but sanctify Christ as Lord in your hearts, always being ready to make a defense to everyone who asks you to give an account for the hope that is in you, yet with gentleness and reverence; and keep a good conscience so that in the thing in which you are slandered, those who revile your good behavior in Christ may be put to shame. For it is better, if God should will it so, that you suffer for doing what is right rather than for doing what is wrong." 1 Peter 3:8-17

A Desolate Wasteland - There are two opposing metaphors concerning salt. It is symbolic of spiritual health, which counteracts the corruption in the world. The prophet Jeremiah describes those who reject God as unfruitful as a desert bush in a barren salt land.

> "Thus says the Lord, 'Cursed is the man who trusts in mankind and makes flesh his strength, and whose heart turns away from the LORD. For he will be like a bush in the desert and will not see when prosperity comes, but will live in stony wastes in the wilderness, a land of salt without inhabitant.'" Jeremiah 17:5-6

In Biblical times, a little salt was used to fertilize the soil. Some armies deliberately ravaged the countrysides of conquered people by adding an excessive amount of salt to the ground, thereby producing an infertile land unable to support life. This desolate wasteland paints a bleak portrait of a life separated from God. Unbelievers have expressed the emptiness as, "I feel something is missing in my life." At this point, they often seek to find a connection with God or attempt to fill the void with whatever temporary pleasures the world offers. Perhaps one definition of hell (an eternity without God) might be living in a barren salt pit in a perpetual state void of hope, peace, or satisfaction of any kind. Praise God that this is not the inheritance He wishes upon anyone; however, the choice is ours. As an abundance of salt spoils the soil, so too a lack of salt in bread-dough affects the outcome.

> "The Lord is not slow about His promise, as some count slowness, but is patient toward you, not wishing for any to perish but for all to come to repentance." 2 Peter 3:9

A Covenant of Salt – Nathan the prophet received a word from the Lord concerning King David and his descendants

(2 Samuel 7:4-17). His message revealed that the right to rule Israel would always remain with David's dynasty as God promised, "And your house and your kingdom shall endure before Me forever; your throne shall be established forever" (2 Samuel 7:16). The book of 2 Chronicles describes the pledge that God made to King David as a covenant of salt. Using salt as a metaphor in connection with this agreement between God and David spoke to the durability and indissoluble nature of this covenant. As salt maintains its flavor, so will the Lord's covenant forever be in force.

> "Do you not know that the LORD God of Israel gave the rule over Israel forever to David and his sons by a **covenant of salt**?" 2 Chronicles 13:5

Moses uses similar words when he recorded God's instructions to the priests concerning grain offerings:

> "Every grain offering of yours, moreover, you shall season with salt, so that **the salt of the covenant** of your God shall not be lacking from your grain offering; with all your offerings you shall offer salt." Leviticus 2:13

Emblematic of purity, cleansing, and durability, salt symbolized the permanent, unbreakable, binding covenant relationship between the God of heaven and His chosen people. Every promise that God makes to us in His Holy Word is an agreement that He plans to keep. For all eternity, the blessings that flow from God's hand will be a sign of His fidelity and friendship towards His children. Praise to God for his patience. Once we belong to God, He will never dissolve the bond He has made with us and **nothing can ever separate us from His enduring, undying love**.

> "But in all these things we overwhelmingly conquer through Him who loved us. For I am

convinced that neither death, nor life, nor angels, nor principalities, nor things present, nor things to come, nor powers, nor height, nor depth, nor any other created thing, shall be able to separate us from the love of God, which is in Christ Jesus our Lord." Romans 8:37-39

Prayer:

Merciful Father, without Your hand of favor upon me, my life feels like hell on earth - desolate, lonely, and without a savory flavor. Teach me to see my situation through Your eyes. Help me focus on You instead of being distracted by my troubles. Capture my attention each day that I might not rest until I add the sweet honey of Your Word of truth to my daily bread. You are incorruptible, Lord, so I know the salt in Your shaker never changes. Let the sweetness of Your goodness transform the unpalatable plate of woes before me into a culinary delight. Let the flavor of Your presence add such a distinctly enjoyable taste that it will be to me like a light which overcomes my darkness. Please make me ever aware of all hints of Your workings in my life, no matter how faint, that I may have the courage to face each new day knowing that I am not alone. And above all, season my words with Your salt that Your wisdom will defend me in the face of unbearable persecution.

Lord, give me the power to refrain from evil. Prevent me from blending the ways of the world into the bread of my life. Guard my mind, heart, and pathway with a thirst for Your righteousness. Stop the impurities of sin from seeping into my daily walk and leaching out the potential power of Your salty witness in me. Satan delights in a diluted form of evangelism because without the flavor of Your loving hand, my testimony is futile. Praise God for the promise that the Holy Spirit, who reigns in the bodies of Your children, is greater than the tug of the world and the tempestuous nature of my own weak flesh.

> "You are from God, little children,
> and have overcome them; because
> greater is He who is in you than he
> who is in the world." 1 John 4:4

Lord, I know that I am a child of the King. Permeate me with Your divine presence that the character of my life may give evidence that we are related. Without Your help, it is impossible for me to get a handle on the sin I battle each day. Evangelism, without the salt of Christ, is as dead as faith without works; so point me in the right direction. Your Word tells me You have a plan and purpose for me, "For [I am, you are] we are His workmanship, created in Christ Jesus for good works, which God prepared beforehand, that we should walk in them" (Ephesians 2:10). Lord, You put the salt in me; You have to keep me salty. Do not let Satan stamp my witness out by luring me into the trappings of sin. Let the power of Your preserving presence be like spiritual smelling salts alerting me to danger and waking me up to the truth. Teach me to tap into Your power source by plugging my energy into reading the Bible, communicating with You in prayer, keeping myself accountable to the fellowship of believers, and following Your leading as I share the gospel. Thank You for continuing to strengthen me, whether I have a thankful heart or a grumbling, discontented spirit. For I know, deep within me, that "I can do all things through Him who strengthens me" (Philippians 4:13). Amen.

Author's personal testimony of the power of God's salt to save a relationship affected by a poor witness:

As a zealous, newly born-again, believing teenager, I bombarded my brother with the gospel message, pounded my limited Bible knowledge firmly on his forehead, and pestered him to choose Jesus at every waking opportunity. Through words and circumstances, we violated each other's boundaries. John lost respect for me and I viewed him as my judge. Our relationship became distant and superficial as we shared little in common. I forfeited my right to speak openly to him of my faith. Miles of emotional space developed between us as I failed to pursue conversations on a deeper level in order to protect myself from the feeling of being on trial. We were both on the defense. Neither one of us had the skill or wisdom to know how to fully understand the other's standpoint. The bridge of love between us hung on by a stubborn genetic link that we both refused to cut. Blood has proven to be thicker than water. The God of the impossible provided a way to reinforce our flimsy foundation and open up the impassable pathway between us by supplying stepping stones of shared interest to bridge the gap.

John and I are as different as honey and peanut butter. Working together to solve a family problem provided an opportunity for two opposites to come together with meaning and purpose. This team effort allowed our relationship to blossom as we gained respect for one another by observing each other's character played out through a real-life experience. Our differences became strengths when we faced our opposing ideas, agreed to disagree, pooled our resources, and discovered we needed each other to accomplish the goal. False thinking and confused notions faded into the background as truth, love, and family devotion stepped forward. God knew that John and I needed to go through this fiery trial together before our relationship could be refined, restored, and defined by love. From this experience I have learned three concepts:

First of all, I must share that my brother is the best thing since peanut butter. In developing a coordinated effort to tackle an impressive mountain of a problem, I discovered there is more than one way to build a sandwich. My natural tendency is to put peanut butter on the bread first and honey second. The problem with this approach is that the peanut butter causes the honey to drip off the edge of the toast. Spreading the honey on first allows it to soak into the bread. The lesson God is teaching me is that in order to reserve my strength for the duration of this trial, I need to allow my brother to be on the top so the honey will not drip out of the sides of the bread and fall to the floor. The Lord is using my brother like glue to hold me together. I can only hope that what I add will be a sweet reflection of God's true love and not my own imitation.

Secondly, I am now more careful to choose an approach to evangelism that best suits each person. If you are about as subtle as a sledgehammer, then either pray that God will send people to you who can handle a strong dose of the gospel truth or ask God to help you lighten your swing. God will use those with the gift of mercy to comfort those who mourn. The hands of a servant can be an instrument to demonstrate the practical reality of God's loving provision in a time of need. One with a teacher's heart can shed light into the mind of a willing pupil. A prophetic word seasoned with salt, presented to a heart prepared by God, and given at the appropriate moment, can turn a life headed in the wrong direction full circle.

Lastly, speaking through the space that God provides is always more effective than pushing farther than both the person we are witnessing to, and God, give us permission to go. Problems arise when God opens a window and we try to break the door down instead!

Prayer:

Lord, when it comes to wooing the lost to Yourself, You are a gentleman. Your love is genuine, unconditional, and never pushy. Your love is true because You want us to be free to love You and not a prisoner forced into a one-sided commitment. Often, I lack wisdom for how to share my faith. Teach me to be a lady of grace and nobility fit to be called Your daughter in Christ. The people in the early church were living, breathing sermons to a lost world because of the way they lived and cared for one another. Show me how to love my neighbor and lift up the name of Jesus in big and small opportunities, so that I can be an attractive, fragrant witness. Praise to You, Oh God, for You are more than able to fix the mistakes of my past and answer my prayer to allow my friends and family to dwell in the house of my Lord forever. May You teach all Your children to be living testimonies of Your love and how to follow the example of the early church. Amen!

"And they were continually devoting themselves to the apostles' teaching and to fellowship, to the breaking of bread and to prayer. And everyone kept feeling a sense of awe; and many wonders and signs were taking place through the apostles. And all those who had believed were together, and had all things in common; and they began selling their property and possessions, and were sharing them with all, as anyone might have need. And day by day continuing with one mind in the temple, and breaking bread from house to house, they were taking their meals together with gladness and sincerity of heart, praising God, and having favor with all the people. And the Lord was adding to their number day by day those who were being saved." Acts 2:42-47

Devotional:

Praise – As Christ dwelt on the earth, He made the invisible attributes of God the Father visible to mankind. Take time to exalt Christ for the perfection of His character. Praise God, for Jesus is Lord of all! Use Colossians 1:15-17 and 2:9-11 as food for prayer.

Confession – Only Jesus is perfect; therefore, this prayer applies to all, "Forgive me for being a poor reflection of the character of Christ." Consider the remnants of sin which resemble life without Christ. Read Colossians 2:12-14 and meditate on this thought: The same power which raised Christ from the dead is available to liberate believers from the bondage of bad habits and patterns which keep the cycle of sin going on and on.

Thanksgiving – Gourmet cooks claim salt draws out the best flavor in foods. Likewise, adding Christ reveals the good which God had in mind when He created us. Think of a believer who displayed the character of Christ in their life in such a way as to impact your life. Give thanks to God for that person.

Intercession – In the making of leavened bread, salt keeps the activities of yeast (symbolic of sin) under control. The book of Colossians uses the metaphor of salt to stress the importance of communicating like Jesus. Words, actions, eyes, body language, and our ability to listen affect our audience. Ask God to use the following insights from the Apostle Paul's letter to the Colossians (3:21 and 4:1-6) to breathe life into your Christian witness. Colossians 3:21 is specific to parent-child relationships, yet the principle stretches beyond the home.

Lord, protect me from the temptation of continually bringing up touchy subjects or making unreasonable demands that irritate, annoy, anger, and discourage loved ones. Holy Spirit, restrain

my voice from preaching and teaching the truth
until God prepares hearts to receive the message.

Read Colossians 4:1-6 and transform Paul's prayer
requests and suggestions into your own petitions:
1. As God, my Lord and Master, is fair and just, help me
   do the same to all.
2. Open doors for me to accurately and clearly preach
   the mysteries of Christ.
3. Fill my public conduct with godly wisdom, so no
   opportunity to be an effective witness will be lost.
4. Jesus always knew how to speak to each person's
   need.

Lord, exert divine influence over my mind and
heart so that my words reflect the grace, purity,
sensitivity, and penetrating quality of Christ.

Submission – In Paul's closing remarks to the
Colossians, he sends encouragement from a fellow Colossian.
"Epaphras, who is one of your number, a bondslave of Jesus
Christ, sends you his greetings, always laboring earnestly for
you in his prayers, that you may stand perfect and fully assured
in all the will of God" (Colossians 4:12). This prayer provides a
definition for what it means for believers to be the "salt of the
earth." Believers are meant to be the image of Christ to the
world. Mature, perfect, always standing firmly in the center of
God's will – has anyone arrived? Submission in this area
requires wrestling and laboring in prayer for self and others.
Pray without ceasing. The enemy rejoices when the salt of our
witness loses its flavor.

Chapter 11: Beauty and the Yeast

Yeast is a one-celled fungus plant, scientifically known as saccharomyces cerevisae, whose pungent smell causes little children to plug their noses. The yellowish, moist mass of yeast plants, cultivated in a media and occurring as a froth on fermenting solutions, are dried in flakes or granules or compressed into cakes for preservation. Fresh cake yeast is highly perishable, must be refrigerated, and will keep for about two weeks. Active dry yeast is sold in a sealed, dated, flat, foil-wrapped packet and need not be refrigerated. Instant dried yeast, purchased in bulk, comes in a dated, vacuum packed container and must be refrigerated once opened. Though yeast is a living organism, it remains in a dormant state until activated by adding a warm liquid. Once activated the "lively" yeast multiply as they feed on the carbohydrate in the dough, thus beginning the process of fermentation. Yeast is described as the "soul" of leavened bread because it spreads throughout, causing a gradual change from a flat lump of dough to a raised puffed-up one. A leavening agent, such as yeast, is a substance used to make batter or bread-dough rise by causing the breakdown of complex molecules and forming a gas.

Just as man's sinfulness and God's holiness are opposites, so is leavened and unleavened bread distinctly different. The consequences of adding yeast to bread and sin to one's life both result in a change. One produces something delicious to eat. The other results in impurity due to the contaminating effects of sin. The process of fermentation and the use of leaven in Scripture as a synonym for sin, provide a key to discovering how those made in God's image can bring forth the beauty and crush the yeasty beast residing in all of Adam and Eve's children.

Someone I once knew thought the phrase, "He saved a wretch like me," should be changed in the famous hymn

"Amazing Grace." To her, it sounded harsh and unreasonable. I could never understand that line of thinking, because even a speck of sin is a wretched thing in the eyes of a Holy God. The power of Jesus, "the Bread of Life," provides the food to fuel the study of the transformation of the beast-like sinner into the beautiful creation God intended from the beginning. For a reflection of our spiritual state, let's look at the factors that affect fermentation and the making of leavened bread.

Illustration of the process of fermentation:

Illustration of the process of creating leavened bread:

Fermentation - During the process of making bread, fermentation is the chemical reaction that causes the dough to rise. For a successful loaf, yeast requires food (honey or sugar), the addition of warm liquids, and properly developed dough. In order to gain energy and multiply, yeast cells absorb carbohydrates in the mixture and decompose them into carbon dioxide plus ethyl alcohol. Once all the ingredients have been added, the warm dough is kneaded by hand or machine and the gluten is further developed. Gluten is a tangled net of protein in wheat.

Once the dough has been kneaded and allowed to raise, a sign that the gluten has been properly and fully developed will be that the dough becomes stretchy like a balloon. In this state, gluten can catch the ever-growing quantity of bubbles distending the dough. Now the baker is ready to flatten the dough, press out the excess bubbles trapped within the stretchy, mesh-like gluten structure, and form the puffing bakery treat into loaves or rolls. Excess bubbles must be pressed out is so the dough will rise evenly without pockets of gas that would mar the end product with annoying holes or a lumpy appearance. Next, the formed loaves/rolls rest in a warm place until they double in size. Since yeast is heat sensitive, it will only continue to feed on the ingredients and grow until the heat of the oven kills the yeast. There are several factors that influence the success or failure of creating a perfect loaf of leavened bread.

For yeast to cause the dough to rise above the rim of the mixing bowl, it must be "lively." Check the expiration date on the package and handle fresh yeast with care. To remain alive, yeast (fresh cake or instant dried) must be stored in the refrigerator. In this state it is like a dormant, sleepy, hibernating bear that survives the winter cold without food to eat. As the warm sun of spring awakens this hungry giant, so too a controlled environment will bring yeast to life. Yeast is so temperamental, that the unused portions must be returned to the refrigerator as soon as possible.

In order to spring to life, the dormant yeast must be placed in a warm, cozy environment. Temperatures of 110° to 115° Fahrenheit are ideal for this purpose. However, if the water is too hot, the poor defenseless yeast quickly dies. This explains why the bread eventually stops rising as it bakes and browns in the oven. Yeast dies at high temperatures and the alcohol evaporates, but the all-invasive effects of fermentation remain.

Both honey and salt affect the rising of bread. Honey is an easily digested, quick source of fuel. Omitting honey will slow fermentation, since it takes longer for the hungry yeast to feed on and process the carbohydrates in flour. Excess honey yields sweeter bread that takes longer to rise. As discussed in Chapter Ten, salt inhibits the rising action of the yeast. Omitting salt gives the yeast free reign to feed its gluttonous appetite. There are three other factors that adversely affect the ability of leavened bread to rise properly. Each of these speaks to the consequences of sin.

The gluten in white, processed flour is already partially developed; therefore, substituting a few cups of white flour in a recipe calling for freshly milled wheat will allow fermentation to proceed more quickly. If care is not taken to decrease the rising time, the gluten strands will break from the pressure. The bread will rise beautifully high in the oven; however, as soon as your hand stretches to remove it from the pan, the loaf will give way and flop to the side. They taste fine, but are chewy, heavy, and funny looking. Likewise, unencumbered sin may look good at first, but the end results speak for themselves.

"There is a way which seems right to a man, but its end is the way of death. A worker's appetite works for him, for his hunger urges him on." Proverbs 16:25-26

Second, many people find baking bread the old-fashioned way therapeutic because the manual labor required is a great stress releaser. Taking this slow way runs the risk of under-developed gluten, while use of modern machines holds the opposite danger. If the dough is placed in a hot oven before it has a chance to fully develop the gluten, it will barely rise. The tedious method of letting the dough "rest," punching it down, allowing it rise again, and then kneading it, is necessary to transform the gluten in wheat into a strong, stretchy substance able to hang on to the gaseous by-product of fermentation. The spiritual parallel warning is to not let sin creep in nor invite it to dwell in your heart long enough to develop. Once the human heart has made a habit of clinging to sin, it takes a lot of work to let go.

Third, my Bosch® mixer is so powerful that in less than seven minutes the machine has completely kneaded the dough. I then form the loaves, let them rise for fifteen minutes, then bake. If I allowed my machine to continue working the dough past the allotted time, or if I later kneaded the dough by hand in child-like play, the gluten strands would break. The severity of the outcome would depend on how long the extra kneading continued. Overly kneading the dough reminds me of the consequences of suffering because of my sins. Sometimes I need to get to the breaking point before I am willing to let go of the by-products of sin, like releasing a prideful lot of hot air. In the hands of man, yeast functions along with the baker to change a flour mixture into an edible loaf. A believer in the hands of Jesus, the slayer of the beast called leaven, will be free to become, in spirit, like the "Passover Bread" (unleavened like Jesus). Though God's anger towards sin is always justified and His punishment fair, the child of God can find comfort from these passages:

"Sing praise to the LORD, you His godly ones,
and give thanks to His holy name. For His anger
is but for a moment, His favor is for a lifetime;

weeping may last for the night, but a shout of joy comes in the morning." Psalms 30:4-5

"...My son, do not regard lightly the discipline of the Lord, nor faint when you are reproved by Him; for those whom the Lord loves He disciplines, and He scourges every son whom He receives. It is for discipline that you endure; God deals with you as with sons; for what son is there whom his father does not discipline?" Hebrews 12:5-7

To Make Sour - In the process of making sour dough, the baker first combines warm water, flour, yeast, and a sweetener (sugar or honey). Next, the mixture rests in a bowl, is unrefrigerated for 5 to 10 days, and is stirred occasionally. Finally, the finished soured dough is refrigerated for later use. This process of perpetual fermentation creates sourdough French bread. A continuous state of fermentation illustrates how sin carries on and on when given free reign.

A belief in Jesus opens the eyes of the spiritually blind to discern truth from error. God sent His Spirit to dwell in His children in order to equip us with the power to say "yes" to God's best and "no" to sin. "If you do well, will not your countenance be lifted up? And if you do not do well, sin is crouching at the door; and its desire is for you..." (Genesis 4:7). If sin becomes my master, the more I bow down, the stronger the pull. Satan delights in turning the sweet, pure fragrance of a faith-walk sour by introducing leaven into the equation.

"Therefore, to one who knows the right thing to do, and does not do it, to him it is sin." James 4:17

An unremorseful heart is fuel to stir the fire of spiritual fermentation. The beauty of repentance turns the key to begin God's transformation process and puts a halt to the state of perpetual sinfulness. Sin is the souring of our lives that is made sweet by God's forgiveness. Unfortunately, the Jewish leaders rejected God's solution and instead clung to that which Jesus called "leaven."

Leadership Laced with Leaven - Jesus repeated the title that John the Baptist gave to the Pharisees and Sadducees. He called these religious men a "Brood of Vipers." This reflected His consistent attitude towards their poisonous doctrines, hypocritical ways, and deceitful yet unsuccessful testing of His authority. Jesus gives stern warnings concerning such men of influence:

> "...Beware of the leaven of the Pharisees, which is hypocrisy. But there is nothing covered up that will not be revealed, and hidden that will not be known. Accordingly, whatever you have said in the dark shall be heard in the light, and what you have whispered in the inner rooms shall be proclaimed upon the housetops. And I say to you, My friends, do not be afraid of those who kill the body, and after that have no more that they can do. But I will warn you whom to fear: fear the One who after He has killed has authority to cast into hell; yes, I tell you, fear Him!" Luke 12:1-5

Beware! Watch out! For the hypocrisy of a group of misguided men will lead any who follow into a dark place. Jesus considered their sins to be 100% leaven. He recognized the circle of influence these leaders had as powerful enough to sway anyone unsure of the truth. Similar analogies are found in the wisdom of King Solomon. The first concerns a legacy of folly. The second is a resolve between husband and wife to prevent anything from spoiling their love.

> "Wisdom is better than weapons of war, but one sinner destroys much good. Dead flies make a perfumer's oil stink, so a little foolishness is

weightier than wisdom and honor. A wise man's heart directs him toward the right, but the foolish man's heart directs him towards the left. Even when the fool walks along the road his sense is lacking, and he demonstrates to everyone that he is a fool." Ecclesiastes 9:18-10:3

"Catch the foxes for us, the little foxes that are ruining the vineyards, while our vineyards are in blossom." Song of Solomon 2:15

Putrefying dead flies are to the perfumer's oil what the casualty of a little folly does to the character of a leader once respected for wisdom and honor. Leaven is to the rising of bread as a little stumble is to a tragic fall. Compromise feeds tolerance of evil. Lies build upon lies until the truth vanishes from sight. Relationships infiltrated with leaven will begin by penetrating their destructive forces from the inside out. In the end, they will plummet like a misguided arrow shot from as high as an eagle's nest and fall all the way to the bottom of the mountain. Therefore, humble yourself and be on the alert for it only takes a little sin to consume a large amount of wise thinking, leaving a tainted heritage of foolishness behind.

"Pride goes before destruction, and a haughty spirit before stumbling. It is better to be of a humble spirit with the lowly, than to divide the spoil with the proud. He who gives attention to the word shall find good, and blessed is he who trusts in the LORD." Proverbs 16:18-20

Fermentation in the Church - The Apostle Paul uses the same analogy to warn two different churches. For one, subtle sins went along with more grievous ones; in the other, false doctrines confused the truth. The tragedy is that the process starts as **we choose** to add yeast to the dough of our life. As time passes, it blends in so completely that its workings

161

act as the microscopic efforts of the yeast unseen by the naked eye. Beware of those trying to persuade you that one measly bite from a forbidden fruit could not possibly affect you the way God said it would! Remember that it only takes three tablespoons of yeast to leaven eight pounds of dough! The world is watching us. If they see we are no different than they are, who can blame them for having no desire to come to Christ! Like the yeast blended into the mixture, man cannot remove the leaven.

"It is actually reported that there is immorality among you, and immorality of such a kind as does not exist even among the Gentiles, that someone has his father's wife. And you have become arrogant, and have not mourned instead, in order that the one who had done this deed might be removed from your midst...Your boasting is not good. Do you not know that a little leaven leavens the whole lump of dough? Clean out the old leaven, that you may be a new lump, just as you are in fact unleavened. For Christ our Passover also has been sacrificed."   1 Corinthians 5:1-2,6-7

"You were running well; who hindered you from obeying the truth? This persuasion did not come from Him who calls you. A little leaven leavens the whole lump of dough." Galatians 5:7-9

A Restless, Fermenting Heart -

In a ferment, I store up unforgiveness, stockpile canceled sins, hide my vast iniquities, and lock up the fruits of the flesh in the seat of my emotions.

In such a heart, hatred, sadness, unrest, impatience, cruelty, evil, unfaithfulness, roughness, and a lack of self-control rule the day and visit by night.

In this wretched state, if the Lord had not rescued me, my sins would have overtaken me, leaving gaping holes inside.

In this desolate place, a heavy, burdensome yoke weighs me down with bitterness, guilt, anger, and shame - pushing those I care about away from my sight.

At the cross, the God of love provided a way to set this captive heart free to beat for joy and find eternal unencumbered peace and rest.

By His Spirit, my transformed heart is cleared of the negative and filled with His love, joy, peace, patience, kindness, goodness, faithfulness, gentleness, and self-control.

Around the Communion table, I remember the pain my sins cost as I ask my Lord to search my heart and remove any specks of leaven with His healing, all-forgiving touch.

In my prayers, I ask God to let every word that comes from His mouth be the fuel that feeds all the activities of my life.

In my life, I desire that living works will stand as eternal proof that God's grace has sustained me and His mercy preserved me.

For all eternity, I exult in the Lord! Thanks be to God for trading my heavy heart for one that is light and free.

"Blessed be the God and Father of our Lord Jesus Christ, who according to His great mercy has caused us to be born again to a living hope through the resurrection of Jesus Christ from the dead, to obtain an inheritance which is imperishable and undefiled and will not fade away, reserved in heaven for you, who are protected by the power of God through faith for a salvation ready to be revealed in the last time." 1 Peter 1:3-5

He Carried our Sorrows - As spoken of by the prophet Isaiah, the sufferings and death of Jesus did more than merely wipe out my transgressions. He also understood and absorbed all of the pain and sorrows that my sins caused others and vice-versa. Praise to Jesus, whose acquaintance with our grief enabled Him to have the power to heal sorrows and infirmities caused by senseless acts infiltrated with leaven. He has stored all of our tears in a bottle. Not one escaped His notice. Someday our Savior and King will dry every eye filled with the tears of sorrow and turn all of our mourning (as at a funeral) into dancing for joy (as at a wedding feast)!

"He [Jesus] was despised and forsaken of men, a man of sorrows, and acquainted with grief; and like one from whom men hide their face, He was despised, and we did not esteem Him. Surely our griefs He Himself bore, and our sorrows He carried; yet we ourselves esteemed Him stricken, smitten of God, and afflicted. But He was pierced through for our transgressions, He was crushed for our iniquities; the chastening for our well-being fell upon Him, and by His scourging we are healed." Isaiah 53:3-5

"Thou hast taken account of my wanderings; put
my tears in Thy bottle; are they not in Thy book?"
Psalm 56:8

Leaven and the Kingdom - Matthew records the
following parable from the teachings of Jesus:

"...The Kingdom of heaven is like leaven, which a
woman took, and hid in three pecks of meal, until
it was all leavened." Matthew 13:33

There is some debate as to the meaning of this verse as
leaven appears to be held in a positive light. Considering that
everywhere else in Scripture yeast is used to illustrate sin, I
have come to the following conclusion: The kingdom of heaven
is filled with God's chosen people, sinners saved by grace.
Just as Jesus did not shrink back when the leper came asking
for healing, so too God will handle our contaminated lives with
care. One cannot make bread from yeast alone. In the three
pecks of meal and the hands of the baker, I found the secret to
create unleavened bread from one infected by leaven. Even
though there is no part of the dough that is not affected by the
leaven, ingredients added and kneading performed affect the
outcome. God will not stop until His children are permeated by
His presence and become like unleavened bread. His patience
extends from our fragile beginnings to our last breath. The
beast of original sin can never overpower the ingredients God
will supply to accomplish the beautiful purpose He has for us.
In spite of our sins, God's kingdom will grow, as surely as
"lively" yeast in a proper environment will cause the bread to
rise. Fortunately, salvation depends on a Holy God and not on
His imperfect people! Our sins will affect us throughout life and
living in this world. However, like the speck of yeast hidden in
the meal, we are under His care. Thanks be to God the Father,
the Son, and the Holy Spirit, for they work together to ensure
our eternal image will be unharmed and intact.

> "For I am confident of this very thing, that He who began a good work in you will perfect it until the day of Christ Jesus." Philippians 1:6

Jesus died for our sins on the cross and stood victorious at the empty tomb; even so, believers are not perfect. We are repeatedly forgiven and will remain "in process" until we meet Him face-to-face. The battle against good and evil is won; but a stubborn attitude of rebellion and a willful rejection of God's best will always place His children in the middle of the battlefield. Jesus is the victorious King who rides on the white horse in the Book of Revelation. He will not idly stand by as His children make evil choices. While we have life and breath, though the enemy lies defeated, the battle still rages on.

Scripture emphatically proclaims a Christian's standing as clean before God because the blood of Jesus erases our sins. The Apostle Paul declares, "There is therefore now no condemnation for those who are in Christ Jesus. For the law of the Spirit of life in Christ Jesus has set you free from the law of sin and of death" (Romans 8:1-2). When we, as new creatures in Christ, choose to sin, it is like transplanting an incompatible foreign organ into our bodies. Likewise, the leavening of bread illustrates the conflict between the spirit and the flesh. In contrast, the making of unleavened bread is the image of an unbroken relationship between a forgiven sinner and a Holy God. As we come to God in prayer and depend on Him for strength, the Lord of the universe will demonstrate His power as only He can tame the beast of sin. Only He can bring forth the beauty that results as He transforms His children into the image of His Son.

> "For in hope we have been saved, but hope that is seen is not hope; for why does one also hope for what he sees? But if we hope for what we do not see, with perseverance we wait eagerly for it. And in the same way the Spirit also helps our weakness; for we do not know how to pray as we

should, but the Spirit Himself intercedes for us with groanings too deep for words; and He who searches the hearts knows what the mind of the Spirit is, because He intercedes for the saints according to the will of God. And we know that God causes all things to work together for good to those who love God, to those who are called according to His purpose. For whom He foreknew, He also predestined to become conformed to the image of His Son, that He might be the first-born among many brethren; and whom He predestined, these He also called; and whom He called, these He also justified; and whom He justified, these He also glorified. What then shall we say to these things? If God is for us, who is against us? He who did not spare His own Son, but delivered Him up for us all, how will He not also with Him freely give us all things? Who will bring a charge against God's elect? God is the one who justifies; who is the one who condemns? Christ Jesus is He who died, yes, rather who was raised, who is at the right hand of God, who also intercedes for us. Who shall separate us from the love of Christ? Shall tribulation, or distress, or persecution, or famine, or nakedness, or peril, or sword? Just as it is written, 'FOR THY SAKE WE ARE BEING PUT TO DEATH ALL DAY LONG; WE WERE CONSIDERED AS SHEEP TO BE SLAUGHTERED.' But in all these things we overwhelmingly conquer through Him who loved us. For I am convinced that neither death, nor life, nor angels, nor principalities, nor things present, nor things to come, nor powers, nor height, nor depth, nor any other created thing, shall be able to separate us from the love of God, which is in Christ Jesus our Lord." Romans 8:24-39

Prayer – As you come to a place of prayer, remember that no matter how much energy, talent, or determination one has to conquer sin's battle, personal resources alone are never enough. Addictions can hold one hostage; sin lures and entices us to fall; misguided desires lead those who follow astray. King Solomon's closing arguments from the book of Ecclesiastes provide a key to breaking the cycle. (A goad is a sharp pointed stick used in driving oxen. The individual spoken of here is called wise because he has mastered the ability to incorporate godly wisdom into his life. Success comes because the source of the wise words is Jesus, the one Shepherd.)

> "The words of wise men are like goads, and masters of these collections are like well-driven nails; they are given by one Shepherd." Ecclesiastes 12:11

> Lord, I am like a stubborn ox when I use my strength to force my desires to rise above Your will. Lead me, oh Mighty Shepherd, to the place where I can clearly discern Your direction. Make it like a sharp stinging goad to prick my hardened heart so I will soften at Your touch.

> The waters of my own making are polluted with the poison of my sins. Lead me, oh Gentle Shepherd, to Your waters of freedom where I will want my sins no more.

> A path full of choices confuses my heart and I know not where to run. Lead me, oh Wise Shepherd, to the straight and narrow way that leaves no room for doubt.

The sins on which I feast empty my pockets, leave my heart aching, and cause my soul to want. Lead me, oh Good Shepherd, to crave the foods from Your banqueting table that is guaranteed to fill my hunger and satisfy my thirst. The fear of death and the chains of sin hold my captive heart. Thank You, oh Saving Shepherd, for breaking the chains that bind me and for keeping my feet homeward bound. Amen.

Jeanette Lavoie, R.N.

Devotional:

Praise – The title for Chapter 11, "Beauty and the Yeast," contrasts the perfect, unblemished image of Christ with the ravages of sin. In John 10:11-18, Jesus describes Himself as the "Good Shepherd." True beauty lies within the heart of Jesus as He demonstrates His goodness towards us. Read this passage, meditate on the following points, and praise Jesus for His absolute and complete goodness.

1. Four times in this passage Jesus expresses His willingness to die for His sheep.
2. As the concerned, committed, caring owner of the sheep, Jesus compares His behavior with the hireling. Consider what happens when a wolf comes and the sheep are under the care of a selfish, uncaring, hireling; the sheep are immediately left alone, some are captured and killed, and others are scattered.
3. Find the verse which describes the intimate relationship which Jesus has with His sheep.
4. Verse 16 demonstrates that His goodness is unlimited; the first group of sheep is the Jews and the second the Gentiles.
5. In verses 16 and 17 Jesus uses the phrase "take up" to predict His resurrection and He declares His sovereign authority over His own destiny. The "Good Shepherd" volunteered to die for the sheep, chose the perfect moment to die, and had the authority to raise Himself from the dead.

Confession – Isaiah 64:6-7 illustrates the power and ugliness of sin as it pollutes any semblance of good. God speaks through the prophet Ezekiel (Ezekiel 33:10-11 NAS) words of comfort along with an understanding of human nature. God knows every person has a fatal attraction to sin, and both our bad choices and the consequences break God's heart. As you bring your sins before God today, reflect on His goodness. God desires that we repent and live. God wants us to know that all sins are forgivable and that He does not delight in the death of the wicked.

Thanksgiving – Understanding the principles of leavened bread paints a picture of a condemned sinner without God in their life. Yeast becomes invisible as it thoroughly blends into the ingredients and becomes one with the dough. Likewise, sin leaves no part of our being untouched. God created us in His image. Sin marred that perfect image. Thank God the Father for sending Jesus to erase our sins so that we can stand free from condemnation and restored in the light of God's goodness. Thank God for the assurance of complete forgiveness.

> "Therefore, there is now no condemnation for those who are in Christ Jesus, because through Christ Jesus the law of the Spirit of life set me free from the law of sin and death." Romans 8:1-2, NIV

Intercession – From Chapter 11, choose the aspects of a restless, fermenting heart (where yeast or sin is alive) that apply to you. Also, review Ezekiel 33:10-11 and focus on these thoughts as you pray.

1. Lord, make me conscious of and sorrowful over my sins.
2. Lord, open my eyes and reveal the consequences of my sins to my mind, and heart. Yeast consumes the sweet ingredients and the waste products create leavened bread. Likewise, today's choices predict tomorrow's future.
3. Lord, do not let me be tempted to allow sin to linger, so I will not become attached it.
4. Lord, the world blurs the lines between good and evil. Educate me so Your truth may remain in my heart, my mind will never forget Your ways, and my actions will accurately represent the goodness of Your character.

Submission – Only in perfect submission can we find rest in God's presence. The challenge which Moses gave to the children of Israel applies to us today. "I call heaven and earth to witness against you today, that I have set before you life and death, the blessing and the curse. So choose life in order that you may live, you and your descendants, by loving the LORD your God, by obeying His voice, and by holding fast to Him; for this is your life and the length of your days, that you may live in the land which the LORD swore to your fathers, to Abraham, Isaac, and Jacob, to give them" (Deuteronomy 30:19-20).

Chapter 12: Taming the Beast

Both honey and yeast were excluded from most offerings to God in Old Testament times because they both fermented. These two elements capture the essence of the battle we face on Earth. Honey embraces all that is good, while yeast stimulates ones appetite to hunger after evil. Everyone knows that sometimes all it takes is the knowledge that something is forbidden to entice one to participate in that, which is tempting. The Apostle Paul expresses this dilemma as a war within that makes him a prisoner:

"For we know that the Law is spiritual; but I am of flesh, sold into bondage to sin. For that which I am doing, I do not understand; for I am not practicing what I would like to do, but I am doing the very thing I hate...Wretched man that I am! Who will set me free from the body of this death? Thanks be to God through Jesus Christ our Lord! So then, on the one hand I myself with my mind am serving the Law of God, but on the other, with my flesh the law of sin." Romans 7:14-15, 24-25

By adjusting the ingredients in bread, the baker can exert power over the outcome. The following experiment is designed to test factors that cause yeast to either thrive, slow down, or die. Spiritually speaking, this study will shed light on God's battle strategy against the beast of sin. Since several people are required to complete this task, it may be something to do as a family or with a group of children.

Fermentation Experiment Using Proofing Method - Proofing is a process used in some recipes whereby a baker activates the yeast before adding it to the flour mixture. Dry or cake yeast is placed into a warm liquid (110oF - 115oF) with 1 tsp. of honey or sugar. Within ten minutes the yeast becomes soft, creamy, and begins to foam, thus signaling that the yeast is thriving.

Objective: To determine what affects the yeast's livelihood and to compare this with the battle between the flesh and the spirit. Adding, subtracting, or changing the ingredients used in proofing, and/or changing the temperature of the liquid will test these variables.

Materials needed: 5 Tbsp. yeast (I use Saf® instant yeast), 6 1/2 Tbsp. honey, 4 1/2 cups water, 1 Tbsp. salt, 1/2 cup buttermilk, 4 Tbsp. oil (plus some extra for coating the funnel neck and the measuring spoon used for the honey), a bread thermometer, 1/4 and 1/2 cup measuring cups, 1 and 1/2 Tbsp. measurements, 10 glass 10-ounce bottles with skinny necks, 2 funnels (one for dry and one for wet ingredients), 10 same-sized large balloons of different colors, one chopstick for stirring, and a tape measure.

General Instructions: Number each bottle according to the following chart. Add the appropriate ingredients to each bottle, with the exception of the liquids or the yeast until you are ready to record the results. Use oil to coat the inside neck of one funnel and the spoons, so the honey will freely slide out and into the bottles. Keep one funnel dry to use for adding the yeast or salt. Make sure the yeast is refrigerated until ready to use. Delegate responsibilities to 3-6 helpers per mixture as each experimental bottle must be mixed and assembled quickly once the yeast and warm liquids are added.

Helper's Instructions: A group of children can take turns adding the honey, oil, or salt to each bottle (see chart). One helper's job is to firmly hold the bottle. Another must be ready with a stopwatch to time and record events as they occur. Someone needs to heat the water/buttermilk (see chart) in the microwave until it is 110oF. Next, one person can add the warm liquids to the bottle. Another must thoroughly stir the mixture with a chopstick. (The bottle with extra honey will take longer to mix. For younger children, you may omit the step of mixing the honey for all the experiments.) One person is designated to hold the lip of the balloon open and be ever ready to secure it over the opening once the contents are ready (let this person practice before you begin). Make sure there is no air in the balloon when you put it on. Once the last ingredient, yeast, is added to the bottle, quickly put the balloon on and then give the bottle a little side-to-side shake to mix. If the neck of the balloon gets stuck together just above the bottle opening, gently pull the sides of the balloon so that the gases can freely flow into the balloon.

Observe Signs of Life: Contents will soften, puff, bubble, foam, hiss, collect gas in the balloon, and sometimes spill up and out of the bottle. This effervescent display indicates that the yeast is flourishing. Record these and other observations. Use the tape measure to determine the circumference of the inflated balloons.

Factors varying the outcome: The accuracy of the experiments will be improved if the following measures are taken: The temperature of the liquid should be right.

Thoroughly mix the honey, oil, buttermilk, and/or salt before you add the yeast. Make sure the yeast used is "lively" (check expiration date). Accurately measure the ingredients. Even a tiny amount of extra honey could change the outcome. Buy balloons that are as close to the same size as possible. Put the balloon over the top of the bottle as soon as the yeast is added to prevent any gas from escaping. Make sure that the balloon does not have any extra air before attaching it to the bottle. Those recording the results should be alert as some of the experiments have immediate results. Some chemical reactions will have observations to record even after many hours. Once the balloon raises on any given bottle, setting a timer for every thirty minutes will help detail the changes in the diameter of each balloon.

Scriptures to Consider: If you do this with older children, divide them into ten groups, let each team do one of the experimental bottles, see the fermentation chart for details, and give them the following verses to consider as they analyze the results.

> Bottle 1 - Galatians 5:7-9 and Ecclesiastes 9:18-10:3
> Bottle 2 - Psalms 119:103-104 and Proverbs 25:16, 27-28
> Bottle 3 - Matthew 5:13-16 and 1 John 4:4
> Bottle 4 - 1 Peter 2:1-3 and Hebrews 5:12-13
> Bottle 5 - 1 Peter 2:1-3 and Hebrews 5:12-13
> Bottle 6 - Proverbs 28:13 and 1 John 1:5-10
> Bottle 7 - John 4:13-14
> Bottle 8 – Matthew 7:21-23
> Bottle 9 - Psalms 23:5 and Job 29:2-6
> Bottle 10 - Psalms 23:5-6 and Philippians 1:6

Chart for the Fermentation Experiment

Bottle Contents	Balloon Rising Time and circumference	Signs of Life	Solution's Activity Conclusion
1.) Control	6 ½ to 7	All the signs of	Perfect

Bottle Contents	Balloon Rising Time and circumference	Signs of Life	Solution's Activity Conclusion
½ cups 110°F Water, ½ Tbsp. Honey, ½ Tbsp. Yeast	minutes. 11-13 inches. 10 hours later, balloon is 9 ½ inches around.	life present until balloon starts to deflate.	environment for fermentation. Yeast is "lively."
2.) Excess honey ½ cups 110°F Water, 2 ½ Tbsp. Honey, ½ Tbsp. Yeast	11-13 minutes. 15 inches. Takes over 24 hours before it begins deflating.	Longest observable signs of fermentation.	Fermentation slowed at the start; however, the yeast remained alive the longest.
3.) Excess salt Same ingredients as the control, plus 1 Tbsp. Salt	Balloon remained flat and without any gas.	No signs of life.	Yeast is dead.
4.) Buttermilk ¼ cup Water and ¼ cup Buttermilk at 110°F, ½ Tbsp. Honey, ½ Tbsp. Yeast.	11-12 minutes. 12-15 inches 10 hours later, balloon is 9-10 inches around.	Besides the usual signs of life, you can see the milk particles actively moving about!	Fermentation slowed a bit at first, but lasts longer than the control bottle.
5.) Buttermilk ¼ cup Buttermilk and ¼ cup Water at 110°F. ½ Tbsp. Yeast No Honey.	Balloon flat with only a slight amount of gas.	No signs of life.	Yeast is dead.
6.) Without food ½ cup 110°F Water, ½ Tbsp. Yeast	Balloon flat without any gas.	Solution creamy. No other signs of life.	Yeast cannot survive long without food.
7.) Hot water Same as control, except make the Water 200°F.	Balloon flat without gas. Balloon gets sucked into the bottle.	Zero signs of life.	(110°F is perfect while 140°F slows fermentation). 200°F spells death to the yeast.

Bottle Contents	Balloon Rising Time and circumference	Signs of Life	Solution's Activity Conclusion
8.) Cold water Same as control except make the water ~60° (Note: honey will not dissolve in cold water.)	2 hours 40 minutes 5 3/4" 4 hours later, balloon is 12 1/2" at its largest	Zero signs of life at first. After ~ 2 hours, a small amount of gas is detected in the balloon. In the end, the yeast consumes all of the honey.	Activity severely delayed. In the end, the circumference of the balloon is not diminished.
9.) Oil Control, plus 1 Tbsp. Canola Oil	7-8 minutes. 10-15 inches. 4 hours later, balloon is 12 inches around.	With 1 Tbsp. oil, the foam bubbles to the top of the bottle's neck.	Almost ties control bottle to start fermenting.
10). Oil Control, plus 3 Tbsp. Canola Oil	12-14 minutes. 6-7 inches.		Activity is severely diminished.

Battle between the Flesh and the Spirit - The control bottle reminds me of the contents of the soul of one who is spiritually dead. Deep down in their heart, the sweet truth of God's love exists from the beginning; however, molecule by molecule the message is destroyed as sin flourishes and grows. Bottle two speaks of those seeking to gain excess knowledge apart from the Holy Spirit's guidance. The power of knowledge without God's wisdom is useless to fight sin. Faith expressed in words only, without evidence of works, is truly dead. Salt embodies the character of Christ played out in the life of a believer. Such faith, empowered by God, can begin to squeeze the life out of our sin nature. The milk of the gospel alone is powerful enough to destroy the hold sin has on us because the message is based on Jesus Christ. Bottle five (buttermilk without honey) illustrates a new believer who looks the same as the bottle with salt (forgiven and freed from sin). Bottle six is a picture of starving our sin nature. If you do not feed the flesh what it wants, sin will have no opportunity to grow. Number seven is a warning to all. Only those hot for Jesus will feel the heat of the Holy Spirit at work to make a difference in our lives. The results from bottle number eight contests the theory that a "good" person who rejects Jesus will slip into heaven. In those cold and unreceptive to the gospel, their sin nature may be hidden at first and their deeds appear to have life. Eventually, the buried dead thing (sin) springs to life. Some of these people call themselves Christians; however, Jesus declares to them, "I never knew you; depart from Me, you who practice lawlessness" (Matthew 7:23). Adding oil to the bottle intrigued me the most. We may be able to shrug off a taste of God's healing touch; however, the lover of our soul does not give up easily. The Master of creation knows how much spiritual oil each one needs to grease the hinges before the door to our heart willingly flies open.

> "Behold, I stand at the door and knock; if any one
> hears My voice and opens the door, I will come in
> to him, and will dine with him, and he with Me."
> Revelation 3:20

In a Ferment - Reviewing the results of the above experiment brings me to the following conclusions:

Living in the flesh, apart from God, looks like the state of agitated unrest apparent any time leaven springs to life. In such a ferment, the sins of the flesh (what I want) create an appetite for the things that please my eyes, appeal to my mind, and temporarily satisfy my emotional needs. As each small, evil thought or deed develops, the effervescence grows inside like a cancer. Sin puffs me up, takes on a power of its own, pushes me towards ungodly places, and leaves a trail of dead works behind. We all start out as the control bottle, spiritually dead and alive to our sin nature. Any "good" deeds we do apart from God are to Him as unworthy, filthy rags. Dead works exclude God, while living works include Him. Faith maintains the truth in all its actions, while sin changes everything around to suit itself. Signs of life in the yeast precipitate death and decay to the sweet elements in the bread dough. Likewise, mix good with evil and the equation never balances out.

> "For all of us have become like one who is unclean, and all our righteous deeds are like a filthy garment; and all of us wither like a leaf, and our iniquities, like the wind, take us away." Isaiah 64:6

Only God can tame the beast of sin. As salt destroyed the yeast in the experiment, so, too, the character that God builds in us will diminish sin's potent touch. Salvation, through Christ, is not a gift to be bought, a thing to be earned, or an object to be admired; it is a present to be opened, a hope that is realized, a faith that is rewarded, and a love to be cherished and shared. Today if you hear God's voice, harden not your heart. His gift will no longer be there if you reject it today and die tonight. All of us, like sheep, have gone astray. We sit on "Death Row" without the hope of a pardon, unless Jesus stands in the gap and bridges our way to eternity.

> "For the wages of sin is death, but the free gift of God is eternal life in Christ Jesus our Lord." Romans 6:23

> "For there is one God, and one mediator also between God and men, the man Christ Jesus, who gave Himself as a ransom for all, the testimony borne at the proper time." 1 Timothy 2:5-6

> "And the former priests [the Levites], on the one hand, existed in greater numbers, because they were prevented by death from continuing, but He

[Jesus], on the other hand, because He abides forever, holds His priesthood permanently. Hence, also, He is able to save forever those who draw near to God through Him, since He always lives to make intercession for them." Hebrews 7:23-25

Prayer:

Lord Jesus, I invite You to come into my life today and give You permission to create the perfect environment to exterminate my appetite for sin. Let the temperature of Your living water sore within me that my sins will remain dead and buried. Lord Jesus, feed my faith with bread from heaven that my doubts might starve to death and my trust in God would flourish. Send mature "spiritually salty" Christians to feed me the milk I need to understand basic beliefs and the honey I crave to expand my faith. Pour the oil of Your presence upon me that whatever I do, think, or say will spring to life and not death. When life gets complicated, it is not easy to say "no" to the flesh and "yes" to the Spirit. Thanks be to God that when I am weak, You are strong enough to tame the beast within me.

Thank You heavenly Father, that our salvation is secured as we put our faith in Christ. Praise You, Lord God, for translating the faith we carry in our hearts into a tangible reality of hope through the comforting, guiding presence of the Holy Spirit. The wages of sin come like a paycheck for a day's work. Your love, oh generous Father, is poured upon us in one lump sum. The value of Your priceless gift never decreases. The more love I receive from Your hand, the more I discover You have already given me. Let the Holy Spirit be the compass to guide my heart, so that I will become all that You desire me to be; not by my might nor by my power, but by God's Spirit.

Jesus, You are my advocate on high upon whose throne the sun never sets. Thank You for continually making intercession for me and effectively silencing the accuser's voice; whether it be my own guilt returning to haunt me or Satan's shrill, desperate, hollow charges against me. The forgiveness of Christ forever changes my status from guilty to innocent! Hallelujah! Our Living Savior takes the decomposed by-products of our foolishness and scatters their ashes to the wind. God exchanges Christ's beauty for our beast and creates a wonder to behold. We are all miracles in-the-making. May You enable us to resist the temptation to get puffed up with pride. Lift us up, all knowing Father, so we can get a clear view of all Your marvelous works. May we live to boast **only** in the Lord! God, we are able to give You the glory when we see ourselves as instruments available for service. Praise You, Lord God, that the tools You provide to accomplish everything good are always within our reach. Amen!

"And my God shall supply all your needs according to His riches in glory in Christ Jesus. Now to our God and Father be the glory forever and ever. Amen." Philippians 4:19-20

Jeanette Lavoie, R.N.

Free
By Sarah Lavoie
4-22-02
Used with Permission

Many times we get entangled in the web of sin
So often that we can never truly win
We may fight
And often with all of our might
To try to flee
From our all encompassing misery

But until the day
We stop, look, and say
That we are not fighting alone
And God's love is truly shone
Only then can we see
That we are truly free

Devotional:

Praise – Christ is risen! He is risen indeed! This familiar Easter Sunday greeting is a celebration of the victory – of light over darkness; of good over evil; of love over hate. The unsurpassed omnipotence of Christ proves He is the conquering king. In Romans 8:37, followers of Jesus share in the victory, as it says, "But in all these things we overwhelmingly conquer through Him who loved us." God's Word is true, yet at times survival and not victory describes the state of affairs. The following quote from my Pastor Dr. Doug Tiffin's 2002 Easter sermon puts things into perspective: "We live in a world that seems like Friday, the day Jesus died. A time when evil flourishes and all that is good is under attack. Jesus' disciples, sealed in their sorrow and hidden away in fear, lost all hope for their cause. Meaning and purpose died with their leader; yet, the dawn of hope rose like the sun on Easter morning. Today we celebrate that while we seem to live on Friday, Sunday does come." Read Romans Chapter 8, use the following outline as a guide, and discover there is a day coming when we will fully realize the reality that we are **overwhelmingly** conquerors through Christ who loved us. Praise the Lord!

1. Romans 8:1-3 – Recounts God's grace in sending Jesus to pay the penalty for our sins.
2. Romans 8:4-17 – God's Holy Spirit enables us to have victory over the power of sin in daily life.
3. Romans 8:18-30 – God's promise for the future; believers will eventually be transformed into the image of Christ.
4. Romans 8:31-34 – The Father declares believers righteous. Jesus intercedes for us like a lawyer defending our character against any that condemn us.
5. Romans 8:35-39 – For those living and remaining without Jesus, the day Jesus died is the end of the story. With Christ alive in us, though circumstances

make us "feel" alone and defeated, we know we are conquerors because nothing can separate us from the unfailing love of Christ.

The resurrection of Christ does not end in a period, it ends with an exclamation point! Each believer's life is a journey to prove that the goodness of God's love overcomes the darkness of evil in the end; therefore, wait with great expectation!

Confession – When yeast is given warm water and food, there are observable signs of life – and so it is with sin. The Apostle Paul captures the essence of the intense struggle of knowing in our spirit what is "right" yet continuing to practice the very thing we hate. Read Romans 7:14-25 and notice the personal nature of these verses suggests Paul wrote from experience. God knows we are all prisoners of war, so He sent Jesus to set us free. As you come to this time of confession, call upon the powerful presence of Christ to bring the battle to a halt today.

Thanksgiving – Though the beginning and middle may be unbearable at times – the ending is secure. Consider the battles before you today. Celebrate each victory – both the battles won and the baby-steps indicating progress.

Intercession – Once awakened from sleep, yeast continues to consume the sweet elements of bread until the heat of the oven ends its life. And so it is with sin – once temptation comes to life as we feed on spiritual junk food (the ways of the world) it spoils our appetite for good. The battle rages in the mind as we weigh our options and come to a crossroad – what we know is right and what "seems" right. Proverbs 14:12 says, "There is a way which seems right to a man, but its end is the way of death." Read Proverbs 14:12-19 and ponder the consequences of the backslider in heart.

Lord, make the evil bow down to the good You have placed within me, so You will call me righteous. Saturate my heart and mind with what pleases my sovereign King, so my soul will be satisfied. Amen.

Submission – Bread bakers use a thermometer to test the water because an accurate temperature is of paramount importance. Hot water kills the yeast, cold water makes yeast slow and sleepy, and lukewarm is the perfect temperature for fermentation to begin. The book of Revelation addresses a message to the church of Laodicea, "I know your deeds, that you are neither cold or hot; I would that you were cold or hot. So because you are lukewarm, and neither hot nor cold, I will spit you out of My mouth" (Revelations 3:15-16). Their actions so displeased God that the words, "to spit you out," literally mean, "to vomit up." According to Revelations 3:20-22, Christ graciously stepped outside of this church, stood at the entrance, and waited for a response as He said, "Behold, I stand at the door and knock; if anyone hears My voice and opens the door, I will come in to him, and will dine with him, and he with Me. He who overcomes, I will grant to him to sit down with Me on My throne, as I also overcame and sat down with My Father on His throne."

The key to victory centers around the intimate atmosphere of dining with Jesus. Our Savior put His "good food" on the table, we put forth our "best effort," and then we talk and eat. This is our life's work, to get closer and closer to Jesus, the source of power; relish it!

To choose what you know is right, you must learn to know Christ – be committed to reading the Bible daily. To have the power to do what is right instead of settling for what "seems" right, take time to pray. To find victory, give up the barriers hindering intimacy with Christ. Let this be our daily bread – to dwell in God's presence now, forever, and always.

Chapter 13: Passover: A Picture of Redemption

Historically, God gave both Passover and the Feast of Unleavened Bread to the nation of Israel. There are a sum total of seven holidays instituted by God. They are called "feasts of the Lord" because they belong to God and are to be entered into according to the terms which He ordained in the book of Leviticus. From the words of Marvin Rosenthal, president of Zion's Hope, "These seven feasts depict the entire redemptive career of the Son of God."1 Mr. Rosenthal explains that the word "feasts" in Hebrew means appointed times. These days tell a perfectly orchestrated story. As defined, these "holy convocations" are intended to be a time of meeting between God and man for a holy purpose.

The first two intimately related solemn, sacred Jewish holidays both commemorate what God did on behalf of the one million people of Israel when He brought them out of the land of Egypt, from bondage to emancipation.

> "These are the appointed times of the LORD, holy convocations which you shall proclaim at the times appointed for them. In the first month, on the fourteenth day of the month at twilight is the LORD'S Passover. Then on the fifteenth day of the same month there is the Feast of Unleavened Bread to the LORD; for seven days you shall eat unleavened bread." Leviticus 23:4-6

The First Passover - Moses told the story of the initial Passover in the book of Exodus. The title of this second book of the canonical Jewish and Christian Scriptures means "way out." The roadway leaving Egypt was not easy for "...the LORD hardened Pharaoh's heart, and he was not willing to let them go." (Exodus 10:27). Passover commemorates the redemption wrought when the Jewish people believed God would exempt them from the tenth, final, and most severe plague sent by the Lord to convince Egypt to let God's people go. According to God's instructions, each household took an unblemished year-old male lamb into their home.

"And you shall keep it [the lamb] until the fourteenth day of the same month, then the whole assembly of the congregation of Israel is to kill it at twilight. Moreover, they shall take some of the blood and put it on the two doorposts and on the lintel of the houses in which they eat it. And they shall eat the flesh that same night, roasted with fire, and they shall eat it with unleavened bread and bitter herbs...Now you shall eat it in this manner: with your loins girded, your sandals on your feet, and your staff in your hand; and you shall eat it in haste - it is the LORD'S Passover. For I will go through the land of Egypt on that night, and will strike down all the first-born in the land of Egypt, both man and beast; and against all the gods of Egypt I will execute judgments - I am the LORD. And the blood shall be a sign for you on the houses where you live; and when I see the blood I will pass over you, and no plague will befall you to destroy you when I strike the land of Egypt." Exodus 12:6-8, 11-13

By faith Moses had the confident assurance in his heart that the God whom he served would bring to pass what the Israelites had hoped for 430 years - FREEDOM! They kept the Passover by applying the blood of the precious lamb as directed by God to the two doorposts and the lintel of each home. By this act of obedience, the one God sent to destroy **passed over** their homes and spared their first-born children. Therefore, the name "Passover" is reflective of God's act of mercy towards His chosen people. As God kept His promise, a joyous relief brought gladness to their celebration table. In contrast, "...there was a great cry in Egypt, for there was no home where there was not someone dead." (Exodus 12:30)

Pharaoh called for Moses and Aaron in the night and gave them permission to leave without insisting on any concessions. Oddly enough, the man whom all of Egypt thought to be divine made only these telling requests:

> "Then he called for Moses and Aaron at night and said, 'Rise up, get out from among my people, both you and the sons of Israel; and go, worship the LORD, as you have said. Take both your flocks and your herds, as you have said, and go, and **bless me** also.'" Exodus 12:31-32

Christ our Passover Lamb - All subsequent Passovers are memorials of this historical event. Looking backwards in time, we can see how this points to Christ. Mr. Rosenthal suggests the most accurate word to describe Passover is "*redemption*." [2] The first lambs redeemed one million Jews from physical bondage. Jesus, the final sacrificial Lamb, died on a subsequent Passover to free all who put their faith in Him from spiritual bondage. John the Baptist called Him, "...the Lamb of God who takes away the sin of the world!" (John 1:29) The Apostle Paul hailed Christ as our Passover. (1 Corinthians 5:7). Peter paints an even clearer correlation between Christ and the Pascal lamb:

> "And if you address as Father the One who impartially judges according to each man's work, conduct yourselves in fear during the time of your stay upon earth; knowing that you were not redeemed with perishable things like silver or gold from your futile way of life inherited from your forefathers, but with precious blood, as of a lamb unblemished and spotless, the blood of Christ." 1 Peter 1:17-19

Blood Sacrifice - Scripture records the first slaying of an animal in the Garden of Eden. Adam and Eve had disobeyed God by eating the forbidden fruit from the tree of the knowledge of good and evil. God listened patiently as Adam blamed Eve and Eve blamed the Serpent. After God pronounced the judgment for their sin, He provided for their need of physical covering by executing the first sacrifice Himself.

> "And the LORD God made garments of skin for Adam and his wife, and clothed them." Genesis:3:21

Forgiveness is never without cost. From the moment the first couple was driven out of Eden, God instituted a system of bringing a sacrifice to cover the sins of the people. Here are a few supporting verses:

> "For the life of the flesh is in the blood, and I have given it to you on the altar to make atonement for your souls; for it is the blood by reason of the life that makes atonement." Leviticus 17:11

> "For if the blood of goats and bulls and the ashes of a heifer sprinkling those who have been defiled, sanctify for the cleansing of the flesh, how much more will the blood of Christ, who through the eternal Spirit offered Himself without blemish to God, cleanse your conscience from dead works to serve the living God?...And according to the Law, one may almost say, all things are cleansed with blood, and without shedding of blood there is no forgiveness." Hebrews 9:13-14, 22

Atonement is like the pitch that Noah applied to make the Ark watertight. Just as it kept the flood of judgment out, so

191

too the blood sacrifices protected each sinner from God's wrath. The Old Covenant or Old Testament system required the process to be repeated over and over because of the constant stream of sin and the temporary nature of the sacrifice. Once Israel became a nation, the priestly tribe of Levi carried out this ritual. The Priests never sat down on the job because their work never ended. One animal was sacrificed for one person or for a whole family. In stark contrast, look what Scripture says about the one momentous sacrifice Jesus made which completely fulfilled God's requirements for the sins of all people for all time.

> "And every priest stands daily ministering and offering time after time the same sacrifices, which can never take away sins; but He, having offered one sacrifice for sins for all time, sat down at the right hand of God, waiting from that time onward until His enemies be made a footstool for His feet. For by one offering He has perfected for all time those who are sanctified." Hebrews 10:11-14

Jesus is both the lamb slain for our sins and the High Priest who performed the ultimate sacrifice. He now **sits** at the Father's right hand because He accomplished what all the other sacrifices could not - He completely wiped out sin and conquered death. To say, "Maybe I need to add some good works to ensure my salvation" is to insult the grace of God!

> "I do not nullify the grace of God; for if righteousness comes through the Law, then Christ died needlessly." Galatians 2:21

One final thought concerning the original Passover sacrifice; God gave these instructions concerning the leftovers:

"And you shall not leave any of it over until
morning, but whatever is left of it until morning,
you shall burn with fire." Exodus 12:10

No specific reason is given for this, but I speculate that
the full consumption of the sacrifice may be a sign of the full
acceptability of the sacrifice to satisfy God's demands. Jesus
gave an even better sacrifice because it never warrants
repeating. His whole work on Earth and death at Calvary fulfills
the promise of the Old Covenant and completes the plan for
forgiveness that no other sacrifice could. If you consider
inviting Jesus into your life today, you must take all or none. If
your Jesus is merely a man who died for his fellow man, then
His sacrifice would fall short because the Bible says, "all have
sinned and fall short of the glory of God" (Romans 3:23). Since
I am convinced that Christ is both fully God and fully man, I
accept the complete spectrum of His sacrifice; from the first
Christmas, to the original Easter Sunday morning, and all that
the Bible says about Christ from the beginning of time. Surely
this man is the Son of God.

"In the beginning was the Word [Jesus], and the
Word [Jesus] was with God, and the Word [Jesus]
was God." John 1:1

Captives - Since Jesus is likened to the lamb, perhaps
the captives of Egypt are descriptive of the world whom God
wishes to set free. The following verses define God's meaning
of freedom:

"Jesus therefore was saying to those Jews who
had believed Him, 'If you abide in My word, then
you are truly disciples of Mine; and you shall
know the truth, and the truth shall make you free.'
They answered Him, 'We are Abraham's
offspring, and have never yet been enslaved to
anyone; how is it that You say, 'You shall become

free?' Jesus answered them, 'Truly, truly, I say to you, everyone who commits sin is the slave of sin. And the slave does not remain in the house forever; the son does remain forever. If therefore the Son shall make you free, you shall be free indeed.'" John 8:31-36

"For if we have become united with Him in the likeness of His death, certainly we shall be also in the likeness of His resurrection, knowing this, that our old self was crucified with Him, that our body of sin might be done away with, that we should no longer be slaves to sin; for he who has died is freed from sin. Now if we have died with Christ, we believe that we shall also live with Him, knowing that Christ, having been raised from the dead, is never to die again; death no longer is master over Him...For sin shall not be master over you, for you are not under law, but under grace...But now having been freed from sin and enslaved to God, you derive your benefit, resulting in sanctification, and the outcome, eternal life. For the wages of sin is death, but the free gift of God is eternal life in Christ Jesus our Lord." Romans 6:5-9, 14, 22-23

"There is therefore now no condemnation for those who are in Christ Jesus. For the law of the Spirit of life in Christ Jesus has set you free from the law of sin and of death." Romans 8:1-2

There is no need to set a captive free unless he/she is in bondage. The Jews were locked into a system of rules and regulations. God gave them basic commandments and instructions that they embellished and took to the extreme. Following the law required human effort which was motivated by fear; however, this system proved futile for no human being could ever perfectly fulfill every point of the law. Jesus came that we might be free to do what is right, able to discern truth from error, and realize God's grace. Man deserves death because of sin; but instead, Jesus offers life eternal and deliverance without exception. A slave could be sold, but as children of God, we will remain His forever. "If therefore the Son shall make you free, you shall be free indeed" (John 8:36). Dwelling in God's grace changes the perspective. The power to live under grace comes from the indwelling of the Holy Spirit. Our motivation to obey God's Word is then transformed from a spirit of fear, "because I have to," to one of love, "because I want to."

Jericho - The last Passover observed before the people of Israel entered the Promised Land prepared them for their first victory at Jericho. Humanly speaking, the obvious military strategy would have been to immediately attack, for Kings of this region had heard, "...how the Lord had dried up the waters of the Jordan before the sons of Israel until they had crossed, that their hearts melted, and there was no spirit in them any longer, because of the sons of Israel." (Joshua 5:1b) Instead, God instructed Joshua to perform the right of circumcision on the sons of Israel; an observance their parents had neglected to do. As the debilitated army moaned and groaned from the pain, God's message warned them against the temptation to follow the same rebellious acts of callous indifference and lack of faith that their parents had.

> "For the sons of Israel walked forty years in the wilderness, until all the nation, that is, the men of war who came out of Egypt, perished because they did not listen to the voice of the LORD, to whom the LORD had sworn that He would not let them see the land which the LORD had sworn to their fathers to give us, a land flowing with milk and honey. And their children whom He raised up in their place, Joshua circumcised; for they were uncircumcised, because they had not circumcised

> them along the way. Now it came about when they had finished circumcising all the nation, that they remained in their places in the camp until they were healed. Then the LORD said to Joshua, 'Today I have rolled away the reproach of Egypt from you.' So the name of that place is called Gilgal to this day." Joshua 5:6-9

The compliance of Joshua's army to God's command and the time of physical healing are viewed as a rolling away of the sins of the past to prepare for the blessings of the future. God gave this place a name with significance, for it means, "the rolling." In an unusual way, God both made these men ready for battle and prepared them to observe their last Passover in the desert.

> "While the sons of Israel camped at Gilgal, they observed the Passover on the evening of the fourteenth day of the month on the desert plains of Jericho. And on the day after the Passover, on that very day, they ate some of the produce of the land, **unleavened cakes** and parched grain. And the manna ceased on the day after they had eaten some of the produce of the land, so that the sons of Israel no longer had manna, but they ate some of the yield of the land of Canaan during that year." Joshua 5:10-12

Passover Dinner - The Passover meal is also called the Seder. This Hebrew word stands for order. Scripture records that the first menu had only three food items: lamb meat, unleavened bread, and bitter herbs. Later, other foods, traditions, and sayings were added to represent various aspects of the Exodus story. Focusing on the original elements of this meal proves rich in symbolism as it paints a clear and revealing portrait of the promised Messiah. How fitting that the last meal Jesus shared before His death, a Seder dinner, was also the first Communion. Let us examine the connection:

In the Passover meal, bitter-tasting herbs reminded the people of the sufferings of Egypt. Eating the roasted flesh of the animal represented the sacrifice of the Passover lamb. Just as God ordained that no bones of the lamb were to be broken (Exodus 12:46), so too, none of Jesus' bones were broken that Scripture might be fulfilled (John 19:33). Partaking the unleavened bread spoke of two points God wanted the people to keep in mind: Never forget how you prepared and ate your meal in haste and how God brought you out of this land of affliction.

> "You shall not eat leavened bread with it; seven days you shall eat with it unleavened bread, the bread of affliction (for you came out of the land of Egypt in haste), in order that you may remember all the days of your life the day when you came out of the land of Egypt. For seven days no leaven shall be seen with you in all your territory, and none of the flesh which you sacrifice on the evening of the first day shall remain overnight until morning." Deuteronomy 16:3-4

Communion is a remembrance in which the elements bid me to never lose sight of the sacrifice that exchanged the bitter bondage of my sins for the sweet pardon of all my iniquities. While communion beckons us to reflect on the cause and cost of Jesus' sacrifice, the Passover dessert proclaims the victorious end result.

> "Bless the LORD, O my soul; and all that is within me, bless His holy name. Bless the LORD, O my soul, and forget none of His benefits; who pardons all your iniquities; who heals all your diseases; who redeems your life from the pit; who crowns you with loving-kindness and compassion;

197

who satisfies your years with good things, so that your youth is renewed like the eagle." Psalms 103:1-5

Aftikomen - Also known as the Passover dessert, the Aftikomen is born of tradition, begins like a drama, and ends up portraying the exclamation point of the Gospel – the resurrection. The father or grandfather of the Jewish family takes three pieces of matzo (unleavened bread) and places them in a special white linen napkin that has three compartments. He than takes out the middle piece, breaks it, leaves one half in the linen, wraps the other half in another linen napkin, and hides the latter portion for the children to find. The father redeems, or buys back, with a coin the Aftikomen or "bread of affliction," from whomever brings it to him. Afterwards, everyone shares a portion of it to eat. The excitement of finding the Aftikomen is a small reflection of what Jesus' disciples went through. Even though Jesus told them He would rise from the grave after three days, they were still surprised when He actually did!

The three matzos are likened to the Trinity. Jesus, the second person of the Godhead, was taken (seized by the Roman guards), broken (beaten, pierced, and killed), wrapped in a white linen, hidden away in a tomb, and raised from the dead. As I think of Jesus holding a bit of matzo bread in His hand that final Passover meal before His death, I believe His eyes were not focused as much on the suffering before Him as on the sweet victory that lay beyond the cross.

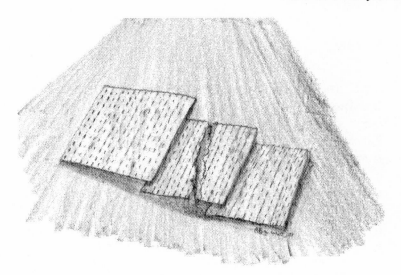

"Therefore, since we have so great a cloud of witnesses surrounding us, let us also lay aside every encumbrance, and the sin which so easily entangles us, and let us run with endurance the race that is set before us, fixing our eyes on Jesus, the author and perfecter of faith, who for the joy set before Him endured the cross, despising the shame, and has sat down at the right hand of the throne of God." Hebrews 12:1-2

To summarize, the basic lesson of the first Passover involved simple faith, trust in God, a willingness to obey God's command, and a belief that lives would be spared as a result. Sincerity, pedigrees, or cultural ties were meaningless if one chose to disobey; without the blood, death came swift and sure. The requirements have not changed for us today - God still demands a blood sacrifice to atone for sin. Is Jesus your Passover Lamb?

"Jesus said to him, 'I am the way, and the truth, and the life; **no one** comes to the Father, but through Me.'" John 14:6

199

Prayer:

Lord Jesus, by faith, the people of Israel applied the blood of the Pascal lamb to the entrance of each home believing that they would be kept safe. By faith, I know that You stand at the door of everyone's heart and invite us to decide to let You set us free or to remain in bondage to our sins. For the Word says, "Behold, I stand at the door and knock; if any one hears My voice and opens the door, I will come in to him, and will dine with him, and he with Me" (Revelations 3:20).

My sins are like bitter herbs whose taste lingers long in my mouth, reminding me of the sufferings my sins have caused. Lord Jesus, I ask You to be my Passover Lamb, to pay the price for all my sins. I acknowledge that I am unable to stand in the presence of a holy God because I am a sinner. Thanks be to Jesus, the only "True Unleavened Bread," who can do what no one else can, "pass over" my sins and set me free!

As the people of Israel continue to remember Passover, let me never forget that when I obey Your instructions, I am always in the safety of Your grace and mercy. Praise the Lord, for all God's children can rejoice knowing that we will remain in God's house, dwell in His presence, and dine at the King's table forever and ever. Amen.

Devotional:

Praise – Genesis Chapter 22 records Abraham's willingness to offer his only son Isaac as a sacrifice to God. Pleased with Abraham's attitude and actions, God's angelic messenger said, "Do not stretch out your hand against the lad, and do nothing to him; for now I know that you fear God, since you have not withheld your son, your only son, from Me." "Then Abraham raised his eyes and looked, and behold, behind him a ram caught in the thicket by his horns; and Abraham went and took the ram, and offered him up for a burnt offering in the place of his son" (Genesis 22:12-13). Abraham called the name of the place where God provided a ram as a substitute, Jehovah Jireh. This phrase means "the Lord sees" or "the Lord will provide." Just like Passover, this story is a picture of redemption. Isaac was set free because the ram took his place. Jehovah Jireh foresees our every need and He is willing and able to meet every need of His people. Romans 8:32 poses a compelling question which has an obvious answer. Look up the verse, meditate on its meaning, answer the question, and praise the Lord!

Confession – Imagine what each Jewish family who obeyed God's instructions experienced the night of the first Passover. With the blood of the sacrificial lamb painted around the door and a feast on the table, the people believed the angel of death would not visit their home – and God kept His promise. If you have invited Jesus into your life, then the same power which kept the Israelites alive is available to keep you, as one of God's children, safe from judgment. As you confess your sins to God, have confidence. When the Father sees the blood of Jesus, the Passover Lamb, like a sign upon you – know that in Him your sins will be forgiven.

> "The next day he [John the Baptist] saw Jesus coming to him, and said, 'Behold, the Lamb of God who takes away the sin of the world!'" John 1:29

Thanksgiving – Daniel Chapter 3 recounts the story of Shadrach, Meshach, and Abed-nego. These three valiant men refused to obey King Nebuchadnezzar's command to bow down and worship a golden image of this same king. As punishment, all three were thrown into a fiery furnace. The blazing heat of the furnace consumed the king's warriors who cast these men into the furnace; however, Shadrach, Meshach, and Abed-nego remained safe; the only thing which burned were the ropes which bound them. The astounded King made an amazing observation and said, "'Was it not three men we cast bound into the midst of the fire?' They answered and said to the king, 'Certainly, O king.' He answered and said, 'Look! I see four men loosed and walking about in the midst of the fire without harm, and the appearance of the fourth is like a son of the gods!'" (Daniel 3:24b-25) As the three men came out of the midst of the fire, the king and his officials inspected them. Not only were their bodies, hair, and clothing unaffected, but the smell of fire was not upon them. "Nebuchadnezzar responded and said, 'Blessed be the God of Shadrach, Meshach, and Abed-nego, who has sent His angel and delivered His servants who put their trust in Him, violating the king's command, and yielded up their bodies so as not to serve or worship any god except their own God.'" (Daniel 3:28)

Do you feel like you are alone in a fiery furnace today? Just as God's protective covering surrounded Shadrach, Meshach, and Abed-nego, so too is Jehovah Jireh with us. Read Psalm 139:7-12 and rejoice with the Psalmist, for there is no place we can go where God is not with us!

Intercession – Bring your petitions to the Lord with a grateful heart recognizing that believers are completely safe and secure in God's grip. See John 10:27-30 for details.

Submission – Concerning the first Passover, Scripture does not give a record of any Jewish family that refused to comply with God's instructions. As a result of their obedience,

God set them free from bondage and spared each firstborn's life. Passover is a picture of redemption, and the story of Jesus' life, death, and resurrection is the reality. As our redeemer, Jesus paid a debt He did not owe (the penalty of our sins), freed us from the bondage of sin, equipped us with the power to make godly choices, and restored our relationship with God the Father. At the moment of salvation, Jesus took something which was worthless (our sins) and granted to us something of infinite value (eternal life). `

When a person accepts Jesus as their redeemer, God places them in the "safety zone." Just as the obedient children of Israel were safe inside their homes on the first Passover, so too are we because of our faith in Jesus. When God sees the blood of Jesus, He extends to us grace (gives us what we do not deserve) and mercy (spares us from judgment), passes over our sins (forgives us), and meets every need (physical, emotional, financial, etc.). Believers who choose to obey God's Word remain in the "safety zone." They enjoy the full coverage and protection granted according to God's perfect plan. As you weigh the choices before you today, consider the following quote from a believer who decided to step outside of God's will for a season:

"Through my time away, God gave me an object lesson about His nature. Though God hates sin, even amidst my rebellion God demonstrated His boundless love, limitless patience, infinite wisdom, and amazing grace. Looking back, I acknowledge that God's hand guarded the hard road I chose like a safety net. If God had abandoned me, my situation could have been worse, but my poor choices never left God without a plan. Even outside of God's will, God knew my need and how to satisfy my hunger and quench my thirst. The greatest lesson I learned is that God never gives up on me. My sins put a strain on the relationship, but my heavenly Father never pushed me away!"

Jesus said, "All that the Father gives Me shall come to Me, and the one who comes to Me I will certainly not cast out" (John 6:37 – Look up the surrounding verses for the whole context.   The theme verse of <u>The Bread Lady's Quest</u> precedes this verse!).

"Jesus answered and said to him, 'If anyone loves Me, he will keep My word; and My Father will love him, and We will come to him, and make Our abode with him.'" John 14:23

Chapter 14: The Feast of Unleavened Bread

The Feast of Unleavened Bread begins the very next day after Passover and lasts for seven days. For the duration of this feast, God commanded that only unleavened bread be eaten. God stressed the importance of following this dietary restriction by passing severe judgment upon those who failed to eat bread made without yeast during this time.

"You shall also observe the Feast of Unleavened Bread, for on this very day I brought your hosts out of the land of Egypt; therefore you shall observe this day throughout your generations as a permanent ordinance. In the first month, on the fourteenth day of the month at evening, you shall eat unleavened bread, until the twenty-first day of the month at evening. Seven days there shall be no leaven found in your houses; for whoever eats what is leavened, that person shall be cut off from the congregation of Israel, whether he is an alien or a native of the land." Exodus 12:17-19

Scripture emphasizes that this week is to be used to keep fresh the memory of the day God freed the people of Israel from bondage. Perhaps the severity of the above judgment is connected to the importance of preserving the sanctity of this holiday and preventing any contamination of the message with the sin symbolized by leaven.

Let there be no mistake, the wonders performed by two men, Moses and Aaron, did not sway Pharaoh's heart to let the people go; however, the handiwork of a Holy God more powerful than the idols of Egypt sent ripples of fear throughout the land.

> "And you shall tell your son on that day, saying, 'It is because of what the LORD did for me when I came out of Egypt.' And it shall serve as a sign to you on your hand, and as a reminder on your forehead, that the law of the LORD may be in your mouth; for with a powerful hand the LORD brought you out of Egypt." Exodus 13:8-9

From the preparation through the duration, no other feast exemplifies God's holy standard of living or the purity of the life and works of Christ more than this feast.

Preparation - Nullification is the ritual performed before the festival arrives and was to be completed prior to the sacrifice of the Pascal lamb. The only specific instruction given to Moses was to remove all food products with leaven from the home. Ellen Parker, a Jewish/Christian missionary in Mexico City, explains: "Ceremonial acts are performed out of tradition to accomplish the above requirement: First, the mother removes all the known hametz (food products with leaven) to begin the cleansing of the household. Next, the father and the children conduct a search by candlelight, the night before Passover. A feather sweeps up any crumb of leaven found into a wooden spoon. Once completed, the feather, wooden spoon, and any hametz is ceremoniously burned; thus ending the process of nullification."[1]

As the Jewish households nullify themselves of all symbolic traces of evil, let believers in Christ take that concept inward. As previously mentioned, feasts are a time of meeting between God and man for a holy purpose. In the same manner, let Christians come to the Communion table with not only clean hands, but also a pure heart, that nothing may hinder us from seeing God's plan for our lives. In the book of Leviticus, God spoke to Moses and declared that He would sanctify His people. Lives defined as unleavened give a tangible reality of what God intended when He said:

"You shall consecrate yourselves therefore and be holy, for I am the LORD your God. And you shall keep My statutes and practice them; I am the LORD who sanctifies you." Leviticus 20:7-8

Prayer:
Lord, I give You the freedom to search every room, closet, and corner of my heart to expose any hidden sin of which I am unaware. Give me the courage to thoroughly examine myself in the light of Your perfect standard and in the warm, forgiving, accepting presence of Your promised mercy and grace. As I come to partake of the elements of Communion, do not let me cling to even a trace of evil for Your Word warns me: "...whoever eats the bread or drinks the cup of the Lord in an unworthy manner, shall be guilty of the body and the blood of the Lord. But let a man examine himself, and so let him eat of the bread and drink of the cup" (1 Corinthians 11:27-28). Therefore, I confess my sins to You. My heart is jubilant over the truth that You are able to destroy my sins and nullify the contaminating effects leaven has had on my life. I praise You and thank You for accepting the bitter sufferings of the cross to make a way for me to enjoy Your sweet fellowship. Amen.

Connected to the Body of Christ - Jesus held a flat bread in His hand, in a room prepared by the traditional mandates of Passover. After giving a blessing, He broke it, and gave it to them, and said, "...'Take, eat; this is My body.' And when He had taken a cup and given thanks, He gave it to them, saying, 'Drink from it, all of you; for this is My blood of the covenant, which is poured out for many for forgiveness of sins" (Matthew 26:26-28).

In applying the image of unleavened bread to His body, Jesus maintained His life contained no sin in order to fulfill the Messianic requirement spoken of in Isaiah 53:9: "His grave was assigned with wicked men, yet He was with a rich man in His death, because He had done no violence, nor was there any deceit in His mouth." Unleavened bread depicts the deity, holiness, and purity of Christ, while leavened bread reminds me of the moment in time when the humanity of Christ absorbed all our sins. The purity of Christ, as reflected by the unleavened bread, and the absence of leaven in the Jewish household in remembrance of Passover, both suggest those under the safety of the shed blood were seen as free from the corruption of sin before a holy God.

> "He made Him who knew no sin to be sin on our
> behalf, that we might become the righteousness
> of God in Him." 2 Corinthians 5:21

Examining Matzo Bread – Matzo is the unleavened bread eaten at the Passover. I purchased a box of kosher (prepared according to Jewish law) matzo bread in order to investigate the contents. The label proclaims: *A fat free, cholesterol free, sodium free food made with only Passover flour and water.* If you want kosher matzo bread that is suitable for Passover – check the label carefully because some boxes said, "Not for Passover use." Passover flour is guarded or watched continually from the time that the grain is harvested until the dough is put into the oven to ensure that no fermentation has taken place. In his article, "Passover," Steve Herzig explained, "To further ensure the absence of even a trace of leaven, special dishes are used, as well as special pots and pans to prepare food, none of which will have any leaven in them."[2] Pure through and through, not a speck of yeast would be acceptable in the end product. The inclusion of the ingredient of water brings a flood of previously covered symbolism summed up in this thought: Jesus is the source of living water that encompasses our hope of eternal life. The square flat bread has holes throughout which appear like windows. When held up to the light, the rays of the sun shine through the openings. The bland taste of the bread did not call attention to itself. Having a dry texture, matzo bread draws attention to the Savior's lowly background as He came "...like a root out of parched ground" (Isaiah 53:2). The likeness of matzo bread to Jesus is fivefold: His purity and sinless nature, His gift of eternal life, the wounds that pierced His flesh, His outward earthly appearance, and the source of His earthly roots. Listen to the prophet Isaiah's physical description of the Messiah's sufferings. Consider the source of His sufferings. Remember the end result. And contemplate what this truth will mean to the people of Israel someday:

> "For He grew up before Him like a tender shoot, and like a root out of parched ground; He has no stately form or majesty that we should look upon Him, nor appearance that we should be attracted to Him. He was despised and forsaken of men, a man of sorrows, and acquainted with grief; and like one from whom men hide their face, He was despised, and we did not esteem Him. Surely **our griefs** He Himself bore, and **our sorrows** He carried; yet we ourselves esteemed Him stricken, smitten of God, and afflicted. But He was pierced through for **our transgressions**, He was crushed for **our iniquities**; **the chastening for our well-being** fell upon Him, and by His scourging we are healed. All of us like sheep have gone astray, each of us has turned to his own way; but the Lord has caused the iniquity of us all to fall on Him." Isaiah 53:2-6

Another prophet, Zechariah, speaks to the Second Coming of Christ as a time when Israel will acknowledge Jesus as their Messiah when they realize He is the one whom their forefathers pierced:

"And I will pour out on the house of David and on the inhabitants of Jerusalem, the Spirit of grace and of supplication, so that they will look on Me whom they have pierced; and they will mourn for Him, as one mourns for an only son, and they will weep bitterly over Him, like the bitter weeping over a first-born." Zechariah 12:10

Set Apart - Just as the matzo bread, made with Passover flour, was kept pure from beginning to end, so too was Christ set apart for purity and incorruptibility from the beginning of His ministry on earth to His ascension back to heaven. In His sermon at Pentecost, the Apostle Peter said this of Jesus:

"And God raised Him up again, putting an end to the agony of death, since it was impossible for Him to be held in its power." Acts 2:24

Then Peter quoted from King David's Psalms the verse that exempted the body of Christ from the divine pronouncement after the fall of Adam and Eve that we shall all become dust from whence we came.

"For Thou wilt not abandon my soul to Sheol; neither wilt Thou allow Thy Holy One to undergo decay." Psalm 16:10

When people die, their bodies undergo a decaying process. For a Jew to touch the body of a dead person made them unclean. In this state, the unclean person could transfer that defilement onto others much like a contagious disease. Just as Jesus must cleanse us from our sins, the unclean person had to undergo a process of purification to become clean once again. Since unclean people could not participate in Passover, God instructed Moses to allow them to observe the feast one month later than the prescribed date. (Numbers 9: 6-12)

> "But there were some men who were unclean because of the dead person, so that they could not observe Passover on that day; so they came before Moses and Aaron on that day." Numbers 9:6

> "The one who touches the corpse of any person shall be unclean for seven days. That one shall purify himself from uncleanness with the water on the third day and on the seventh day, and then he shall be clean; but if he does not purify himself on the third day and on the seventh day, he shall not be clean. Anyone who touches a corpse, the body of a man who has died, and does not purify himself, defiles the tabernacle of the LORD; and that person shall be cut off from Israel. Because the water for impurity was not sprinkled on him, he shall be unclean; his uncleanness is still on him." Numbers 19:11-13

The body of our Lord never experienced the ravages of death while in the grave; therefore, according to Marvin Rosenthal, the second feast instituted by God proclaims the sanctification of Christ. For He was set apart for a holy purpose.3

Closing Ceremony - The Feast of Unleavened Bread ends as it began, with a decree similar to a Sabbath day's rest.

> "On the first day you shall have a holy convocation; you shall not do any laborious work. But for seven days you shall present an offering by fire to the LORD. On the seventh day is a holy

211

convocation; you shall not do any laborious work."
Leviticus 23:7-8

During this time the people ceased from the laborious work of the day such as reaping the harvest, threshing the wheat, grinding grain to flour and so on. Similarly, to create the heavens, the earth, and all that is in the universe, God, seeing all that He had made, praised Himself by calling it, "very good." When God completed His work of creation, the seventh day became representative of the perfect satisfaction He felt with the results. The Feast of Unleavened Bread celebrates the finished work of God as He fully moved the people out of the land of Egypt and defeated their enemies; thus, having a cessation of their normal activities gave a fitting end to this holiday by building in some time to rest and focus on what a marvelous feat God had accomplished.

A Family Matter - As individuals, both Communion and the Feast of Unleavened Bread remind us of the importance of taking the time to reflect on and beware of any error or evil in our personal lives, for we are called to holy living.

> "As obedient children, do not be conformed to the former lusts which were yours in your ignorance, but like the Holy One who called you, be holy yourselves also in all your behavior; because it is written, "YOU SHALL BE HOLY, FOR I AM HOLY." 1 Peter 1:14-15

Turning from a private, intimate, personal sphere, let us now take a look at the corporate level and see how the life of the church body should operate. In the Apostle Paul's chastisement to the Church of Corinth for openly tolerating the sin of incest, he used the first two feasts to make his points:

> "And you have become arrogant, and have not mourned instead, in order that the one who had

done this deed might be removed from your midst...Your boasting is not good. Do you not know that a little leaven leavens the whole lump of dough? Clean out the old leaven, that you may be a new lump, just as you are in fact unleavened. For Christ our Passover also has been sacrificed. Let us therefore celebrate the feast, not with old leaven, nor with the leaven of malice and wickedness, but with the unleavened bread of sincerity and truth." 1 Corinthians 5:2,6-8

First Paul reminds them of the known fact that welcoming a believer engrossed in his/her sin to remain in the assembly is like inviting a little leaven to ferment in the church pews. If undealt with, the souring effects will permeate the entire Church family. Allowing such a one to partake of the bread and wine of Communion in an unworthy state would create an atmosphere of hypocrisy and confusion, which are breeding grounds for discord. The hearts of the leadership need to beat with the spirit of openness to God's leading and bleed with the brokenness of an attitude of grieving over their own sin and that of others. Then they will be given the power to act in a united effort to deal with the residual sins (old leaven) of our life before Christ, so that the members can function in their new position in Christ (unleavened). Trying to bake unleavened bread in a pan labeled wickedness will never yield a loaf worthy of illustrating the power of Jesus as our Passover Lamb; nor will it demonstrate the purity of walking in holiness as did our sanctified Lord. How can the world know what Jesus looks like if we never learn how to bake heavenly bread!

Prayer:

Lord, purify the hearts of the pastors, elders, and leaders of our church. Revive, renew, and equip them to guard over the hearts of their people like the orthodox Jews guarded the Passover flour. Bless them with wisdom, humility, and love that they may gain the respect of the people. Teach them how to become aware of any speck of sin and act swiftly with boldness and grace before iniquity is allowed to ferment and spill out among the congregation. From the moment a new believer is harvested from the field of the world and throughout their maturing of faith, give the leaders a tender heart to participate in this process.

Protect Your people from becoming disillusioned when leaders fall. Let Your Holy Spirit burn like a hot oven to stop the fermenting action of sin and set in motion a holy fire to light the way for love, forgiveness, restoration, and revival. Empower us with the wisdom to leave the ashes of disappointment in man behind. Prevent us from dipping our fingers into the ashes of another's sins for the purpose of spreading gossip. Teach us to focus on the stability, holiness, and unchanging nature of Jesus, our best example of living an unleavened lifestyle. Through the power of Your unconditional love, bond Your children together that our members may remain a family and not forsake assembling together in peace and unity.

The purity of Your church is at stake, Lord. Let the changes You inspire begin at the top and filter all the way down to the babes in arms. Blessed Holy Spirit, take command of the bakery You have entrusted to Your church. Throw out the batches of good works tainted with the leaven of fleshly effort. Praise to You for Your patience and forgiveness regarding our half-hearted efforts. Create in us a new lump of dough, a fresh start. Let the product be bread so full of sincerity and truth that no one can discount its tasty flavor and fragrant, blameless nature.

Lord, save Your church from the humiliation of baking lifeless bread. You alone can teach us how to produce genuine life-giving bread because You hold the key that unlocks the secret ingredient. When the world asks me why I refuse to add to, omit, or change God's design, my answer never changes, "Jesus is 'the Bread of Life' and I can never improve on His recipe to sanctify His church!" Amen.

"Blessed be the God and Father of our Lord Jesus Christ, who has blessed us with every spiritual blessing in the heavenly places in Christ, just as He chose us in Him before the foundation of the world, that we should be holy and blameless before Him..." Ephesians 1:3-4

Devotional: Since this devotional is too long to absorb in one sitting, it has been divided into sections. Take time to allow God's Holy Spirit to move in your heart as you pray.

Praise – The name, Jehovah M'kaddesh, means "the Lord who sanctifies." One who is sanctified is set apart for a holy purpose. Scripture testifies that God's Holy Spirit empowers us to live holy lives, thus enabling us to fulfill God's plan. Fire is a symbol of God's holiness. The Lord our God is called a "consuming fire, a jealous God" (Deuteronomy 4:24). God desires to enjoy our company for all eternity; however, we will not be fit for heaven until He consumes all traces of sin and fills us up with His holy presence.

> "Now may the God of peace Himself sanctify you **entirely**; and may your spirit and soul and body be preserved complete, without blame at the coming of our Lord Jesus Christ. Faithful is He who calls you, and He also will bring it to pass." 1 Thessalonians 5:23-24

Can believers attain complete sanctification this side of heaven? Humanly speaking, that is impossible! A blameless person is one with no legitimate ground for accusation. Every person falls short of God's perfect standard (Romans 3:23). Only Jesus fits the definition of holy, which is: spiritually perfect or pure, sinless, deserving awe, reverence, and adoration (see 1 Peter 1:17-19). If God's people, the bride of Christ, stand blameless at Jesus' second coming, it will not be a reason for man to boast; God alone could perform such a miracle! Praise the Lord!

Confession – The activity of the Holy Spirit is likened to a fire. Just as hot water kills yeast, so too will God's holy, unquenchable fire completely burn up all the chaff of wickedness on the Judgment Day (See Luke 3:16-17). Scripture warns, "Do not quench the Spirit" (1 Thessalonians 5:19). The Spirit is quenched whenever His ministry of sanctification is stifled in an individual or a church. By comparing the effect of temperature on yeast with the spiritual thermometer of the seven churches addressed in the book of Revelation, and concepts from the parable of the sower, we can test how free the Holy Spirit is to work in a believer's life. (If you want to visualize this principle, follow the instructions for the fermentation experiment in Chapter 12. Add ½ cup water, ½ Tbsp. Honey, and ½ Tbsp. Yeast to each of four bottles, but vary the temperature in each; 200° for hot, 140° for warm, 110° for lukewarm, and 60° for ice-cold water.)

Yeast	The seed is God's Word. The soil is the human heart.	The seven churches
Boiling hot water kills yeast instantly.	The seed planted in a responsive heart bears lasting fruit (see Matthew 13:23).	Church of Smyrna (Revelations 2:8-11) and Church of Philadelphia (Revelations 3:7-13)
Warm water slows fermentation.	The seed planted in the shallow heart has no firm roots to their faith (see Matthew 13:20-21).	Church of Pergamum (Revelations 2:12-17) and Church of Thyatira (Revelations 2:18-29)
Yeast placed in ice-cold water appears lifeless until the water comes to room temperature hours later and it springs to life.	The passive, unresponsive heart does not allow God's Word to penetrate; thus, their faith is without growth (see Matthew 13:19).	Church of Sardis (Revelations 3:1-6) and Church of Ephesus (Revelations 2:1-7)
Lukewarm water provides the perfect environment for yeast to quickly grow and thrive.	The cluttered, preoccupied heart crowds out the right response (see Matthew 13:22).	Church of Laodicea (Revelations 3:14-22)

217

The beauty of heaven resides in the heart of those who are **spiritually hot**. The Churches of Smyrna and Philadelphia were the only ones receiving no rebuke and only commendation. Those who are spiritually alive hear God's Word, understand it, act on it, and bear "good" fruit. God's refining fire has swept through their being and their heart's desire is to be holy, to answer God's call, and to be ready to do their Master's will. Their eyes are open; they are not naïve. Their mind is sharp; the division between right and wrong is clear; sin is not tolerated. No matter what the cost, their aim is to draw as close to God as humanly possible. Quiet moments sitting at the Savior's feet in prayer can be as difficult as sitting at length very close to a blazing hot fire. When my son Zack was nine years old, he invented a "heat shield," a cardboard mask covered with aluminum foil, to protect his face. This invention allowed him to sit by a hot burning fireplace longer. In the same way, once sins are confessed, sitting by God's holy fire feels pleasant.

Believers who are **spiritually warm** mix the beauty of heaven with the ugliness of the world. I classify the Churches of Pergamum and Thyatira as warm since they are exhorted to repent of their sins, yet are given some commendations. The fire and zeal of those spiritually warm has diminished. They hear the Word, but confusion enters in causing gray areas to form between right and wrong. Their spiritual eyes are half-mast; thus, they are unable to see things clearly at times. Sin is either hidden or openly tolerated. When persecution arises, some fall away.

In a state of **spiritual hypothermia**, the Church of Sardis is rebuked for being dead. The Church of Ephesus is commended for not tolerating wicked men, yet they are rebuked for allowing their love for the Lord to grow cold. The spiritually cold hear God's Word without understanding it, their foundation is weak, and they are unable to defend their faith. They are spiritually passive and apathetic. Without a passion for God, missing church, failing to read the Bible, and skipping prayer becomes a way of life. Their sleepy senses are dull, not sharp, and the enemy finds no challenge in snatching the truth away. Sin may be dormant, but can quickly spring to life. With small embers of life flickering, the exhortation to a cold believer sends a challenge, "Wake up, and strengthen the things that remain, which were about to die; for I have not found your deeds completed in the sight of My God. Remember therefore what you have received and heard; and keep it, and repent. If therefore you will not wake up, I will come like a thief, and you will not know at what hour I will come upon you" (Revelation 3:2-3).

The beauty of heaven has vanished from the heart of the **lukewarm Christian** and their passion for God extinguished. A fire not properly tended will die down. Dousing a warm fire with cold water or adding moisture-filled logs causes the fire to sputter and spit as it sends smoke into the air and embers flying. No longer able to enjoy the fire, windows must be opened and fresh air let into the room. Even the next day, a smoky scent permeates the house making breathing labored. The Church of Laodicea is the only church that received no commendation and only rebuke. Scripture describes them as "wretched, miserable, poor, blind, and naked" for they have quenched the Spirit. They are backsliders who hear the Word, but the worries of the world and the deceitfulness of riches make this the home of compromise. Truth is perverted and ethics are the invention of man. Their eyes are blind; thus, they have lost sight of what God has ordained is right and wrong. With choices clearly influenced by the world, sin is accepted and thriving. They are deceived and unfruitful. The smoky remnants of their deeds make them miserable, yet God tenderly offers them relief (see Revelations 3:18-21).

As believers, we can all slip through times where we are spiritually hot, warm, lukewarm, and cold because salvation does not remove our free will. The phrase that ends each message to the seven churches applies to all: "He who has an ear, let him hear what the Spirit says to the churches" (Revelations 3:22). During this time of confession, look inward and answer these questions: "How is your spiritual fire burning?" If Jesus reigns in your heart, consider this promise, "Sin shall not be master over you" (see Romans 6:5-14). What benefit have you derived from the things of which you are ashamed (see Romans 6:21)? What benefit is there in submitting to God (see Romans 6:22-23)? What happens when you choose to overcome evil with good (see Romans 12:9-21)? The good deeds you heap on your enemy are described as burning coals. God uses these burning coals to start a holy fire in others, but cold coals are useless.

Let go of sin; lay hold of God's grace; secure His mercy; let God stoke your spiritual fire. It is never too late to invest your life in the kingdom. God's goal is to sanctify His church and this process begins with a repentant heart, receptive mind, and willing spirit.

Thanksgiving – If the process of sanctification depended on the works of man, no one would cross the finish line. Read the following verses and rejoice, for God is able to complete what He starts! Each believer's story will have a happy ending; all will be transformed into the image of God's Son.

> "For I am confident of this very thing, that He who began a good work in you will perfect it until the day of Christ Jesus." Philippians 1:6

> "For our citizenship is in heaven, from which also we eagerly wait for a Savior, the Lord Jesus Christ; who will transform the body of our humble state into conformity with the body of His glory, by the exertion of the power that He has even to subject all things to Himself." Philippians 3:20-21

Intercession – The image of Christ, like unleavened bread, is a picture of one who is spiritually on fire for God and has a blameless, peaceful conscience. The image of sinful man, like leavened bread, is a picture of one who is lukewarm in faith, willfully resisting God's plan, puffed up with self, quenching the Spirit's ministry, and **never** able to rest! Bread dough can only truly rest when there is no yeast to make it rise. In this intercession time, focus on asking for a spirit of holiness and a life full of Christ-like behavior. Pray without ceasing, for the battle is fierce! God will sanctify His church, but the enemy's goal is to keep sin alive as long as possible. When the enemy accuses you of wrong doing, pray you will be able to honestly echo the defense the Apostle Paul used when persecuted:

> "In view of this, I also do my best to maintain always a blameless conscience both before God and before men." Acts 24:16

Submission – Read 1 Peter 1:14-16 and decide: be conformed to the world or allow God's Holy Spirit the freedom to sanctify your body, soul, and spirit. Are you standing on holy ground or unholy ground? Let God's standard be the judge. Jesus fed 5,000 with five loaves and two fish. How much of Jesus, "the Bread of Life," do you have in your hand to offer a dying world? Whether you have little or much, God desires to cause it to multiply. Are you ready to do His will?

Chapter 15: Communion: God's Recipe for Peace

As a child of seven, I remember feeling like a bride as I wore a homemade white dress and donned a lace-trimmed veil for the celebration of my first Holy Communion. A matching white purse hung from my arm and held a tiny white prayer book with a shiny, colorful picture of Jesus and a little girl like me on the front cover. Marching down the aisle with child-like faith, I believed the basic truth that Jesus died for my sins and rose again. When I arrived at the front of the line the Priest repeated the words, "The Body of Christ." I responded as taught by saying "Amen" and receiving the host on my tongue.

To say "Amen" is to give hearty approval to what has been said. Then I could comprehend only the simplicity of the teaching. Now that I have studied the ingredients of bread as they relate to Christ and pondered the cup of suffering He drank for me, the depth of meaning fills my thoughts far longer than it takes for the round flat white Communion wafer to dissolve in my mouth. From the preparation and celebration of the first three Feasts instituted by God, to the sacrifice on the cross, past the doorway of the empty grave, the elements of Communion represent the principles needed to discover God's recipe for finding a peaceful connection between a Holy God and a sinful man. Baked together like a perfectly-formed loaf of fine homemade bread, the story brings the Jew and the Gentile together for a more complete picture. God is the Master Baker. His message is complete and pure; thus, I could find no gaping holes. His news is not only good to hear, but it fills all my senses with wonder. God's Word compels me to examine myself, the bread, the wine, and the art of baking bread as we come to the Lord's Supper Table.

Personal Identification: To identify with the death of Christ is to realize that because of His self-sacrificing love, He gave up His life for me and for you. During His Last Supper, just prior to the cross, Jesus spoke these words to His disciples:

> "Greater love has no one than this, that one lay down his life for his friends." John 15:13

> "And while they were eating, Jesus took some bread, and after a blessing, He broke it and gave it to the disciples, and said, 'Take, eat; this is My body.' And when He had taken the cup and given thanks, He gave it to them, saying, 'Drink from it, all of you; for this is My blood of the covenant, which is poured out for many for forgiveness of sins." Matthew 26:26-28

Personal Examination: Unconfessed sin represents a portion of the pain and suffering each one of us added to Jesus when He took upon Himself the past, present, and future sins of all mankind. Clinging to our sins with one hand and partaking of the elements of Communion with the other is the same as inviting our guilt and shame to dine with our Savior. Jesus never refused to eat a meal with a sinner; yet, His character did not allow Him to participate in their sins. Jesus mastered the art of loving, made the sinner feel welcomed, and hated the sin at the same time.

> "For as often as you eat this bread and drink the cup, you proclaim the Lord's death until He comes. Therefore whoever eats the bread or drinks the cup of the Lord in an unworthy manner, shall be guilty of the body and the blood of the Lord. But let a man examine himself, and so let him eat of the bread and drink of the cup." 1 Corinthians 11:26-28

King David's closing remarks in Psalm 139 read like a poetic song beseeching God to cleanse his heart. To me, this proclaims the essence of how God wants us to prepare ourselves to receive the symbols of remembrance.

"Search me, O God, and know my heart; try me and know my anxious thoughts; and see if there be any hurtful way in me, and lead me in the everlasting way." Psalm 139:23-24

Come With a Humble Heart: At the evening meal before Passover, Jesus quietly rose from supper, laid aside His garments, took a towel, filled a basin with water, and in a dramatic display of humility, He washed the feet of His disciples as well as those of His betrayer, Judas. Confused, Peter watched His master switching roles by taking on a servant's job and blurted out, "Never shall You wash my feet!" Jesus warned, "If I do not wash you, you have no part with Me" (John 13:8). Once the job was done, Jesus explained His baffling behavior as a lesson in servanthood and a command to His followers to pattern their lives according to His attitude.

Jesus said, "If I then, the Lord and the Teacher, washed your feet, you also ought to wash one another's feet. For I gave you an example that you also should do as I did to you." John 13:14-15

The Apostle Paul further clarified, "Have this attitude in yourselves which was also in Christ Jesus, who although He existed in the form of God, did not regard equality with God a thing to be grasped, but emptied Himself, taking the form of a bond-servant, and being made in the likeness of men. And being found in appearance as a man, He humbled Himself by becoming obedient to the point of death, even death on a cross. Therefore also God highly exalted Him, and bestowed on Him the name which is above every name, that at the name of Jesus EVERY KNEE SHOULD BOW, of those who are in heaven, and on earth, and under the earth, and that every tongue should confess that Jesus Christ is Lord, to the glory of God the Father." Philippians 2:5-11

Sincere confession requires self-examination and humility for forgiveness to be genuine. Once the heart is made ready, the ears are open to hear God's voice, and the individual is ready to receive the bread and wine.

The Elements: Jesus commanded us to take and eat of the bread and drink of the cup. The Communion food is symbolic of internally taking in the words Jesus spoke. The bread embodied the purpose of His first coming, while the wine demonstrates the means and method for achieving His redemptive goal. I believe Jesus is asking us to swallow the whole message He came to give by digesting the meaning and letting the truth pour into our bloodstream, in order to infiltrate every part of us. Without blood in our veins we have no life. Unlike the physical food we eat, the spiritual food Jesus offers contains no waste products. All that Jesus holds out to us to receive is completely useful to nourish our soul and never leaves us wanting.

He teaches us His message through His true, true Word.
He fills my hunger to know Him with His sweet, sweet Word.
He feeds me true bread from heaven until I want no more.
Thank You Jesus, thank You Jesus for You fill my cup.
Blood of Jesus, blood of Jesus, wash me, wash me,
till the stain of sin I see no more.

The Art of Bread-baking: While we were yet like leavened bread, Christ died for us so that we could become unleavened like Him. Christ, the perfect, Unleavened Bread from heaven, willingly took the leaven of our sin upon Himself in order to defeat our wickedness which causes enmity between ourselves and God. Let us consider the art of bread baking and how it relates to the Easter story.

First the wheat is **crushed** to make flour, then all the ingredients are mixed together and a warm liquid is added. The dough is then **kneaded** (pounded, punched, and worked over), placed in a **hot oven**, baked, and then **broken** and **eaten** by people.   Listen to the words of the prophet Isaiah describing the passion of the suffering Servant of God (Jesus) and meditate on the similarities:

> "Surely our griefs He Himself bore, and our sorrows He carried; yet we ourselves esteemed Him stricken, smitten of God, and afflicted. But He was pierced through for our transgressions, He was crushed for our iniquities; the chastening for our well-being fell upon Him, and by His scourging we are healed. All of us like sheep have gone astray, each of us has turned to his own way; but the Lord has caused the iniquity of us all to fall on Him." Isaiah 53:4-6

When the broken body of our Savior lay in a borrowed tomb, the message of His unselfish, *agape* (a New Testament Greek word for unconditional love) love rang clear. He died not just for His chosen disciples and friends, He died to give the enemies of God a chance to be redeemed; yet, our sins were not powerful enough to hold Him in the grave. The Good News is that just as surely as leavened bread rises, so too did Jesus burst forth from the spiced tomb on the third day, just as He foretold that He would.   Jesus lives; therefore, we can be assured that our faith is not in vain and that eternal life is the guaranteed inheritance of every child of the King.

The Cup of Suffering: There is a contrast between the intimate way Jesus addresses God the Father in His prayer from the garden of Gethsemane and the anguish-filled cry from Calvary. In the garden He said, "My Father, if it is possible, let this cup pass from Me; yet not as I will, but as Thou wilt" (Matthew 26:39). On the cross He cried out with a loud voice,

227

"...My God, My God, why hast Thou forsaken Me?" (Matthew 27:46)

I believe the struggle to drink Gethsemane's cup did not lie in the torture that He faced, for the Father had sent the Son for the purpose of suffering in our place. His love for us willingly drew Him to this task. Rather, Jesus knew that once He drank the cup and took all of the sins of the world upon Himself, the intimate, unbroken fellowship He enjoyed with the Father would be broken until the goal had been accomplished. Put yourself in His place: if your best friend were forced to sever their relationship with you for a time, how would that feel? Jesus went farther than any man could ever go to conquer Satan, sin, and death. The physician Luke documents Jesus' last words, which indicate a restored intimacy between Father and Son. John's record of this final moment reflects the status of the work of Christ.

> "And Jesus, crying out with a loud voice, said, 'Father, into Thy Hands I commit My spirit.' And having said this, He breathed His last." Luke 23:46

> Jesus said, "...'It is finished.' And He bowed His head, and gave up His spirit." John 19:30

In Remembrance of Him: Communion is a picture of the gospel and an image of the bridge of love that God constructed to remind me of His personal, unbreakable commitment to all who draw near to Him. Using the essentials of prayer as a guide, I have formulated an outline that I use when partaking of the elements of remembrance. By pooling together the ingredients that make Jesus my life-giving bread, using what I have learned about the process of baking bread, sifting these concepts through Scripture, and correlating them to the Last Supper, I have a place to bring my broken dreams, wounded body, and sin-infested soul. There I can dwell awhile and then leave feeling like a whole, complete, new, fresh lump of unleavened dough. As a believer in Christ, I know that I can come to God in prayer at any time and be assured of the same effect; yet, there is something unique about this sacrament instituted by Christ which puts life into perspective as I review the magnitude of what Christ has done on my behalf. Progressing through these prayerful steps allows Communion to become a quiet moment interrupting the confusion and pressures of daily living in order to bring hope-filled "Good News."

Praise: Praising God for who He is lays a foundation on which to base my prayers of faith.

* Egg: I acknowledge that You are my Creator and I am Your child. (Read Genesis 2:7)

* Oil: Praise to You my loving Shepherd and able Caretaker. Your provisions for me are perfect because, as my Creator and Father, You alone know me best and are intimately acquainted with all of my wants, needs, and desires. (Read Psalm 23)

* Water: Jesus, my Lord and Savior, You are my source of eternal life. (Read John 4:13-14)

Confession: Examining what I have done begins the process of clearing my conscience by providing an opportunity for humility and repentance.

* Yeast: I acknowledge my sins to You, Lord. Without Your help, I cannot win my war against sin. (Read 1 John 1:6-10)

*Water: Lord, Jesus, I ask You to let the waters of Your salvation cleanse me of all of my sins. Thanks be to Jesus for placing this sinner in the position to be under divine construction that I may begin the process of becoming transformed into a holy vessel. (Read 1 John 1:9)

　　* Salt: I lay my sins before Your throne of mercy and grace; I accept the power You offer me to fight this daily battle. All praise and glory goes to You, my Father, for the weakness of my flesh is no match for Your sovereign majesty. (Read Philippians 4:13)

　　Thanksgiving: My gratitude brings me to my knees as I survey all that God has done for me.

　　* Wheat: Thank You, Lord, for sifting through the vast silo of humanity in search of the kernel bearing my name. You plucked me out of the world, placed me in the palm of Your hand, and bestowed upon me the honor of being Your child. (Read Luke 3:17)

　　* Water: Praise You for the Living Water that quenches my thirst for God, satisfies my life with joy, and gives me a peace that surpasses all understanding. Dear Jesus, Your claim to be able to completely satisfy my needs is a promise that only God could make; therefore I praise You for Who You are - God the Son. (Read John 4:13-14)

　　* Milk: I praise You for the security of Your Word and the dependability of Your promises that nourish my faith. (Read 1 Peter 2:1-3)

　　* Oil: Thanks be to Your Holy Spirit, who showers me with Your boundless love and proves each day that Your unlimited power is always available to help me cope with all that life would bring my way. Pull me up on Your lap, Daddy. Open my finite mind to view my joys and sorrows through Your eyes. I know You promise that all things will work out for my good. Let the knowledge of Your character plant seeds of courage in my fainting heart. Remind me often of the truth of my Pastor Doug Shiplett's words, "God is God, and I am not."

You hold the key to the mysteries; let this thought be satisfaction enough that I might sleep in peace and find rest in the day. (Read Job 37:5 and Romans 8:24-28)

Intercession: Honest expressions of our feelings, needs, and concerns are encouraged by our God, for in asking we are only repeating what He already knows. For Scripture declares, "O Lord, Thou hast searched me and known me. Thou dost know when I sit down and when I rise up; Thou dost understand my thought from afar. Thou dost scrutinize my path and my lying down, and art intimately acquainted with all my ways. Even before there is a word on my tongue, behold, O Lord, Thou dost know it all" (Psalm 139:1-4).

* Milk and honey: Help me to be faithful to daily search the Scriptures for the answers to my questions and comfort for my soul. Feed me the bread of angels and fill me with the gospel truth that the knowledge of Who You are will guide me in Your wisdom. Make Your face shine upon me and enlighten me so that I can come to know You better. (Read Psalm 119:11, 33-35)

* Yeast: Help me to stay within the walls of Your will that I might enjoy the security of Your boundaries of protection. (Read Romans 12:1-2)

* Oil: Lord, I lay my needs before You and trust You for my provisions, protection, healing, salvation, and comfort. (Read Psalm 23)

* Salt: Let the labor of my hands be permeated with the character of Christ, so that the world will know that I can do all things through Christ who **continually** strengthens me. When Satan points out my weaknesses, teach me to increase my dependence upon You so that the strength of Your power will grow in me more and more as a testimony that I am an heir to Your kingdom. Give me the wisdom to speak and act in

accordance to Your will, so that unbelievers who observe my life will become thirsty for Jesus. (Read Matthew 5:13-16)

* Seeds: Help me to cooperate with You, Lord. Equip me with all I need to be an effective fellow worker in the field you have chosen for me, so that the works of my life may bear fruit. (Read Psalm 1:1-3 and 1 Corinthians 3:6-9)

Submission: Teach me to think like Jesus when He said, "...yet not what I will, but what Thou wilt" (Mark 14:36b). Lord, sometimes my desires are at war with Your will and often Your path of choice for me is not immediately obvious. Help me to surrender to Your will, so that I will be prepared to listen to Your voice of instruction.

* Water and Wheat: Your words pierce as deep as the division between the bone and marrow when You tell me: "If you love Me, you will keep My commandments" (John 14:15). Soften my heart with the waters of Your love, cleanse me with the fiber of Your Holy Word, and rub away any residual chaff from my life, so that nothing will prevent me from walking in the center of Your will. (Read Psalm 139:23-24) As I now eat the bread and drink the wine, I thank God for saving me from my sins. On the first Passover, when the angel of death saw the blood of the lamb on the homes of the Jews, the people inside were saved from physical death. Lord Jesus, thank You for shedding Your blood so that God would pass over my sins, allow me the privilege of becoming a child of God, and permit me to live in heaven forever upon my physical death.

"And being found in appearance as a man, He humbled Himself by becoming obedient to the point of death, even death on a cross. Therefore also God highly exalted Him, and bestowed on Him the name which is above every name, that at the name of Jesus EVERY KNEE SHOULD BOW, of those who are in heaven, and on earth, and under the earth, and that every tongue should confess that Jesus Christ is Lord, to the glory of God the Father." Philippians 2:8-11

Partaking of the Lord's Supper: Communion contains one element that is fermented (wine) and one that is not (unleavened bread). Wine is produced by yeast cells feeding on the sugars in grapes. The release of the waste product alcohol is the basis for this industry. Likewise, sin is the waste of man's valuable God-given resources that precipitated Christ's first coming. Jesus, the unblemished bread of life, shed His pure blood to reverse the effects of our foolish fermentation. As I eat the bread and drink of the cup, my soul bears witness to the truth that Jesus and His redemptive work of love made this peaceful friendship with my Father God possible. My friend Ellen Parker, a Christian and a Jew, concludes my thoughts with these final words: "Many Jews commemorate Passover without having a real Communion, and many Christians participate in the Lord's Supper without considering sharing a Passover meal. The Jews celebrate Passover in joy, remembering what God has done freeing them from slavery. Christian friend, never forget that the Messiah has freed us from the slavery of our sin. Christ says, 'Do this in remembrance of me.' Shalom!"[1]

Jeanette Lavoie, R.N.

Thank You Jesus

Words by Jeanette Lavoie
Music by Mary Mc Sweeny

Prayer: The Lord's Prayer, in Matthew 6:9-13, is the perfect model as it contains all the essential elements.

Praise: "Our Father who art in heaven, hallowed be Thy name." Verse 9

Submission: "Thy kingdom come. Thy will be done, on earth as it is in heaven." Verse 10

Thanksgiving (when one recognizes that all gifts come from God): "Give us this day our daily bread." Verse 11

Confession: "And forgive us our debts, as we also have forgiven our debtors." Verse 12

Intercession: "And do not lead us into temptation, but deliver us from evil. [For Thine is the kingdom, and the power, and the glory, forever. Amen.]" Verse 13

Devotional: Since this devotional is too long to absorb in one sitting, it has been divided into sections. Take time to allow God's Holy Spirit to move in your heart as you pray.

Introduction: Isaiah chapter 53 is a Messianic prophecy written to enlighten Israel and to inform them that the Christ would come, suffer, and die on their behalf. This passage records the people's future rejection of the Suffering Servant, as they were instead on the alert for one who looked more like a reigning king. As you analyze the communion bread, read through Isaiah 53, and review the following notes, ask the Holy Spirit to reveal the portraits of both the Jesus and the people for whom He suffered, died, and rose again.

Praise: Isaiah 53:1-2 expounds on the person of Christ the Servant. The **plain, bland, spice-free taste** of communion bread reflects the outward appearance of Christ and the **dry texture** draws attention to His earthly roots. How amazingly wonderful and comforting that Jesus did not look like a "supermodel!" The Jews stumbled over the "ordinary" person of Christ and gossiped over His lowly background (see Matthew 13:54-58, John 1:46, and Acts 2:22-36) for nothing grand or mighty is expected to grow out of a parched ground! Someday Israel will mourn over their rejection of God's Servant, for they still fail to believe His extraordinary miracles came from the powerful "arm of the Lord." Who is the person of Christ the Servant to you? Take time to praise Him.

> "...they will look on Me whom they have pierced; and they will mourn for Him, as one mourns for an only son, and they will weep bitterly over Him, like the bitter weeping over a first-born." Zechariah 12:10

Praise: Read Isaiah 53:3, underline the attitudes of the people towards Him, and recognize His emotional pain. Jesus understands loneliness, rejection, sorrow, and grief; yet, some people did not recognize His worth! Praise Jesus for He is worthy!

Praise: Read Isaiah 53 in its entirety. Circle the words (our, us, all, their, etc.) that indicate who caused Christ to suffer and why? Clearly, mankind is the object and our sins the cause as the Suffering Servant willingly bore our griefs and carried our sorrows. Focus on Isaiah 53:4 and discover the opinion of the people. Our Savior understands those who are misunderstood. Even today there are those who falsely believe God was causing Him to suffer for His own sins! Praise Christ for enduring the punishment and persecution with a patient, willing spirit and for His loving attitude towards each undeserving, judgmental, confused, disrespectful sinner. Christ did not die for the perfect, for there are none, He died for the helpless, hopeless, ungodly sinner (See Romans 5:6-8). Praise Jesus for He loves us just as we are sinners in need of a Savior!

Confession: The **flat shape** of communion bread indicates that it is made without yeast and thus symbolizes the purity and sinless nature of Christ. Jesus is "the Bread of Life;" therefore, since **bread is the food** we eat at communion, it reminds us that He is the source of eternal life. When dry communion bread similar to Passover matzo bread is used, the **crunching sound** made as this food is chewed reminds us of Isaiah 53:5 which states, "He was crushed for our iniquities." Wine or grape juice, the communion drink, tells the story of the blood that literally spilled from Jesus' wounds as He died for our sins. Read Isaiah 53:5 and circle in red the descriptive words that paint a picture of the passion or sufferings of Christ. Jesus knew that believers continue to sin even after He died and rose again, for Isaiah 53:6 was written before Jesus walked as a man on the earth; yet, He deemed His suffering worth the price as He knew that "...by His scourging we are healed." Isaiah 53:5-6 depicts the essence of our gratitude and the reason we feel peace, comfort, and healing after a time of confession. Once sins are confessed, we are prepared to receive communion. **Swallowing the elements** is an audible sound that each person can privately hear. Like a sigh of relief, it echoes a sweet song in our hearts: "I sinned and now I am forgiven!" "I am free of this burden forever!" Now, we are ready to give thanks.

Thanksgiving: Isaiah 53:7-9 speaks to the passivity of the suffering Servant. The Messiah is described as an innocent, gentle, quiet, submissive, sacrificial lamb willing to be led to slaughter ("cut off") for the benefit of those who would believe. Imagine the life of Christ as a perfect lump of bread dough, the exact image of a holy God. As Jesus willingly poured out Himself to death, **He added our sins** into the recipe of His life. The sin Jesus absorbed is a foreign ingredient contrary to His person and nature. The following verse has been paraphrased to illustrate this point:

> 2 Corinthians 5:21 says: "He made Him who knew no sin to be sin on our behalf, that we might become the righteousness of God in Him." The author's paraphrased version reads: God the Father made Jesus who had no trace of yeast (sin) to become leavened bread on our behalf, He took our sins away and soaked them up into the dough of His body so that we may be transformed into unleavened bread in His power.

As the sins of transgressors contaminated the body of our Savior, **He allowed His dough to be poured out from the Father's holy hands into the hands of wicked men.** For as Jesus literally became our sin and took the punishment we deserved, He experienced what the lost sinner feels as he/she is separated from God. Look up Psalm 24:3-4 to understand that our holy God cannot allow sin in heaven. Do you now understand the anguish-filled, loud cry spoken by Jesus as he hung on the cross? "...MY GOD, MY GOD, WHY HAST THOU FORSAKEN ME?" (Matthew 27:46, Jesus took this quote from Psalm 22:1)

First **a baker's hands** place a formed lump of bread dough **into a pan,** next he/she puts it into a **hot oven,** and finally the baker **shuts the oven's door.** These movements of the baker parallel the following events: Wicked men nailed Jesus to the cross. After His death, a rich man named Joseph

239

took the lifeless body of Christ. He placed Him in a tomb he had reserved for himself and sealed the entrance with a large stone. This prophecy from Isaiah 53:9 came true as recorded in Matthew 27:57-60.

Yeast in leavened bread continues to live and raise the dough until the heat of the oven causes it to die. The analogy holds that as Christ bore our sins and carried them to the grave, this process destroyed the power of sin and removed the sting of death. With potholders protecting his hands, a baker retrieves the **finished, fragrant, warm bread** from the oven and allows it to cool on a rack. If the **opening of the oven** is symbolic of the resurrection and the finished bread a picture of the risen Lord, this analogy takes a spiritual twist for mortal hands did not play role in this drama!

> "And God raised Him up again, putting an end to the agony of death, since it was impossible for Him to be held in its power" (Acts 2:24, look up surrounding verses for more details).

Like **a timer** that alerts the baker when the bread is ready, Jesus rose with the sun on Sunday morning for the grave could not silence His victory celebration. The **shelf life** of warm, fresh, homemade, preservative-free bread is limited. Unlike earthly bread that grows cold and stale with time, Jesus went into the grave cold and emerged warm and radiant with life never to taste death again! The heat of His sufferings destroyed our sins and baked the dough of His life to the point of perfection! He shares this Bread, His life, His story, and His Words through the pages of the Bible. This food that Jesus supplies always makes available something new and fresh daily to nourish us spiritually. This is why I call Him "the Bread of Life."

Many have said, "If you (<u>insert your name</u>) were the only person that ever accepted Jesus as Savior, He still would have agreed to go through this misery for you!" Think of a loaf of leavened bread sitting tall and proud as the image of your life before Christ. Compare it with a flat, humble, piece of unleavened bread that represents who you are in Christ today. At the Last Supper, Jesus took some unleavened Passover bread, gave thanks to the Father, broke it, offered it to His disciples, and commanded them do to this in remembrance of Him. When we **receive the communion bread** into our mouth, this represents the acknowledgment of the truth of His testimony, an acceptance of His gift of salvation, and the joy of knowing that our sins are forgiven. A baker cannot squish the yeast bubbles out of the dough and force it to stay flat. Once yeast is in the dough, the invisible creature cannot be found and removed. Likewise, only Jesus can deflate the puffy, fleshly lumps of human bread dough we hold up to Him and extract every trace of sin.

When Adam and Eve first sinned, Satan robbed them of a piece of their soul; this is the part patterned after the image of Christ. This treasured lump of dough, precious in God's sight, represents each person's potential and is filled with meaning, purpose, and God's plans for us. The enemy tries to keep this piece of our soul under lock and key for without it we can never be victorious! This pearl of great price is the object that Jesus purchased at the cross and brought back to heaven for safekeeping. Jesus holds out this lump of potential as a gift for you today; as you receive your daily portion, it plugs up the hole in your soul allowing you to realize your potential for today. If you have never asked Jesus to come into your heart and fill the empty, torn, weeping hole in your soul, all you need to do is ask Jesus to give you back what the enemy has stolen, and it is yours to keep. Once you have invited Jesus into your life and received His gift of salvation, no one can ever steal it away from you again! Once a believer enters into the gates of heaven, God examines his/her lump of potential and places it in heaven's oven. As surely as Jesus rose triumphantly from the grave, each believer can be confident that his/her lump of dough will emerge looking, smelling, and tasting like the bread Jesus holds in His hands!

Give thanks to our sovereign God for His amazing plan of salvation and for the wealth of potential we each have in Christ! If you are still breathing today, then thank God that you still have time to reach your potential. For we are not baked, until God says we are finished!

Intercession: In Isaiah 53:10-12, we see the portion of the Servant and His claim to greatness. With every ounce of His being, Jesus rendered Himself as a guilt offering. Isaiah foresaw the death of Christ as "a guilt offering" which atones for the damage or injury done by sin. Jesus willingly complied with God's plan of salvation and is exalted for His obedience. These are the consequences of Christ's sacrifice: God the Father is pleased; Jesus will see His offspring (many unbelievers will come to believe in Christ); God will prolong Jesus' days (this required His resurrection after the completion of His suffering); the hand of Christ will prosper (His suffering will bear fruit); Christ will justify many; like a general who wins a battle, Jesus earned the privilege to share the goods taken from the enemy with believers. As you read Isaiah 53:10-12 and consider Christ's attitude, use the following outline as a guide to pray:

1. Pray that whatever God asks you to do today, that you will do it with your whole being (mind, heart, body, and soul) so that God will be pleased with the results.
2. Ask God to open your spiritual eyes to discern whether the things you desire will be worth the price.
3. Pattern your attitude after the Suffering Servant, and the labor of your hands and the anguish of your soul will see the results and be satisfied.
4. When God's plan is hard to face, say a little prayer: "Lord, make my mind as still and peaceful as a lump of unleavened bread dough, able to relax and rest knowing that my life is in the Master Baker's hands."
5. The kneading process develops the gluten in bread dough and enables it to become stretchy like a balloon and capable of holding on to yeast-bubbles; thus, this process allows leavened bread to rise. In a similar way, our extraordinary God often uses unexpected means to stretch ordinary

people exceedingly, abundantly beyond what they thought possible in order to achieve incredible results.

Prayer:

Lord, give me a vision of my potential, stretch my faith to expand my horizons, and develop my character to make me willing to go beyond my comfort zone in order to accomplish the plans You have for me. Amen.

Submission: A matter of attitude.

When we come to this place of submission with no agenda of our own, we follow Jesus' example. Compare your life to the following four lumps of bread dough. Consider which of these extremes best paints a picture of your attitude, faith, and works? (See James 2:14-26 for more details.)

1. **A bowl full of puffing leavened bread dough** is alive with life as the yeasty beast has one goal, to satisfy it's own appetite as it rises to the top. Once the food supply is depleted or the dough is placed in a hot oven, the life of the yeast ends. The result of its life's work, feeding its gluttonous appetite, creates a fluffy, tall loaf of bakery bread. **Blind Faith** is this person's name and self-centered is his/her attitude. Sin is the poisonous gas that inflates their ego resulting in self-destructive dead works. In the end, their tombstone reads, "What you see is what you get. I did what seemed best for me!"

2. **Sourdough starter** rests in a cold, dark refrigerator, in a continuous state of perpetual fermentation, waiting for the baker to take a portion of its dough to create a loaf of sourdough French bread. (See Chapter 11 for details) This soured dough represents the image of a willful, premeditated, rebellious spirit seeking every opportunity to recreate his/herself in the life of another individual. The motto of this person's life's work is, "spread the wealth and multiply myself." **Arrogant, Self-absorbed Faith** suits this person as a name for he/she has no need of God to successfully promote their personal agenda. Their spiritually dead works are not a dead end, for they carry on well after this person is gone. As they take a few secret ingredients to

245

the grave, their legacy grows as others gossip, wonder, and write books in a quest to discover just how their bread recipe multiplied into the millions! Interviewing family, friends, and enemies provides a taste of his/her memorial of remembrance: "Dynamic, charismatic, passionate, a born leader, he/she was my hero!" "My mentor, my friend, my role model!" "My worst nightmare!"

3. **Without a leavening agent** such as yeast, bread dough cannot rise on it's own. This lifeless, paralyzed lump of dough is determined to fulfill it's perceived destiny to sit, to rest, to remain alone, to never multiply, and to be content to do nothing but remain flat. Once baked, this unproductive lump takes on the noble, characteristically flat shape of communion bread; however, the hidden attitude behind the end result strips this lump of it's royal potential. In this state of passive rebellion, a man, woman, child, or adolescent does not dare to dream the impossible or care to realize their potential. Unmotivated and apathetic, they stay the same, never growing or changing, and remain dead in their spiritual life. If their tombstone could speak, it would say the following without an exclamation point, "Whatever." Lamenting, woeful weeping pour out from those mourning the loss of one christened as **Faith with a Near-death Experience**. Oh what he/she could have become if only they had eyes of faith to catch a vision of all they could have accomplished with the power of the Lord as their guiding strength. (See James 2:17-18 if thirsty for more.)

4. **Unleavened bread dough with a twist!** A faith renowned as alive and ready for action has the nickname**, Moving and Grooving in Jesus' Name**. The core ingredients that give testimony

of this believers life and work include all the essentials required to free God's Holy Spirit to bake heavenly bread, even when Moving and Grooving makes a mess in the kitchen. He/she feasts on "the Bread of Life," drinks every drop of gospel milk, washes it down with living water, dips his/her fingers often into the honey of God's Word, adds salt to spice situations up by imitating Jesus, spits out anything with a trace of leaven, invites the oil of God's presence to leave fingerprints on every piece of work, and faithfully believes that the seeds God provides will reap a mighty harvest! A still, pure, undefiled lump of unleavened bread dough, quietly resting in the Master Baker's hand, is ready, waiting for action, pliable, easy to mold into a shape, and willing to take on any form: a loaf, a slice, a roll, a lowly cracker, a minuscule crumb, or the mere fragrance of Christ's heavenly bread. This lump of potential is free to dance and jump for joy for it represents a believer in full surrender to Jesus Christ, bubbling over with a zest for life and overflowing with a passionate, unquenchable desire to proclaim the gospel message.

If these lumps of dough have given you a headache as your struggle to decide where you fit, then say the following prayer, and carry on. Do not get discouraged; life is a journey, God makes sure to get all the kinks out of the recipe along the way, and He saves the baking of your dough until the very end!

Prayer:
Lord Jesus, I surrender my weak, ordinary, lifeless lump of dough, teeming with the yeast of sin, into Your care. You willingly died between two robbers (See Matthew 27:38), remain unashamed to handle any flawed bread recipe,

247

and pray without ceasing for sinners just like me. Lord, teach me to be like You.

When my human, self-centered, arrogant, self-absorbed dough tempts me to makes some moves You do not approve of, rain the salt of Christ's character on my parade to remind me of the consequences while I still have time to decide my fate.

I am like an unruly lump of salt-free leavened bread dough full of myself. As I humbly admit the pride of my heart and sheepishly knock on heaven's door, I expect thunder and lightening and instead receive a shower of forgiveness to cleanse my soul. My jubilant heart bubbles over with glee, as I examine the dough of my life now transformed by the hand of God. Thank You, for this is my gift and my portion of unleavened bread dough patterned after the image of Christ.

Heavenly Father, I hold up to You my ordinary, still, lump of potential which You made alive in Christ, for it is all I have to offer today. Please pour in more Jesus and stretch the capacity of my dough that I might fill up to overflowing with the power of the Holy Spirit. For when it is my time to die and I awake in heaven, it is my wish and hope that the people of earth remember me as the one who was always moving and grooving to the sound of God's voice calling. And with my mouth I will sing, "Glory to God in the Highest!" If my bread dough speaks once it is removed from heaven's hot oven, I hope it will say, "MMM...Good! Tastes just like Jesus' Bread!" Amen!

Submission: To share in the inheritance of Christ, we must be willing to accept our portion as a servant of the Lord. Do you feel God is asking too much of you today? Do you feel too weak to bear the cross you have been given? Is the enemy holding you back by reminding you of your transgressions? Reread Isaiah 53 and take courage!

1. Jesus died for your sins, will justify His children, and is well equipped to carry your burdens, for His arms are strong!
2. He will share His inheritance with His children.
3. Though we are sinners, Christ is not ashamed to stand next to His children.
4. Christ promises to intercede for us because He knows that we desperately need Him to pray for us. For we are all transgressors that fall short of God's perfect standard.

Scripture assures us that we will advance in His certain triumph towards our destiny and we will not be disappointed when we arrive at our destination. (See 2 Corinthians 2:14) This promise is a true fact for Titus 1:2 says, "...God,...cannot lie..." As a soldier in God's army, God sets a plan before you today. These are the full gamut of your choices: retreat, sit and watch, sleep, eat, work a little, run aimlessly in various directions, grumble and complain about the plan, stand at attention while God gives directions, listen carefully for the details, be ready to serve at a moments notice, defend the faith without shame in your eyes, exercise effort as you use the sword of God's Word as your defensive weapon, pray without ceasing, and/or advance victoriously towards God's kingdom with the power of His Holy Spirit as your guide.

Now the question stands, what will you do today? The ground you stand on has been bought with a price, and the victory secured by the blood of Jesus; yet, it is still a battlefield, not a playground! God holds the gift of an abundant life out to you today. Whether in days of plenty or in times of wanting, you will find joy in the Lord no matter what your situation; however, the satisfaction you feel at the end of the day will depend on your attitude. Philippians 2:1-11 demonstrates the humility of Jesus, our role model, whose passion to serve His heavenly Father is the picture of perfection.

As you advance towards the finish line, heaven, and come boldly with confidence towards God's throne, He smiles at each of His children with arms open wide anticipating your homecoming! In heaven you will finally experience Psalm 16:11 fully, completely, forever, and always! The angels are watching! Heaven is waiting for you! Why do we hesitate to actively serve in God's victorious army? Are you scared? Then look up Ephesians 6:10-20 to learn all about the armor of God that you may proudly wear. Your shoes are a symbol of the gospel of peace, so they must carry the power to make war cease. As a final note, tuck these promises into your belt for quick reference:

"I can do all things through Him who strengthens me." Philippians 4:13

"The LORD will march out like a mighty man, like a warrior he will stir up his zeal; with a shout he will raise the battle cry and will triumph over his enemies...I will lead the blind by ways they have not known, along unfamiliar paths I will guide them; I will turn the darkness into light before them and make the rough places smooth. These are the things I will do; I will not forsake them." Isaiah 42:13,16 NIV

Take it or leave it: After you finish praying and reading scripture for today, take your daily portion of Jesus with you; forget your burdens as they now belong to Jehovah Jireh; be ready to share "the Bread of Life;" be willing to go wherever He leads. Prayer is an intimate, reflective, quiet time that prepares us for the day's events by providing our daily bead. Philippians 2:12-18 reads like a benediction to send us on our way:

> "Therefore, my dear friends, as you have always obeyed—not only in my presence, but now much more in my absence—continue to work out your salvation with fear and trembling, for it is God who works in you to will and to act according to his good purpose. Do everything without complaining or arguing, so that you may become blameless and pure, children of God without fault in a crooked and depraved generation, in which you **shine like stars** in the universe as you **hold out the word of life**—in order that I may boast on the day of Christ that I did not run or labor for nothing. But even if I am being poured out like a drink offering on the sacrifice and service coming from your faith, I am glad and rejoice with all of you. So you too should be glad and rejoice with me." Philippians 2:12-18 (NIV)

The shining stars in the preceding verse represent believers, and the "word of life" they hold, is Jesus, "the Bread of Life." God turned the bright lights off at night to reveal the beauty of a star lit sky. Believers who pattern their lives after the image of Christ walk as points of light towards a dark and dying world. God's holy fire is the passion in one's soul with which to blaze the trail.

With the oven of our heart full of Jesus and the Holy Spirit free to adjust the thermostat, the enemy will run for cover! At the name of Jesus, "the Bread of Life," the enemy trembles for therein lies the secret of living the abundant life. As this powerful, life-giving bread absorbs into the dough of our lives, our hope will magnify as our faith multiples. The difference between a wish and a hope is the faith to believe what is hidden from sight will someday be revealed. The dreams an unbeliever can only wish for is the hope a believer knows he/she will possess someday.

> "Now faith is the assurance of things hoped for, the conviction of things not seen." Hebrews 11:1

The following poem, written by my daughter Sarah, captures the essence of a heart longing to be satisfied:

Stars in the Sky
By Sarah Lavoie
1999
Used with Permission
It is the most beautiful thing in the sky.
Up so very, very high.
Every time I see it I wish upon it.
Will it ever come true?

You fill the sky on dark nights.
Your beauty shows forever more.
If only I could reach it.
I'd wish for a whole lot more.

In prayer we ask, "Give us this day our daily bread." As you leave this quiet time and go on your way, ask yourself a few questions: "Do I have enough of "the Bread of Life" to share with a searching, hurting soul longing for a taste of God's goodness?"

One sweet day I only had time to ponder one verse, John 6:35, and fourteen years later my heart still bubbles over with wonder! The choice of ingredients that Jesus includes, the feel of dough as I place it in the oven, the smell His Bread that commands attention, and the taste of His goodness. How can anyone resist? Whether you read only one verse today or many chapters, God's Word always provides something sensational on which to chew.

To those who ask, God will gladly send bread from heaven to come alive through the pages of the Holy Scriptures. The menu is His choice; the decision to eat is yours alone. Take it or leave it? Toss it or let it go way down deep? Share it or keep it for yourself? Watch it sit and catch dust or use it and see it multiply? Which recipe will you follow His or yours?

Jeanette Lavoie, R.N.

Poem Inspired by Psalm 139:13-16:

A Lump of Potential
By Jeanette Lavoie

How much potential is in your dough?
Only the Lord God truly does know.
To Him our frame was never hidden.
Yet for some daylight would be forbidden.

God treasures each tiny lump of beginning.
To Him each life was meant to be thrilling.
Each life is fearfully and wonderfully made.
And this skillful design isn't meant to fade.

A gift to keep is the image of Christ in me.
This is the potential that longs to be free.
Rejecting the design God created us to take.
By this man fails to recognize what's at stake.

And the hole deep down in my soul weeps.
As my emptiness from place to place leaps.
And the enemy rejoices over his stolen prize.
As he captures my potential every angel sighs.

Over the loss of my potential Jesus willing dies.
To regain this promise is the reason he did rise.
Jesus died once to restore His image in us.
And that is why the enemy makes such a fuss.

My lump of potential will never ever be lost.
For Jesus knew His victory was worth the cost.
God knows each and every lump by name.
To Him this fight for our life is not a game.

In His book each one's name is recorded.
As the world twists and turns meaning is distorted.
We add, we change, we fix, and we mix.
The dough of beginning changes by our tricks.

Jesus came to give life to the empty soul.
But without Him inside, life takes its toll.
We try to live by God's perfect decrees.
Yet success in this is a matter of degrees.

Rejoice in the oil of God's powerful presence.
For this is better than a thousand presents.
When in me God's Spirit cranks up the heat.
My heart shall surely never skip a beat.

On the days I never fail to sit at Jesus' feet.
The enemy knows for sure that he is beat.
Each gift received from "the Bread of Life."
Is a means to put an end to all the strife.

To reach my potential is not just a dream.
For by God's power I will never lose steam.
And when in the end I shall see God's face.
For His child, I know, He reserves a space.

Epilogue: What Is *Your* Calling?

Hearing about any one of the ingredients used to bake bread starts a chemical reaction in my brain and ignites my heart with a passion to speak that cannot be silenced. Weaving the Gospel into everyday conversation becomes effortless once you have found a place to start. What about you? Are you a carpenter? Then you have insights into passages describing Jesus as the cornerstone and God as the Master Builder that others miss. Are you a grocer? Upon examining a bag of persimmons, you notice that the farmer slipped in a few small green ones that will remain bitter and never ripen. As you read passages talking about the fruit of the Spirit, God can use your expertise in handling produce to broaden your understanding of these truths. God does not expect us to be good in areas where we lack knowledge; rather, He delights in using familiar items in our life to teach us His ways. That is one of the reasons why Jesus spoke in parables.

Where do you fit in God's kingdom? What perfect niche has God prepared for you? To find your calling, the task upon which God has put your name, brings meaning, purpose, and a reason for living. A calling can be a relationship you are born into such as a daughter, sister, mother, or friend. It may grow out of a hobby or job you go back to day after day, or it may be a God given talent you are destined to use. When God's fingerprints cover each step you take towards completing a task or carrying out a role, the joy of cooperating with God and the fulfillment of being a part of His team is an indescribable gift. Do you realize that God has a plan for your life? Did you know He prepared what you needed long before the time to carry out the deed arrived? Take a look at your life and consider how God would use the blessings He has bestowed upon you.

"For by grace you have been saved through faith;
and that not of yourselves, it is the gift of God; not
as a result of works, that no one should boast. For
we are His workmanship, created in Christ Jesus
for good works, which God prepared beforehand,
that we should walk in them." Ephesians 2:8-10

Hobby - In my life, bread baking is obviously one hobby
God used as a springboard to a teaching ministry. God used
gardening in my mom's life for a different expression of His
love. For her, it brings comfort in times of distress, fills her day
with enjoyment, and is a place where she says, "I can always
find God in my garden even when I cannot see His face
anywhere else." Whenever she visits a friend, her hands are
never empty - they are always overflowing with the beautiful
products of her labor. There is joy in giving and greater
pleasure in knowing the gifts are welcomed. After a tour
around mom's garden or sharing a garden-fresh meal at her
table, no one ever leaves hungry.

Workplace - Working as a Registered Nurse brought me
joy beyond measure. I told my husband before we were
married, "Ask me to give up anything except Nursing." Working
in a Christian hospital gave me the freedom to minister to the
whole person (physical, emotional, and spiritual). I thrived in
this atmosphere, and my career felt more like a mission field
than a regular, boring job. As life changed and the children
came, I spent fewer hours at work and more at home. When
my calling, Nursing, became a job, it lacked the excitement and
opportunities for which I once lived. At that time I willingly set
aside this role. A job is just a job, but a calling gets me out of
bed in the morning and gives me a reason to plow through my
day. Some callings remain for a season, and we may or may
not visit them again.

Where to look? - As you scan through the daily
schedule or peruse a list of hobbies, talents, skills, and
resources, a variety of ministry opportunities will emerge.

257

Trying to turn each one into a calling will be attempting a superhuman feat. You cannot fight in every battle. Choosing to use God's gifts where and when He directs will teach the value of what God treasures. Time spent on what God calls important and doing the "good works" that He prepared for each one to do, is never a wasted resource. Before his martyrdom, missionary Jim Elliot said, "He is no fool who gives what he cannot keep to gain what he cannot lose."[1]

How to choose? - First, spend time in prayer, read the Bible, and ask God to orient your heart towards His will. Invite others to pray with and for you. Seek wise counsel. Look for God's direction and listen to His calling. No matter how qualified you think you are to accomplish a task, if God has not chosen you, you are not the right one to meet the need. Signs of a green light are:

* After time spent with God, you feel a peace to move forward.

* When the plan is supported by your spouse, or by the leadership of your church, if your ministry falls under their authority. When others who know you well think the idea is a good fit for you.

* When you realize that the motive for serving is driven by commitment, love, compassion, and a tender heart towards the recipients of the ministry's efforts.

* When your gifts and abilities match the need.

* Positive responses of those affected by your efforts lend affirmation and confirm your effectiveness in the position.

Wrong reasons to join would be out of guilt, just because there is a need, or with unrealistic expectations for personal benefit. If the ministry shoe fits, but you are not sure you want to put it on, consider this old Ben Franklin poem: [2]

"For want of a nail a shoe was lost; for want of a
shoe a horse was lost; for want of a horse a rider

was lost - and for want of a rider the war was lost!"

My own personal prayers concerning my desire to write this book have sounded like this at times:

Lord God, let me not boast regarding my gifts. Help me remember that every "good" gift comes from You. I have often wondered why You chose me to write this book. Someone else could have completed this task much faster. The challenges in my life have made me realize how much I depend on You, my Lord. When I doubt I can go on, You send me courage. When I feel weak, You give me strength. When I am at a loss for words, You find creative ways to end my "writer's block;" like the time I struggled with the opening paragraph to Chapter Seven and the answer came as I dipped my tea bag into the steaming hot water! Thank You Lord, for giving me areas of weakness so that I might learn to find my strength in You. Blessed am I when I hunger, for in You alone shall I be satisfied. Lord, if Your favor rests upon me as I attempt to carry out Your plan, then and then alone will I enjoy the blessings that stem from the fruits of my labor. Praise to the Lord, for the Scriptures give me hope as they speak to my need:

"For consider your calling, brethren, that there were not many wise according to the flesh, not many mighty, not many noble; but God has chosen the foolish things of the world to shame the wise, and God has chosen the weak things of the world to shame the things which are strong, and the base things of the world and the despised, God has chosen, the things that are not, that He might nullify the things that are, that no man should boast before God. But by His doing you are in Christ Jesus, who became to us wisdom from God, and righteousness and sanctification, and redemption, that, just as it is written, 'LET HIM WHO BOASTS, BOAST IN THE LORD.'" 1 Corinthians 1:26-31

Overcoming Stumbling Blocks - On a gray, overcast day in February of 1996, I passed a Wonder Bread® truck on the freeway on my way to present my "*Jesus is the Bread of Life*" class to some grade-school children. It had been a while since I had done this, and I felt like Moses when God called him to bring the people out of Egypt: "Aren't I the wrong woman for this job?" Fear threatened to lead me back home. As I thought of the truck God had placed within my field of vision, my imagination whirled around in my head. God exchanged my nervousness for laughter. "How silly of me to worry! Jesus, the real live "Wonder Bread" is with me!" God's faithfulness enabled me to complete the task that, for a fleeting moment, I thought would be difficult. Going home from this event, sweet smiles of contentment danced across my face for I had found my place amongst the ranks of God's soldiers that day. If you are starting to tremble at the thought of where God's call might lead you, notice the **all** in the following verse. It is there for a reason.

"I can do **all** things through Him who strengthens me." Philippians 4:13

Answer the Call - Once you have answered the call, plans may not always proceed smoothly. Filled with a sense of awe and wonder, I have learned to echo Job's understanding of the omnipotence of God as he stated, "I know that Thou canst do all things, and that no purpose of Thine can be thwarted" (Job 42:2). Long before the desire to be a writer entered my thoughts, God prepared people to be a part of the fourteen-year process of completing my first book. If I took the time to share the story of how each person helped me, the length of this book would be greatly multiplied. If I carefully sifted through all the days of my life, I would discover other names that I forgot. The quest to search for the words to express what Jesus, "the Bread of Life" means to me, appeared like a puzzle that has now come together; thanks be to God! At first, the completed puzzle lay upside-down. The vague outline could be seen only as a few ideas on paper, disconnected thoughts that fit perfectly somewhere, and the excitement on the faces of little children as they listened intently to my story and played with their own mound of bread dough. As I formulated my thoughts, words flowed as smooth as oil. Other times, the labor seemed to fall short of honey sweet. Always, God provided people with words, actions, and deeds sprinkled with salt, to turn another piece of the puzzle right side up. One by one, section by section, God set the stage to reveal the hidden picture. On September 20, 1996, I wrote this note, "I desire to finish my book," next to this verse:

"However, I consider my life worth nothing to me, if only I may finish the race and complete the task the Lord Jesus has given me - the task of testifying to the gospel of God's grace." Acts 20:24 (NIV) [3]

That same month and year, Gigi Whitt, a gifted artist went back to church, quickly came to know the Lord, and before the end of the year, God put a desire in her heart to use her gift for God. Three years later, a mutual friend introduced us and she became my illustrator.

In June 1998, I completed my first draft, gave it to eight friends to edit, and dreaded the prospect of finding a publisher. The next four years brought delays and disappointments mixed with joys and steps in the right direction. Time is not the enemy, that foe is our own impatience. As I struggled with this truth, pieces slowly fell into place: words were set to music and poems written, artwork sprang to life, and the idea for two versions of the same book emerged (an adult devotional and a teacher's edition). The value of waiting patiently became God's gift to ensure the end result would be what God had in mind. The following quote from our 2001 Christmas letter prompted friends to pray, revived my enthusiasm, and opened new doors of hope that the finish line was close: "Jeanette still pursues her dream of completing her first series of books called, <u>The Bread Lady's Quest</u>. Her publishers abruptly closed the publishing side of their business last Spring, which left Jeanette on her own. She forges on at a snail's pace, believing the truth of these words, 'Let us not be weary in well doing: for in due season we shall reap, if we faint not.'[4] Pray Jeanette will not 'faint,' so that she will complete this project which began when she baked bread with Sarah's kindergarten class. Sarah is now nineteen years old!"

Have you heard God's voice calling? Did you give God an answer? Do you feel overwhelmed by the task before you? Are you troubled by missing pieces, frustrated by delays, and puzzled by sections that do not seem to fit? Is there no end in sight? Relax! Be still and know that God has every piece under His watchful eye. Nothing will be lost. Everything hidden will be revealed in the proper time. All that you need to complete each step is ready and awaiting God's orders. "Delight yourself in the LORD; and He will give you the desires of your heart. Commit your way to the LORD, trust also in Him, and He will do it. And He will bring forth your righteousness as the light, and your judgment as the noonday. Rest in the LORD and wait patiently for Him." (Psalm 37:4-7a). While you wait, take the time to say a little prayer.

Prayer:
Lord, please give me a drink of Your living water, the journey has made me thirsty to know You better. Send me a tall glass of gospel milk to remind me that I belong to You. Can You hear my growling stomach, Lord? I would love to partake of a honey sandwich made from the bread of angels, to fill my hunger; however, I must first bow my head, humble myself, and allow You to cleanse me of all traces of leaven. Thank You for forgiving me of my sins. Praise You for Your patience as You add the salt of Christ's character to flavor my life. Pour the oil of Your presence upon me, Lord, that all I do may be guided by Your will. I will never be able to joyfully embrace the fruits of my labor unless You are pleased. All praise, glory, and honor belong to You, my Lord; for each puzzle that tells a story of my life will fall into place and be held together by the glue of Your love. As I look at each one in heaven someday, and watch You fill in the last few pieces, all the mysteries will be solved and the questions answered. Oh Jesus, my "True Bread" from heaven, on that wonderful day my hunger and thirst will be satisfied forevermore! Amen.

"The mind of man plans his way, but the Lord directs his steps." Proverbs 16:9

"All the ways of a man are clean in his own sight, but the LORD weighs the motives. Commit your works to the LORD, and your plans will be established." Proverbs 16:2-3

"Thou wilt make known to me the path of life; in Thy presence is fullness of joy; in Thy right hand there are pleasures forever." Psalm 16:11

Devotional:

Praise – God is the source of every gift and He deserves all the glory. Without God's help, we are powerless to accomplish anything of eternal value. Meditate on Ephesians 2:8-10 and Philippians 4:13 as you spend time praising God.

Confession – Read Acts 20:24, Psalm 37:4-7, and Proverbs 16:2-3. Ask yourself these questions: Is my delight to do God's will? Are my motives for serving pure? Allow moments of silence for the Lord to speak to your heart. Perhaps you could begin your prayer like this:

> Lord, examine my heart and help me face with honesty the things which stand in my way of being obedient to Your will and plan for my life.

Thanksgiving – Before we took our first breath, God prepared a special place for each of His children to serve Him. Everything we need to carry out God's plan will be provided as needed. Review Ephesians 2:8-10. The definition of the word "workmanship" is the skill of a workman, or the quality of his work. Verse ten begins with the words, "For we are God's workmanship." This means the salvation we enjoy is a product of God's workmanship not from man or his works. We are God's masterpiece! Think of a time God gave you the ability to accomplish a "good work." Like salvation, the ability to do "good works" is a gift from God. Thank God for your gifts and talents.

Intercession – As you read 1 Corinthians 1:26-31 and consider your calling, here are a few suggestions for prayer:
1. Lord, teach me how to use and develop my time, gifts, talents, and resources to share Christ with people.
2. Lord, where do I fit in Your Kingdom? Show me this and I will find the meaning, purpose, and the joy of being alive!

3. If you believe you have nothing to offer God and are too weak for any job – God has a plan for you; do not lose heart.

   Submission – Add your own thoughts as you submit your life to God and read the prayer of the Bread Lady's heart, "Lord, give me the passion and drive to obey You. Prepare my heart and mind. Make me ready to serve You. Guard against discouragement, procrastination, and distractions so I will complete the task according to Your timetable. Amen!"

Appendix

Jeanette Lavoie, R.N.

Betty's Seven Grain Recipe
Used with permission of Betty Watson.

Mill:
7 cups Hi-protein wheat berries (hard spring or hard winter)
1 cup soft wheat berries
1/3 cup whole oats
1/4 cup each of rye, barley, millet, brown rice

OR: IF YOU ARE NOT MILLING YOUR OWN GRAIN USE THE FOLLOWING AMOUNTS OF FLOUR:
12 cups whole wheat bread flour
2 cups whole wheat pastry flour
2/3 cup oat flour
1/2 cup each rye, barley, millet, rice flours

SET ASIDE MILLED OR BLENDED FLOUR TO BE USED LATER.

ADD THE FOLLOWING INGREDIENTS TO YOUR BOWL EQUIPPED WITH DOUGH HOOK:

1 quart Buttermilk plus 2 cups water (or substitute with 6 Tbsp. Tofu milk powder and reduce liquids to 5 ½ cups of water if allergic to milk products)- Heat water & buttermilk to 135oF - 140oF.
1/2 Tbsp. salt (opt. salt is for flavor, leaving it out will cause bread to rise faster as salt is a retardant to rising)
1/2 cup oil
1/2 cup honey (Tip: Measure oil and then honey in same cup and honey will slide right out)
1 egg (opt.)
3 Tbsp. Dough Enhancer (purchase from Betty) OR 200 mg. vitamin C crushed (helps to keep bread fresh longer)
8 cups of milled or blended flour above
1 cup of a mixture of seeds (millet, sesame seeds, sunflower seeds, or poppy seeds).

1 1/2 cup gluten flour (This is a commercially-produced flour that is the protein portion of the whole grain. We use it to supplement the wheat gluten when we use nongluten flours such as we are using in this recipe).

NOW USE SPRING - SWITCH ON MACHINE TO FOLD THE FLOUR INTO LIQUIDS. WHEN ALL FLOUR IS MOISTENED, TURN TO SPEED 1 AND BLEND FOR 1 MINUTE.

NOW ADD: 3 Tbsp. dry active yeast and blend to moisten.

NOW ADD: 3 cups more flour and pulse to quickly blend in. Turn to speed 1 and continue to add flour until dough is very soft but is beginning to form and come up center post and down sides of bowl about halfway. It will be beginning to pull away slightly from sides, but will still be very sticky. When dough looks like this…STOP ADDING FLOUR even though dough is still soft and sticky. This process of adding the last 2 - 5 cups of flour should take no longer than 2 minutes.

SET TIMER AND KNEAD ON SPEED 1 for 4 - 7 minutes until gluten elasticity is developed. Since children love to play with the dough, and often over-knead it, you may wish to keep the timer to 5 minutes. Otherwise the bread will not rise as well. Gluten can be overdeveloped when kneaded by the machine.

THE UNIQUE KNEADING PROCESS OF THE BOSCH® IS WHAT DEVELOPS THE GLUTEN SO THOROUGHLY FOR A HIGH, LIGHT LOAF OF BREAD THAT RISES IN 15-25 MINUTES.

Oil four - 2 # bread pans (4"x 8") or six - 1 1/4 # bread pans (3"x 7") with a mixture of lecithin/oil. (Mix 2 parts oil with 1 part lecithin liquid). If using this recipe to teach a group of children about Jesus as "the Bread of Life," let each child make his own small bread roll and place on baking sheet lined with parchment paper! Write the name of each child under his/her roll.

Lightly oil hands and work surface (such as a Tupperware® mat or Formica® countertop). Turn dough out onto surface and roll dough over to oil both sides. Divide into 4 - 6 portions depending on pan size. Form loaves. Be sure to work out all air bubbles. Place loaves in oiled pans. Place loaves into preheated (150oF) oven and allow to rise to double (oven should be turned off while loaves rise). When double in size, turn oven to 350oF and bake for 25 - 45 minutes. The length of time varies greatly oven to oven. Remove from pans to cool on racks.

Tip: If your oven has a preheat element in it that comes on in the top of your oven, you will need to remove bread while oven preheats.

HIGH ALTITUDE: FOR ALTITUDES OVER 4,000 FEET, BAKE BREAD AT 425oF FOR 10 MINUTES, REDUCE HEAT AFTER FIRST 10 MINUTES TO 350oF AND CONTINUE BAKING FOR 25 - 35 MINUTES.

NOTE: THIS RECIPE IS DESIGNED FOR THE BOSCH® KITCHEN MACHINE TAKING ADVANTAGE OF ITS LARGE CAPACITY AND ITS UNIQUE ABILITY TO TOTALLY DEVELOP THE GLUTEN IN JUST A FEW MINUTES OF KNEADING, THEREBY REQUIRING ONLY ONE RISE PERIOD. YOU MAY FIND THAT YOU WILL NEED TO REDUCE THE RECIPE SIZE TO HALF VOLUME IN ORDER TO MAKE BY HAND OR IN ANOTHER TYPE OF BREAD MAKER (SUCH AS A KITCHEN AID® FOR INSTANCE). ALSO, BECAUSE OF THE UNIQUE KNEADING DESIGN OF THE BOSCH® WHICH COMPLETELY DEVELOPS AND ELASTICIZES THE GLUTEN GIVING A LIGHT, TENDER LOAF OF BREAD, YOU MAY FIND THAT THE FINISHED LOAF OF WHOLE GRAIN BREAD WILL NOT BE AS LIGHT AS YOU WOULD LIKE IT TO BE. USING HALF WHITE FLOUR WITH HALF-WHOLE GRAIN FLOUR WILL HELP YOU ACHIEVE A LIGHTER LOAF.

271

Jeanette Lavoie, R.N.

About the Artist: Gigi's Testimony

Gigi Whitt was born in the Philippine Islands. She is a Fine Arts graduate of the Philippine Women's University where she majored in Graphics. At first, her playful and vibrant watercolor paintings were just a hobby. In September of 1996, a renewed interest in attending church and a willingness to learn more about the Bible brought new meaning and purpose to her artwork. Inspired by His Word, God put the desire in her heart to use her artwork for the glory of the Lord. Three years later, on a quiet morning in March of 1999, Gigi prayed, "Lord, please show me how I may use my art in your kingdom!" The phone rang interrupting her thoughts and the answer came as her friend Melodee spoke, "My friend Jeanette is writing a book and she is interested in inviting you to illustrate her work." Later, Gigi and Jeanette discovered how both of their lives were tied together in time to complete this task.

One clear testimony is the beautiful painting on the back cover of <u>The Bread Lady's Quest</u>, "Golden Harvest", which Gigi was inspired to create even before she met Jeanette! The two old-fashioned ladies wearing hats and admiring a whimsical field of wheat must be Gigi (with the black hair) and Jeanette (with the light hair). All the hopes and dreams both artist and writer hold in their project, <u>The Bread Lady's Quest</u>, are represented by the field. The playful butterflies, warm, glowing sun and wheat ripe unto harvest are reminders that God's plans for us will take to wing and fly if only we believe that prayer changes things. Gigi discovered that when hearts and lives are transformed, as the Lord allows us to use a God given gift, it is a miracle! Gigi said, "Living for God is the best thing that ever happened to me and my family!"

Gigi lives in California with her husband Don and her two children, Angelo and Anthony. They attend Calvary Life Church in Petaluma. She teaches an after-school Art

Jeanette Lavoie, R.N.

Enrichment program and, as an illustrator, assists Christian writers on children's and inspirational books. To contact Gigi, send her an email at beautedreamer57@hotmail.com

Notes

Prologue
1. Don Moen, "I Just Want To Be Where You Are." Integrity's Hosanna Music. Copyright 1989.

Chapter 1
1. Lorna Simcox, "The Woman's Relationship to Her Home and Family," Israel My Glory (August/September 1996): 11. The Friends of Israel Gospel Ministry, Inc. Bellmawr, NJ.
2. Marvin Rosenthal, "Israel's Spring Feasts," Zion's Fire (May/June 1995): 3-8. Zion's Hope, Inc.,Orlando, FL.
3. Rosenthal, 6.
4. Charles F. Pfeiffer, Howard F. Vos, and John Rea, Wycliffe Bible Encyclopedia (Chicago: Moody Press, 1976) 1498.
5. Rosenthal, 8.
6. Charles Ryrie, The Ryrie Study Bible (Chicago: Moody Press,1978) 1577.

Chapter 2
1. Kenneth Wuest, The New Testament: An Expanded Translation (Grand Rapids: William B. Eerdmans Publishing Company, 1959) 536.
2. Eddie Espinosa, "Change My Heart, Oh God." Mercy Publishing. Copyright 1982.
3. Jeanette Lavoie, Bev Ristow, and Greg Newlon, "May I Be Like You." Copyright 1999 by Jeanette Lavoie, Greg Newlon, and Bev Ristow.

Chapter 3
1. F. Nigel Hepper, Pharoah's Flowers: The Botanical Treasures of Tutankhamun (London: HMSO, 1990) 7.

Chapter 4

1. John F. Walvoord, and Roy B. Zuck, <u>The Bible Knowledge Commentary</u> (Wheaton: Victor Books - a division of SP Publications, Incorporated, 1978) 394.
2. <u>The Holy Bible: New International Version</u> (Grand Rapids: Zondervan Bible Publishers, 1984) Acts 20:24.

Chapter 5
1. Mark Robinson, "The God of Israel: One God or Three?" Bellmawr: The Friends of Israel Gospel Ministry, Inc.) 9.

Chapter 7
1. Sir Winston Churchill.

Chapter 8
1. Josh McDowell, <u>Evidence that Demands a Verdict</u> (San Bernardino: Campus Crusade for Christ, Incorporated, 1972) 18.
2. Edwin Way Teale, <u>Adventures in Nature and Science: The Bees</u> (Chicago: Childrens Press, Incorporated, 1967) 1.
3. Ed Brinkman, personal interview, 18 June 1999. Owner of Apiary: San Jose, California. (interview)
4. "Perfect." <u>Webster's New Collegiate Dictionary</u> (Springfield:G. & C. Merriam Company, 1981) 844.

Chapter 9
1. Philip Keller, <u>A Shepherd Looks at Psalm 23</u> (Grand Rapids: Zondervan Publishing House, 1970) 116.

Chapter 10
1. Reggie Coates, "Make it Shine." Reggie Coates, P.O. Box 113, Mount Hermon, California 95041. Copyright 1982. All rights reserved. Used by permission. www.heartfeltmusic.org

Chapter 13
1. Rosenthal, 4.
2. Rosenthal, 6.

Chapter 14
1. Ellen Parker, "Passover Haggadah" (Notes from her Seder Dinner Class)
2. Steve Herzig, "Passover," Israel My Glory (April/May 1992):
3. Rosenthal, 8.

Chapter 15
1. Parker
2. Jeanette Lavoie, and Mary McSweeney, "Thank You Jesus."
   Copyright 1999 Jeanette Lavoie and Mary McSweeney.

Epilogue
1. Susan Martins Miller, Jim Elliot: Missionary to Ecuador
   (Uhrichsville: Barbour Publishing, Incorporated, 1996)
   Back face cover of book.
2. Ben Franklin
3. The Holy Bible: New International Version, Acts 20:24.
4. The Holy Bible: King James Version (Chattanooga: AMG
   Producers, 1994) Galatians 6:9

Note: Unless otherwise stated, all Bible passages are from the New American Standard Translation®. Copyright© 1960, 1962, 1963, 1968, 1971, 1972, and 1977 by The Lockman Foundation, a corporation not for profit. Used by permission of Producers of Amplified Translations.

Jeanette Lavoie, R.N.

.

About the Author

Jeanette Lavoie, R.N. is a freelance writer whose hobby of bread-baking and passion to know more of Jesus, "The Bread of Life," inspired this honest, transparent book. She lives in Sunnyvale California with her husband Marty and their two children Sarah and Zack.

Printed in the United States
1289200004B/1-48